# Dimensions of Aesthetic Encounters

SUNY series in American Philosophy and Cultural Thought

Randall E. Auxier and John R. Shook, editors

# DIMENSIONS OF AESTHETIC ENCOUNTERS

Perception, Interpretation,
and the Signs of Art

ROBERT E. INNIS

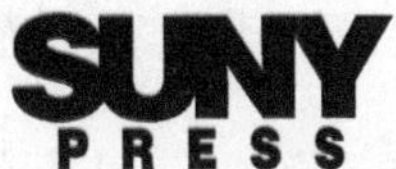

Published by State University of New York Press, Albany



For information, contact State University of New York Press, Albany, NY
www.sunypress.edu

Library of Congress Cataloging-in-Publication Data

Names: Innis, Robert E., author.
Title: Dimensions of aesthetic encounters : perception, interpretation, and the signs of art / Robert E. Innis.
Description: Albany : State University of New York Press, [2022] | Series: Suny series in American philosophy and cultural thought | Includes bibliographical references and index.
Identifiers: LCCN 2021038626 | ISBN 9781438488257 (hardcover) | ISBN 9781438488264 (ebook)
Subjects: LCSH: Aesthetics. | Art—Philosophy. | Dewey, John, 1859-1952. | Peirce, Charles S. (Charles Sanders), 1839-1914.
Classification: LCC BH39 .I55 2022 | DDC 111/.85—dc23
LC record available at https://lccn.loc.gov/2021038626

10 9 8 7 6 5 4 3 2 1

# CONTENTS

# ILLUSTRATIONS

ACKNOWLEDGMENTS

I wish to thank the following publishers for permitting the revised and reconfigured use of the following materials in a new form and format:

Chapter 1 is a reconfiguration of two basis texts: "Dimensions of an Aesthetic Encounter," originally published as a chapter in *Semiotic Rotations: Modes of Meaning in Cultural Worlds*, edited by SunHee Gertz, Jaan Valsiner, and Jean-Paul Breaux, 113–134 (Charlotte, NC: Information Age Publishing, 2007), and "Perception, Interpretation, and the Signs of Art," originally published in the *Journal of Speculative Philosophy* 15, no. 1 (2001): 20–32, and used by permission of the Pennsylvania State University Press.

Chapter 2 is based on, and extends with new examples and analyses, my essay, "Energies of Objects," which was originally published as a chapter in *Das Entgegenkommende Denken*, edited by Franz Engel and Sabine Marienberg, 21–38 (Berlin: de Gruyter, 2016).

Chapter 3 selectively merges material from two essays as well as, in part, their titles: "Dewey's Peircean Aesthetics," originally published in *Cuadernos de Sistemática Peirceana*, no. 6 (2015): 139–160, and "Peirce and Dewey Think about Art: Quality and the Theory of Signs," originally published in a special issue on Peirce's later theory of signs in *Semiotica*, no. 228 (2019): 103–133 (Berlin: De Gruyter; https://doi.org/10.1415/sem-2018-0079).

Chapter 4 was originally published as "Aesthetic Naturalism and the 'Ways of Art': Linking John Dewey and Samuel Alexander," in *Rivista di Storia della Filosofia*, no. 3 (2017): 513–532 (Milan: FrancoAngeli srl).

Chapter 5 combines two texts: "Between Nature and Art: Analytical Exemplifications of Dewey's Aesthetics," originally published in *American Aesthetics: Theory and Practice*, edited by Walter Gulick and Gary Slater, 111–134 (Albany: State University of New York Press, 2020), and "Between the Thinking Hand and the Eyes of the Skin: Pragmatist Aesthetics and Architecture," originally published in *Cognitio* 20, no. 1 (2019): 77–90.

Chapter 6 combines two texts: "Pragmatism and the Challenge of a Cosmopolitan Aesthetics," originally published as a chapter in *Cosmopolitanism and Place*, edited by Jessica Wahman, José M. Medina, and John J. Stuhr, 60–75 (Bloomington: Indiana University Press, 2017), and "Peirce's Aesthetics and the Way of Beauty," published in a volume in honor of Ivo Assad Ibri, *Sementes de Pragmatismo na Contemporaneidade*, edited by Eluiza Bortolotto Ghizzi, Lucia Ferraz Nogueira de Souza Dantas, Marcelo S. Madeira, Maria Eunice Quilici Gonzalez, and Monica Aiub, 47–57 (São Paulo: FiloCzar, 2018).

Chapter 7 originally appeared as "Filling the Hole in Sense: Between Art and Philosophy" in *Journal of Speculative Philosophy* 32, no. 1 (2018): 50–69, and used by permission of the Pennsylvania State University Press.

# Introduction

Let no one say that I have said nothing new; the arrangement of the material is new. In playing tennis both players use the same ball, but one plays it better. I would just as soon be told that I have used old words. As if the same thoughts did not form a different argument by being differently arranged, just as the same words make different thoughts when arranged differently!

—Pascal, *Pensées*

This is a book of seven linked chapters that examine the varied imports, dimensions, and sources of aesthetic encounters. The chapters are directed toward diverse audiences with different disciplinary backgrounds and interests, encompassing philosophers, cultural psychologists, literary theorists, sociologists, and art historians. They are not mainly expository but rather dialectical, exploratory, and programmatic. They do not make up a treatise, nor are they meant as a "review of the literature." The analytical linkages and frameworks of the chapters oscillate in a kind of swing and sway in the conceptual and hermeneutical space defined by a broad and open pragmatism and an equally broad and open semiotics.

But the chapters are not *about* pragmatism, or semiotics, or hermeneutics. They are about ways in which pragmatist analytical tools (especially those of Dewey and Peirce), semiotic analytical tools (specifically those of Langer and Peirce), and other complementary conceptual resources with philosophical import can throw new light on, and extend in various directions, the conceptual kernel and complex backgrounds of the theme of the opening chapter, "Dimensions of an Aesthetic Encounter," which interlinks perceptual, hermeneutical, and semiotic frameworks.

The chapters proceed by a kind of "method of rotation and exemplification." While each of the chapters can stand on its own, they are internally related to one another and intersect, overlap, or extend each other in multiple ways. The inevitable repetitions and recurrences of themes, while due to each chapter having its own distinct purpose and point of origin, reinforce their cumulative heuristic effect and the intertwined thematic threads running throughout. The chapters bring into play a range of materials that are not otherwise combined. Their main purpose is to illustrate aesthetic linkages in new ways and to avoid committing the deadly fallacy of false alternatives, instead pursuing a core philosophical task of seeing connections.

Although the chapters could be read in any order, the order in which they are placed in the book is by no means arbitrary. The first chapter, "Dimensions of an Aesthetic Encounter: Encountering Giorgione's *Sunset*," which supplies the theme and sets the analytical task of the volume, begins with the analysis of an aesthetic encounter with Giorgione's painting *The Sunset*, as fictionally portrayed in Iris Murdoch's novel *The Sacred and Profane Love Machine*. The episode exemplifies in rich detail the multidimensional perceptual, hermeneutical, and semiotic nature of the encounter. This chapter introduces categories that will be exploited and developed in different ways in later chapters: the relations, implicit and explicit, between John Dewey's and C. S. Peirce's foregrounding of the category of quality and the qualitative matrix of perception; the aesthetic relevance of Peirce's theory of interpretants; the role of the material and bodily nature of the medium in art, as illustrated in the phenomenology of painting with the help of the work of James Elkins and Nigel Wentworth; the centrality of embodied memory; Gadamer's hermeneutical use of the play model of aesthetic encounters; and other issues and examples.

The second chapter, "Energies of Objects: Between Dewey and Langer," examines the notion of energies of objects and their organization, a core theme in Dewey's *Art as Experience*. It links Dewey's pragmatist aesthetics, with its recognized fusion of Peircean and Jamesian categories, to Langer's cognate yet different semiotic approach to art and the aesthetic dimensions of experience. This chapter engages a wide range of concrete examples: Siri Hustvedt's account of her long-term engagement with Giorgione's *The Tempest*, a foregrounding, in light of the theme of the energies of objects, of some different aspects of Murdoch's fictional Giorgione encounter episode, and paintings by Pierre-Auguste Renoir and Hans Hofmann. It follows the theme of artworks as organized energy fields that are embodied in material sign-configurations with distinctive qualities. The chapter takes up the central notion of rhythm in Dewey and its relation to Langer's idea of livingness, which Dewey also discusses as the animating power of an artwork. Rhythm and livingness are shown to be expressive properties that have experiential force in their dynamic forms as gradients that permeate, not just artistic structures, but our experience as a whole.

The third chapter, "Quality and the Theory of Signs: Dewey's Peircean Aesthetics," takes up in more detail the role, both implicit and explicit, of Peirce's theory of quality in Dewey's aesthetics. The argument is that Dewey developed a "Peircean" aesthetics without explicitly developing Peirce's aesthetic hints in the systematic semiotic ways interpreters of Peirce's work have projected that Peirce would have employed, according to the fragmentary hints strewn throughout his writings. While Dewey does not systematically exploit Peirce's theory of signs in the development of this aesthetic theory, his aesthetics nevertheless mirrors its main lines. Dewey's aesthetics is not to be taken as an alternative to Peirce's but rather as one of its possible, indeed necessary, exemplifications and extensions. Thus, to speak of Dewey's "Peircean" aesthetics is to claim that there is a deep complementarity or congruence between them on multiple levels. In order to give concreteness to the discussion, the chapter examines the diverse engagements with Michelangelo's "Moses" by Robert Browning, Dewey, Sigmund Freud, and Giorgio Vasari.

The fourth chapter, "Aesthetic Naturalism and the 'Ways of Art': Linking Dewey and Samuel Alexander," discusses, with both historical and systematic intent, a potential hidden source in Dewey's aesthetics. This source is quite different from the implicit and explicit roles played by Peirce and James, as well as many others whom Dewey acknowledged to some degree. Alexander, the author of *Space, Time, and Deity*, also wrote extensively on aesthetics. Dewey was familiar with two of Alexander's rich essays, "Art and the Material" and "Artistic Creation and Cosmic Creation," and had corresponded with him but never met him in person. Nevertheless, notwithstanding that there is only one explicit reference to Alexander in *Art as Experience* and in letters to Sidney Hook and Corinne Chisholm and a passing allusion in his *Ethics*, there is evidence of Alexander's work in Dewey's *Art as Experience* that substantiates the deep naturalism of Dewey's approach to art and aesthetic experience. This chapter traces, with close attention to parallels, the shared thematic threads of (a) embodiment in a medium, (b) the notion of quality, (c) the materiality of inspiration, (d) the open nature of experiencing, and (e) metaphysical aspects of artistic processes.

The fifth chapter, "Between Nature and Art: Analytical Exemplifications of Dewey's Aesthetics," foregrounds the relations between examples and aesthetic theory in *Art as Experience* and examines further the theme of nature as the matrix and medium of aesthetic experience and self-formation and of artistic creation. Dewey's lifelong philosophical project can be characterized as grappling with "the immense variety of interactions between the live creature and his world" ([1934a] 1989, 317). This world encompasses nature as immediately experienced in its dynamic variety and the human world arising out of nature's transformations by art and technics. Dewey shows nature's aesthetic import by means of texts from W. H. Hudson, Ralph Waldo Emerson, George Eliot, George Santayana, and others on their experience of nature's multiple forms. This chapter passes in review Dewey's remarks on the openness of nature in Chinese painting, the parallel sense of this open domain in van Eyck's *Jean Arnolfini and Wife*, and the bearing of Dewey's notion of such a background on a startling interpretation of the *Mona Lisa*. The analytical triad of representation, expression, and abstraction that runs throughout *Art as Experience* is illustrated by means of Dewey's comments on the Albert Barnes–motivated examples of Paul Cézanne, Henri Matisse, Renoir, and others. Dewey's distinctions between space, spatiality, and spacing as qualities of space-time in shaping nature in art and life lead to a consideration of Dewey's remarks on architecture and its links to and confirmation by the work of the Finnish architect Juhani Pallasmaa. A discussion of architecture reveals in concrete detail the correspondences of qualities of space-time in art and life, and thereby raises critical questions about the nature of the design processes of the built world and the individual and social effects on the human sensorium.

The sixth chapter, "Pragmatism and the Challenge of a Cosmopolitan Aesthetics: On Theory beyond Borders," takes up the nature and scope of a remark in Ben-Ami Scharfstein's *Art without Borders*: "Art is not a single problem, nor does it have a single solution, rational or mystical." Art's multiple contexts, and its various types of contexts, are, he argues, the sources of this radical plurality, which characterizes thought itself. In this, art mirrors life. Nevertheless, in spite of the admitted plurality, Scharfstein issues a call for an "open aesthetics" (366) and an "aesthetic pluralism" (367) and asks, "Is there really an aesthetics that cuts across all human cultures?" (2009, 404). This chapter offers some elements for answering this question. I show how Dewey's notion of an encompassing nonobjective whole has deep affinities with the Taoist aesthetic vision presented in François Jullien's *The Great Image Has No Form*. Jullien's further formulation, in his *In Praise of Blandness*, of paradoxical aspects of the "circle of the perceived" in Chinese aesthetics, is examined in light of, and intersects with, the application and extension of the role of Peirce's theory of quality in aesthetic perception. At the end of chapter 6 I trace further some remarkable parallels between Peirce's cosmological vision and the Taoist way of beauty put forth by François Cheng. The upshot is that while analytical concepts from Dewey and Peirce may not be sufficient on their own to frame a cosmopolitan aesthetics, they certainly can be used as paving stones for constructing pathways to an aesthetic pluralism and open aesthetics.

The seventh chapter, "Filling the Hole in Sense: Between Art and Philosophy," follows up on Dewey's argument in *Art as Experience* that the significance of art as experience is of incomparable importance for the adventure of philosophical thought. Dewey claimed that while both art and philosophy move in the medium of imaginative mind, art provides a "unique control" for the "imaginative ventures of philosophy" ([1934a] 1989, 309). This chapter explores some supplementary and supporting ways of showing how this is the case by taking up (a) Raymond Tallis's core idea that art's central task is to heal an "incurable wound in the present tense" (2014, 46) or "hole" in sense that leads us to substitute a conceptual scheme for experience itself, making it difficult to be present to one's experience "on the far side of use" (47); (b) Susanne Langer's authentication of presentational abstraction and symbolization as essential processes that makes being present semiotically possible; (c) Vladimir Jankélévitch's (2003) analysis of music's ineffability and its epiphanic and nonargumentative nature as a paradigm for philosophical practices; and (d) Michel Henry's (1988) seemingly paradoxical claim, based on reflections on Wassily Kandinsky, that art, especially abstract art, makes possible an affect-drenched experience of "seeing the invisible" and grasping of the essence of being alive. These are challenging exemplifications of ways of formulating, presenting, and critically engaging focal issues, both methodological and substantive, of art's challenge to the tasks of philosophy. The originary agonistic context of philosophy is wresting meaning from the noise of meaninglessness or discerning order in a seeming world of chaos. It is not merely that of winning an argument or composing treatise-like discursive arguments, goals that it also pursues. But philosophy can be pursued in multiple manners. Jankélévitch shows us that just as short forms in music should not be measured by the model of symphonies nor artworks measured by their monumentality, so philosophical reflections can and should be measured by their mediation of insight, their revelatory power, independent of monumentality. Both philosophy and art attempt to fill a "hole in sense" by various practices, which are discursive in the case of philosophy and nondiscursive or presentational in the case of art. Artworks and the forms of philosophical writing can, by their very finiteness, nonetheless bear on the infinite or plenum of sense without claiming to encompass it. The fascinating multiplicity of artworks offers us nonreductive models that challenge philosophy to take on new forms in a conjoined task of enabling us to maintain and restore our existential and experiential balance and to make us be present to our experience, within what Dewey called, in *Experience and Nature*, the "moving unbalanced balance of things" ([1925] 1988, 341).

# CHAPTER 1

# Dimensions of an Aesthetic Encounter

### Encountering Giorgione's *Sunset*

In Iris Murdoch's 1974 novel, *The Sacred and Profane Love Machine*, Harriet Gavender, the wife of Blaise Gavender, the psychological and narrative pivot (and even butt) of the novel, is visiting the National Gallery in London and has been viewing a famous Giorgione painting, fictionally called *St. Anthony and St. George*, which is actually *The Sunset / Il Tramonto* (see figure 1.1). Murdoch writes:

> She had felt very strange that afternoon. . . . An intense physical feeling of anxiety had taken possession of her as she was looking at Giorgione's picture. . . . There was a tree in the middle background which she had never properly attended to before. Of course she had seen it, since she had often looked at the picture, but she had never before felt its significance, though what that significance was she could not say. There it was in the middle of clarity, in the middle of bright darkness, in the middle of limpid sultry yellow air, in the middle of nowhere at all with distant clouds creeping by behind it, linking the two saints yet also separating them and also being itself and nothing to do with them at all, a ridiculously frail poetical vibrating motionless tree which was also a special particular tree on a special particular evening. . . .
>
> Hypnotized by the tree, Harriet found that she could not take herself away. . . . Harriet recalled having suffered when young in the Louvre and the Uffizi and the Accademia. The last visit on the last day, as

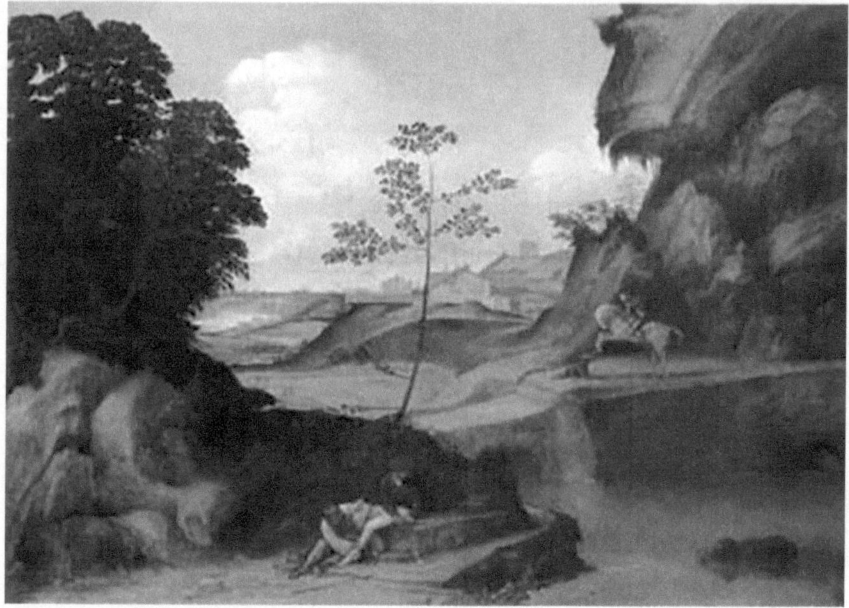

Fig. 1.1. Giorgione, *The Sunset*, 1508. *Source*: National Gallery, London.

closing time approached, indeed the last minutes of any day, had had this quality of heart-breaking severance, combined with an anxious thrilling sense of a garbled unintelligible urgent message. (1974, 52–53)

This is a remarkable description—of a full and deep encounter with a remarkable painting. For Harriet, the body-mediated encounter with this painting—what John Dewey called the art product on the way to becoming the *work* of art—is first and foremost a work of embodied perception, just as the actual production of the painting was. Its enigmatic significance, however, elicits a work of interpretation, just as the painting itself is an interpretation of a complex spiritual relationship conveying a vital message. But in spite of its explicitness, indeed its absurd precision, what it means seems to slip away beyond the bounds of discourse, even though the configuration of marks on the canvas was as articulate as possible and consummately beautiful. Harriet finds a deep affective affinity (although not necessarily a harmonious one) between herself and the world projected in the painting. The affective quality or tone that structures the painting offers her a source both of self-recognition and of a kind of shattered, even undefined and undefinable, self-completion. The painting speaks to her even though she is not able to say or fully comprehend what it is saying. At the analytical level, Murdoch pinpoints the distinctive features of the existential meeting between Harriet and the painting. Both the literary description and the painting that is described are clearly correlative and mutually defining; they are perceptually "thick" and hermeneutically engaging and nuanced, and they exemplify the diversity and complexity of signifying powers of the various material elements that carry the perceptual qualities, objects, and significances embodied in, represented by, and expressed in the painting.

Murdoch's schematization highlights the essential moments in our encounter with works of art quite generally, and not just visual works. These inseparable and internally related dimensions are the perceptual, the hermeneutical, and the semiotic. In Murdoch's novel, the work itself is not presented or reproduced, but rather accessed through a linguistic presentation of an encounter with it. But it is immediately clear that the text itself has certain features that distinguish it from an art historical analysis, which, indeed, make it an instance of literary discourse. One could see the interplay of moments in Murdoch's text itself as giving rise to such an experience and exemplifying the dimensions of an aesthetic encounter. A rich schematization of these features on the basis of a plethora of literary examples is given a masterful discussion in Johansen's *Literary Discourse: A Semiotic-Pragmatic Approach to Literature* (2002; see also Innis 2007b).

Murdoch focuses on the embodied perceiving, meaning-making, and sign-reading interpreter, that is, on the receptive side of the encounter. These dimensions within which Harriet's meeting with the artwork takes place are parallel with the productive dimensions within which the artist works. As Nigel Wentworth, in his *The Phenomenology of Painting* (2004), has illustrated in a particularly rewarding way, there is a fusion and mutual reinforcing of the dimensions from both the productive and receptive sides. The whole logic of his book, which is a kind of extended meditation on and application of the insights of Merleau-Ponty, is aimed at uncovering "the pre-reflective realm of painting," which is a matter of "lived-experience" (19; see also G. Johnson 1993). The viewer of any painting, as well as the reader of his book, Wentworth claims, needs to gain an understanding of this prereflective activity. To do so, they must "live the experience involved in it, and this can be achieved through learning to look at paintings in certain ways, ways that reveal something of how paintings come into being" (19). His discussion of the *material,* the *plastic,* and the *figurative* elements is shot through with echoes of

the dimensions alluded to previously: the perceptual, the hermeneutic, and
the semiotic. Think also of Harriet's experience of the Giorgione painting in
light of Wentworth's two following remarks: (1) "A painting does not merely
express a certain feeling, but also embodies a world" (242) and (2) "When
a viewer looks at a painting, and has the experience of entering the world
expressed within it, this world also enters him" (243).

Differently pitched theories of interpretation intersect in the interweav-
ing and weighting (or valorizing) of perceptual, hermeneutic, and semiotic
strands in their approaches to art. Perception-based models, which are rooted
in our bodily-being; hermeneutical approaches, which are rooted in, but
clearly not restricted to, the primordiality and universality of our relation to
language; and theoretical semiotic frameworks, which are rooted in the "spiral" of unlimited semiosis carried out in the production and interpretation
of signs quite generally, are not really alternatives or in irresolvable conflict.
They are rather different ways of foregrounding and scaling permanent features of our encounter with texts or sign-configurations of all sorts, whether
explicitly or thematically aesthetic or not. Artworks are configurations of perceptible qualities and hence must be perceived in some modality. As having a
content, as world-opening or bearing on a world, these configurations must
be interpreted; that is, they set us a hermeneutic task of self-understanding,
of orienting ourselves to and within a world (cf. Ricoeur 1976, esp. 36–37;
Johansen 2002, 113–174; Innis 1998b, 2007b). Furthermore, the perceptual
configurations and contentful meaning-structures have a distinctive makeup
as artifacts: they are combinations of sign-functions with distinctive logics or
grammars, the investigation of which is the task of a philosophical semiotics,
something that can take, and has taken, different forms (see Innis 1985, 1994,
2002, 2009, 2013; Nöth 1990).

The aesthetic domain—or in Hans-Georg Gadamer's anti-Kantian way of
putting it, which was confirmed by John Dewey, the domain of the experience
of the work of art (see Gadamer [1960] 1991, 1977b, 1986e)— can function
as a kind of laboratory wherein the adequacy as well as the complementarity
of differently oriented interpretative strategies and theories of interpretation
can be fruitfully assessed. Keeping constantly in mind the concrete instance
of Harriet's fictional experience in the National Gallery, I would like to indicate, briefly and schematically, how conceptual tools taken from representative or paradigmatic philosophical, or philosophically relevant, positions (to
be developed in other chapters) can illuminate, in specific and powerful ways,
essential dimensions of aesthetic experience and aesthetic reflection.

While these conceptual tools are derived from sources that have a deep affinity with one another, they were in some cases (though not all) developed without explicit connections. Their choice, of course, reveals a broad set of value judgments and theoretical commitments on my part, which are grounded in the work of Peirce, Langer, Cassirer, and Dewey, as well as many others. I will try to show that a sufficiently sober semiotics can thematize the perceptual sphere, but it also intersects with the more florid phenomenological tradition in aesthetics, culminating in the types of investigations undertaken by Merleau-Ponty and Mikel Dufrenne. In this chapter the hermeneutical dimension is represented first by the valuable work of Gadamer, but it will become clear from the discussion that semiotics and hermeneutics are not competitors, but rather collaborators, in a properly configured account of the dimensions of an aesthetic encounter. At any rate, my programmatic intention is both to initiate a discussion about the dialectic of methods and to exemplify the heuristic fertility of doing so with these conceptual resources.

## Perception and the Qualitative Matrix

Any interpretation theory adequate to the experience of art must find some way of thematizing the perceptual dimension. Gadamerian hermeneutics, which stems from and extends Heidegger's project while clearly opposing the "principle of the empty head" and insisting on the tradition-laden and prejudice-informed nature of our understanding quite generally, starts high for the most part. The body-subject, in whom, in Dewey's words, "action, feeling, and meaning are one" ([1934a] 1989, 22), plays little role in Gadamer's thought, although it is foregrounded in another context in his rich essays in *The Enigma of Health* (1993), with its development of the core notion of a body-based existential balance. Perhaps we could say that his language-based hermeneutical theory, rich as it is, suffers from a certain blind spot, which we could call the "principle of the empty body." Because, as Dewey says, the self is a "force, not a transparency" (251), its transactional relation to the experiential field itself is intrinsically problematic. The enigmatic nature of texts of all sorts, which for hermeneutically oriented theories of interpretation elicits the labor of interpretation, in fact prolongs the original (and originary) labor of perception, a point developed by Louise Rosenblatt's extension of Dewey's pragmatist positions into a theory of reading (Rosenblatt 1994, 1995; Innis 1998b), as well as by Thomas Alexander (1987), who foregrounds the actional nature of an organism's transactions with its "situation." Shusterman (1997, 2000, 2002) engages Dewey's positions by focusing in novel fashion on what lies "beneath interpretation," namely, the lived body, the autoaesthetic implications of which are to be studied, practiced, and promoted by a new discipline, termed *somaesthetics* (Shusterman 2008, 2012, 2018). The "opening" that Gadamer rightly ascribes to texts, following Heidegger's analytical lead, marks the field of perception itself, which has, if we follow Dewey ([1934a] 1989), no greatest upper bound.

> We unconsciously carry over [a] belief in the bounded character of all *objects* of experience (a belief founded ultimately in the practical exigencies of our dealings with things) into our conception of experience itself. We suppose that experience has the same definite limits as the things with which it is concerned. But any experience, the most ordinary, has an indefinite total setting. Things, objects, are only focal points of a here and now in a whole which stretches out indefinitely. This is the qualitative "background" which is defined and made definitely conscious in particular objects and specified properties and qualities. (196)

Art explores or makes manifest in a distinctive way the forms in which this qualitative background comes to appearance. This background, Dewey asserts, is a "bounding horizon," which moves as we move ([1934a] 1989, 197). It is a field that can never be expanded out to definite margins, which themselves "shade into that indefinite expanse beyond which imagination calls the universe." Thus, Dewey writes, "About every explicit and focal object there is a recession into the implicit which is not intellectually grasped" (198) but rather functions as a frame that is qualitatively defined and revealed. This is the field that Harriet finds herself embodied in, willy-nilly, as she is grasped by the painting's "aura." There is an allusion here to William James's distinction between the focus and the fringe of the field of consciousness. The fringe makes up a vast web of interconnected links and nodes, in multiple sensory modalities, which are not the thematic object of consciousness, but which surround, emerge out of, flow into, expand, and modify it. The richer the fringe, the richer is the matrix of the given focal object. The fringe, however, is not stable. It is constantly "in motion," although it is clearly not "going any place." The dynamism and time-conditioned character of aesthetic apprehension is deeply conditioned by this fringe, as the embodied interpreter is caught up in the to and fro of the relational field, which cannot be surveyed all at once. James's great image of conscious experience being structured like the alternations of the flights and perchings of a bird, with the periods of transitions composed of transitive parts and the period of rest composed of substantive parts, is of great aesthetic importance.

Donald Dryden (2001) has explored this theme, connecting, not James and Dewey, but rather James and Langer. He points out, with startling clarity, that for James, naming—language and discursive forms—that is oriented toward the substantive parts of consciousness can capture only, in James's words, "the very smallest part of our minds as they actually live" ([1890] 1983, 255). It is the role of art—what Langer calls the realm of presentational forms—to capture and express the "innumerable relations and forms of connection between facts of the world." So numberless are these relations, James writes, that "no existing language is capable of doing justice to all their shades" (244–245). Thinking about the stream of thought, James speaks, in a powerful metaphor, of the "free water of consciousness" that is resolutely overlooked by psychologists. However, in his view, which is confirmed by art, "every definite image in the mind is steeped and dyed in the free water of consciousness that flows round it. With it goes the sense of its relations, near and remote, the dying echo of whence it came to us, the dawning sense of whither it is to lead. The significance, the value, of the image is all in this halo or penumbra that surrounds and escorts it" (255). It is the artistic image that valorizes and makes present to awareness this vague, yet rich, domain. Dryden shows in detail how Langer's aesthetic theory speaks to these issues.

This penumbral field is defined by a distinctive quality or affective tone, by what Mikel Dufrenne calls "dim evidences" ([1953], 1973, 67). Dewey would say that Harriet interacts with the painting as a "whole organism" ([1934a] 1989, 127). The "total response" charted in Murdoch's description is mediated by the senses in their diverse ways, as Dewey is at pains to affirm:

> It is not just the visual apparatus, he writes, but the whole organism that interacts with the . . . environment in all but routine action. The eye, ear, or whatever, is only the channel *through* which the total response takes place. A color as seen is always qualified by implicit reactions of many organs, those of the sympathetic system as well as of touch. It is a funnel for the total energy put forth, not its well-spring. Colors are rich and sumptuous just because a total organic resonance is deeply implicated in them. (127)

The "limpid sultry yellow air" and the "ridiculously frail poetical vibrating motionless tree" illustrate the intersensory—indeed, total-sensory—nature of Harriet's reading of the configuration of signs inscribed on the canvas. As I have written elsewhere, "This organic resonance makes up the body of semiosis, objectified in systems of perceptual signs which have their own intersensory 'feels'" (Innis 1994, 62).

Russell Epstein (2004) has pointed out many instances of this phenomenon in Marcel Proust and its connection with the work of James. Taking the simple example of how wiping one's mouth with a starched napkin can bring a whole past situation back to consciousness, Epstein notes how Proust speaks of reexperiencing "not only . . . the sight of the sea as it had been that morning but . . . the smell of my room, the speed of the wind, the sensation of looking forward to lunch, of wondering which of the different walks I should take" (Proust 1982, 3:909). Involuntary memory is, in fact, a kind of paradigm of what happens to us when we encounter or are interrupted by a work of art, although the contingency of such an episode of memory in real life is replaced by the necessity or "felt rightness" of the artistic form. A work of art can condense and make manifest a "tissue of dimly-felt associations" with a force and power beyond normal experiencing (Epstein 2004, 9). But what Proust (1982) says about involuntary memory in life also applies to the complex artistic image that combines, in dialectical fashion, the voluntary and the involuntary.

> An image presented to us by life brings with it, in the single moment, sensations which are in . . . fact multiple and heterogeneous. The sight, for instance, of the binding of a book once read may weave into the characters of its title the moonlight of a distant summer night. The taste of our breakfast coffee brings with it that vague hope of fine weather which so often long ago, as with the day still intact and full before us we were drinking it out of a bowl of white porcelain, creamy and fluted and itself looking almost like vitrified milk, suddenly smiled upon us in the pale uncertainty of the dawn. An hour is not merely an hour, it is a vase full of scents and sound and projects and climates, and what we call reality is a certain connection between these immediate sensations and the memories which envelope us simultaneously with them. (3:924)

It is the skilled artist who knows how to capture these felt significances—and the skilled critical perceiver who is sensitive to them; indeed, who is captured by them.

Aesthetic perception, as Dewey works it out, is characterized by a kind of "unbalancing" preanalytic apprehension of meaning or significance that defines a kind of dialectic of "original seizure and subsequent critical discrimination" ([1934a] 1989, 150). Rosenblatt (1994, 1995) makes much of this dialectic, considering it a cornerstone of her practice-oriented theory of literary interpretation. The unbalancing nature of Harriet's encounter with the painting is exemplified in the following passage from Dewey's *Art as Experience* ([1934a] 1989).

> The total overwhelming impression comes first, perhaps in seizure by a sudden glory of the landscape, or by the effect upon us of entrance into a cathedral when dim light, incense, stained glass and majestic proportions fuse in one indistinguishable whole. We say with truth that a painting strikes us. There is an impact that precedes all definite recognition of what it is about. As the painter Delacroix said about this first and preanalytic phase "before knowing what the picture represents you are seized by its magical accord." This effect is particularly conspicuous for most persons in music. The impression directly made by an harmonious ensemble in any art is often described as the musical quality of that art. (150)

The preanalytic phase (or stratum) progresses to the analytic or interpretative (or hermeneutic) phase.

The *phasal* structure of the aesthetic encounter, as John Armstrong (2000) has shown, is the experience of first being markedly lured or drawn to a work, our being "affected" by it, a process that cannot be forced and is not, first and foremost, dependent on information or objective knowledge in any technical sense. A work of art whose "magical accord" has quickened our sensibility and enlivened our reveries, as in Harriet's case, leads us to deep contemplation. Armstrong charts and concretely exemplifies the rhythmically phasal structure of contemplation—*animadversion*, or noticing of details; *concursus*, or seeing the relations between the details; *hololepsis*, the seizing of the work as single, complete entity; the *lingering caress*, the "holding on to our perceptual holding of the object" (98); and *catalepsis*, the mutual absorption of self and object. Absorption, he notes, "is not a quick or simple process. It depends upon what is already there within us: our pre-formed digestive capacities, our already existing manner of feeling and behaving" (101). Such is clearly Harriet's situation.

Murdoch's presentation of Harriet's experience of the artwork is focused on the meaning of being moved. Hermeneutics, as exemplified in the Gadamerian mode, is first and foremost interested in the "movement of meaning." In fact, the Giorgione painting, as it functions in Harriet's lifeworld, is paradoxically a symbol as defined by both Gadamer and Susanne Langer. The symbolic nature of art for Gadamer, following Goethe's claim that "everything is a symbol," is that certain pregnant forms complete us by giving us a means of self-recognition and a sense of being connected in a vast interlocking realm of references and meanings that assemble us. "This 'everything' is not an assertion about each being . . . but an assertion as to how it encounters man's understanding. There is nothing that cannot mean something to it. . . nothing comes forth in the one meaning that is simply offered to us" ([1964] 1977, 103) This notion is ultimately derived from Goethe's concept of an *Urphänomen*, or "primary phenomenon," which Cassirer made a focal point of his *Philosophy of Symbolic Forms* ([1923–29] 1953–57), especially part 2, chapter 5, in volume 3.

But why do we recognize certain forms as deeply revelatory of ourselves and our sense of existence? According to Langer, who was writing far from the Heidegger-inspired tradition of Gadamer and much closer to Cassirer, to whom she dedicated *Feeling and Form* (1953), it is because they articulate a particular morphology of feeling. Writing in her last work, she asserted that "all levels of feeling are reflected, explicitly or implicitly, in art" (1967, 208). These forms are "symbols of feeling" or formulations of a peculiar and distinctive "logic of sentience." They *body forth* their sense. As Langer sees it, the response of the perceiver or interpreter encompasses an awakening to all those dimensions of sentience that are differentially articulated in the form, which is their symbol: order, pattern, rhythm, growth and diminution of energies; sense of effort and release; dynamism and relaxation; and so forth. "Gradients of all sorts—of relative clarity, complexity, tempo, intensity of feeling, interest, not to mention geometric gradations . . . —permeate all artistic structure" (Langer 1967, 211).

James Bunn has given a remarkable exemplification of issues surrounding the importance and pervasiveness of gradients, rhythms, tempos, and so forth, focusing on the linguistic domain, but with sensitive awareness of the similarities and differences between linguistic and visual forms, in his *Wave Forms: A Natural Syntax for Rhythmic Language* (2002). Consider the bearing of the following passage on our discussion.

Why should literary and artistic people interest themselves in the sometimes recondite theory of symmetry? In every art form one finds a rhythmic pattern as a base. These patterns, though formal, are everywhere evidence of material in action. Principles of symmetry provide a way of explaining how aesthetic patterns are enactments of the very principles that structure the universe in rhythmic patterns. Every artwork, whatever its nature, is constructed of materials that make the patterns develop at the same deep level as the laws of physics and biology. Perhaps the most important thesis is that the principles of symmetry can help explain the ways that nature distributes patterns as *stabilizing* structures. If symmetry conserves structures in rhythmic patterns of material, works of art also should enact those same kinds of harmonic principles but in wonderfully strange and sometimes discordant harmonies of form. So a fair answer to the question is, I believe, that symmetry theory can explain why the arts are not just an "add-on," but that they demonstrate in different media and by different enactments the ways that the world works, moves, and stabilizes itself in rhythms. What I have called *natural syntax* is a way of describing these physical transformations of pattern. (xii–xiii)

While Gadamer, for his part, leaves the lower threshold of the symbol relatively unthematized, concerned as he is with tracing the web of symbolic connections and reverberations in which we are caught up—that is, their "play"—Langer, following Cassirer and others, wants to indicate the rootedness of the symbol and the roots of interpretation in that lower threshold and in the grasp of form and formal significance; in, that is, "the basic symbolic value which probably precedes and prepares verbal meaning" (1953, 378; see also Innis 1994, 2009).

In this endeavor Langer is supported by psychoaesthetic investigations, which likewise, but with different emphases, push the originating stratum down to a stratum that is pregnant with meaning, constitutive of Dufrenne's realm of dim evidences. This stratum is not coded or, at least, not easily codable. David Maclagan (2001), in his *Psychological Aesthetics*, has vigorously discussed the role and status of this stratum for an adequate aesthetics (see also Tinio and Smith 2017). He points out, relying on such writers as Anton Ehrenzweig (1965) and Marion Milner (1957), that while artworks emerge as structures, as gestalts, out of the material transforming processes of sense giving, their originating matrix is a complex mix of prestructural, presymbolic, and prethematic elements and factors. The key notion, according to Maclagan, is that of an "inarticulate" or "Gestalt-free" form and its continuing effects in the objectified artwork (2001, 62). Here "vagueness, fluidity and superimposition" rule, and they appear, as characteristics, in the completed form. In any articulate form there is "a dynamic and rhythmic interplay between depth and surface," between "instinctual pressures and their sublimation" (66). It is precisely the dialectical tension, not just between surface and depth, but also between ways of understanding surface and depth that Maclagan shows we should be concerned with. Already existing unconscious processes are not necessarily to be thought of as represented in consciousness, where depth content defines or "insinuates itself into surface form." Indeed, it could be the case that "it is not just the artist who consciously or unconsciously imbues his or her work with certain psychological content, but that the work itself, both in process and in its final form, suggests or dictates these, both to the artist and to the spectator" (69).

Cassirer calls this prethematic semiotic basic value "symbolic pregnance." Its fundamental stratum is that of "expression" (*Ausdruck*), on which supervenes the stratum of perceptually grounded "representation" (*Darstellung*) and the stratum of "formal or pure signification" (*Bedeutung*). Symbolic pregnance, what Cassirer, echoing Goethe, calls the "primary phenomenon" (*Urphänomen*), reveals "the true pulse of consciousness," (1957, 203), the secret of which, according to Cassirer, is "precisely that every beat strikes a thousand connections. . . . No conscious perception is merely given, a mere datum, which need only be mirrored; rather, every perception embraces a definite 'character of direction' by which it points beyond its here and now. As a mere perceptive *differential*, it nevertheless contains within itself the *integral* of experience" (203).

The notion of a definite character of direction allows Cassirer to claim that consciousness in all cases takes on a "specific directional meaning—a vector, as it were, pointing to a determinate goal" (203). But the content of consciousness may, Cassirer notes, "assume very different shades of signification" by a process of differentiation, each dimension of which exemplifies and further concretizes the principle of symbolic pregnance, the indissoluble wedding of form and content in every phenomenal unity or configuration of consciousness. That is, the phenomenal content of consciousness is always "torqued," and in the case of a work of art, this "torquing" involves the exploitation of all the differential vectors that the perceived form contains and makes possible. Here Cassirer's analysis joins hands with the insights of James and Proust.

For his part, Merleau-Ponty, who mined Cassirer's work deeply at crucial times, pointed out in his *Phenomenology of Perception* ([1945] 1962) that "we must recognize as anterior to 'sense-giving acts' (*Bedeutungsgebende Akten*) of theoretical and positing thought 'expressive experiences' (*Ausdruckserlebnisse*); as anterior to the sign significance (*Zeichen-Sinn*), the expressive significance (*Ausdrucks-Sinn*), and finally as anterior to any subsuming of content under form, the symbolical 'pregnancy' of form in content" (235). Semiosis is here pushed down, with an explicit reference to Cassirer, to the emergence of meaning in the lowest dimensions of the perceptual field itself, which permeate its higher dimensions without reducing them. Cassirer (1979) wrote a passage that exemplifies this polydimensionality of the phenomenon of art.

> The sphere of art is a sphere of pure forms. It is not a world of mere colors, sounds, tactile qualities—but of shapes and designs, of melodies and rhythms. In a certain sense all art may be said to be language, but it is language in a very specific sense. It is not a language of verbal symbols, but of intuitive symbols. He who does not understand these intuitive symbols, who can not feel the life of colors, of shapes, of spatial forms and patterns, harmony and melody, is secluded from the work of art—and by this he is not only deprived of aesthetic pleasure, but he loses the approach to one of the deepest aspects of reality. (186)

The notion of an *intuitive symbol* is crucial, as perception, interpretation, and semiosis are interpenetrating "dimensional planes" of the total phenomenon.

Langer (1953) highlights (her italics) the intertwining of dimensions in an important way: "The comprehension of form itself, through its exemplification in formed perceptions or 'intuitions,' is spontaneous and natural *abstraction*; but the recognition of a metaphorical value of some intuitions, which springs from the perception of their forms, is spontaneous and natural *interpretation*. Both abstraction and interpretation are intuitive, and may deal with non-discursive forms. They lie at the base of all human mentality, and are the roots from which both language and art take rise" (378). Langer points out that the logical, that is, semiotic, distinction between discursive and presentational forms (one of the permanent themes of her work), accounts in a pivotal fashion for the different ways meaning emerges and is symbolized in our experience of any form. Discourse, she asserts, "aims at building up, cumulatively, more and more complex logical intuitions." The sudden emergence of meaning that marks discourse is "always a logical intuition or insight." However, Langer contends, the art symbol, even the linguistic work of art, "cannot be built up like the meaning of a discourse, but must be seen in toto first; that is, the 'understanding' of a work of art begins with the intuition of the whole presented feeling. Contemplation then gradually reveals the complexities of the piece, and of its import. In discourse, meaning is synthetically construed by a succession of intuitions; but in art the complex whole is seen or anticipated first" (379).

Langer is not denying the temporality of an aesthetic intuition—that it is a sequence of syntheses, a position that lies at the heart of a Gadamer's theory of interpretation. Intuition as interpretation takes time, and indeed is taken up into time. But the result is the grasp of a *unique whole*, however complex, held in the unity of "vision." Langer (1967–82, 1:208) speaks of "the inviolable unity of a total form." This wholeness is the semiotic (and, for Langer, "logical") key to art's inexhaustibility and inability to be formulated in or translated into discursive concepts. While Gadamer treats this issue by constant references to a central thesis of Kant's aesthetics, Langer's semiotic proposal for a hermeneutic practice is to indicate how to escape what she calls "a real epistemological impasse" deriving from the fact that *verbal meaning* and *artistic import* differ in how they can be accessed. Artistic import must be "exhibited," as Justus Buchler (1966, 1974, 1979) richly showed within a systematic theory of judgment. The art symbol cannot be separated from its sense, since for Langer there are no "equivalent symbols" or "semantic units with assigned meaning" to effect either a translation or a paraphrase. The mode of accessing the feeling-content of a work of art, its character as an affective whole, is "to present the expressive form so abstractly and forcibly that anyone with normal sensitivity for the art in question will see this form and its 'emotive quality'" (1953, 380).

But it would seem that even the artist as the original creative interpreter is bound to the expressive form itself. All critical analysis, all attempts to dismember and segment the form into parts, must return, ideally enriched, to the original whole and its sui generis feeling and significance. Polanyi (1958, 50–52), in another context, speaks of "destructive analysis" of wholes into parts and of subsequent "reintegration" as part of the hermeneutical and critical enterprise. If the carrier of the form is, as semiotic theory teaches, sign-bearing matter, and if we avoid the logocentric trap of thinking of signs along the model of language, then the significance of the prime symbol that makes up the work of art can be ascribed to the material quality that is resident in and projected in it. This significance is the multidimensional *semiotic feel*, which can be differentiated into "interpretation-spaces" attendant on Peirce's essential contention that every sign gives rise to an equivalent sign—an interpretant-sign—in the interpreter.

The Play of Interpretants

Every prime symbol unfolds its significance within these interpretation-spaces, the actual contents of which we become aware of in our engagement with the sign-configuration, which, as Mikel Dufrenne has pointed out and Gadamer echoes, puts a *demand* on us. Peirce's schematization of interpretants—the proper significate effects of signs—supplies us with a semiotically derived framework that allows us to situate the event of interpretation in a way that is not too closely tied to grasp of content in any, however attenuated, purely intellectual sense. Indeed, Peircean semiotic theory allows us in the semiotic key to foreground with precision and nuance our *being grasped* by a content, of being caught up in a play of signs (Innis 1994, esp. chap. 2).

In Peircean terms, and avoiding, on this occasion, any contentious discussion of the ultimacy and relative priority of the various typologies of interpretants (see Liszka 1996, 120n12; Johansen 2002, 42–49; Innis 2014), every sign, or every structural-logical dimension of a sign, gives rise to an equivalent sign—the interpretant—in the mind of the interpreter. Indeed, for Peirce the mind of the interpreter is a topos (place or space) where the "play" of thought-signs that are interpretants takes place. We are in the play, Peirce remarks, rather than the play being in us. That is Gadamer's position exactly, as extensively developed in the aesthetic context in his indispensable "The Relevance of the Beautiful: Art as Play, Symbol, and Festival" (1986d). The implications of play as an analytical category are much wider, as I have tried to show (Innis 2001, 2005). The differentiation of types of meaning spaces or interpretants is due to the semiotic structure of the artwork, which, in any case, must be sensuously present, and hence perceptible and perceived, in some way, as Dufrenne incessantly argues. The nuances of meaning, as found in the complex play of signs in any artwork, will have their counterparts in the distinctive and unique configuration of sign-factors, in their unique patterning and balancing.

The Peircean affective interpretant (I prefer *affective* to *emotional*) corresponds to the form of feeling or significate effect that the distinctive *quality* embodied in the artwork as a sign-configuration engenders. This defining quality is not an object *qua tale*, but rather the qualitative feel of the object, what Langer called its "morphology," that is made present by the artwork, as Murdoch's fictional framing showed. Dewey saw this and made it the cornerstone of his pragmatist aesthetics, as I discuss in chapter 3. This feel is first of all bound to the *material quality* of the artwork, to the particular way the constituent signs of the artwork become palpable and are not transparent, as Jakobson (1988), following a long tradition, famously argued.

Using the language of alchemy, James Elkins (1999) has given a strong—at times bewildering but certainly challenging—meditation on the materiality of painting. His focus, like Wentworth's, is on "the act of painting, and the kinds of thoughts that are taken to be embedded in paint itself. Paint records the most delicate gesture and the most tense. . . . Painting is an unspoken and largely uncognized dialogue where paint speaks silently in masses and colors and the artist responds in moods" (5). Indeed, Elkins continues, the meanings embedded in paintings preserve the motions that generate them. "Painters can sense those motions in the paint even before they notice what the paintings are about" (5), and so can the perceivers of the paintings. Wentworth (2004, 43) gives a nuanced and convincing defense and illustration of the thesis that "each material has its own qualitative nature." His analysis of the intertwining of brush, paint, and gesture, as material supports of pictorial meaning, is complemented by a fine account of the plastic elements—color, line, tone, texture, form, and composition—that function on the border between the semiotic and the only seemingly nonsemiotic as well as between expression and figuration. Verbal art, though admittedly with a different feel, is also embedded in and permeated by language's paradoxical materiality, which is wedded to the power of abstract distancing (Burnshaw 1979).

In fact, on Peircean grounds there are no purely transparent signs, since even transparency, in the case of language as a discursive system, has a distinctive feel. Polanyi's theory of tacit knowing, the aesthetic aspects of which I have discussed elsewhere (Innis 1977; 1994, 36–43; 2002, 149–163), specifies this feature of consciousness by distinguishing a "phenomenal" aspect of the universal *from-to* relation of parts to wholes that Gestalt theory has studied. Wholes change their "face" by a spontaneous reconfiguring of their supporting features. Polanyi extends the scope of the gestalt concept by assimilating meanings to ordered contexts quite generally. Ordered contexts, especially aesthetic contexts, are qualitatively defined structures.

Peirce's affective interpretant covers the domain of *Befindlichkeit* or, following Dreyfus's suggestion, "affectedness," in Gadamer's Heidegger-influenced project. It is developed extensively by Dewey's philosophical and aesthetic potentiation of the ramifications of Peirce's theory of quality, based on resemblance, or what I think could also be called a *qualitative* affinity between a feeling and a sign form (Innis 1998a, 2011). This is the starting point of Langer's independent semiotic expansion and development of aesthetics and of J. H. Randall's own stimulating critical reflections (which are Dewey-influenced, but with reservations) on the adverbial—and antiessentialist—nature of aesthetic experience in his "Qualities, Qualification, and the Aesthetic Transaction" (1958, 271–295). Recognizing the qualitative matrix and adverbial dimension of the aesthetic transaction is protection against reification of qualities without denying the real powers of artworks as iconic signs to discover and define pathways to distinctive, specific forms of feeling. Johansen (2002), using the Peircean subdivision division of icons into images, diagrams, and metaphors, has also perspicuously shown how reading a literary text is a tridimensional process of imagining, diagramming, and allegorizing (Peirce specifies the metaphorical aspect) (326–341), something that Dewey also saw (discussed in chapter 3). Murdoch's literary image of Harriet's encounter or aesthetic transaction with the Giorgione exemplifies such a process.

The Peircean energetic interpretant, functioning in what he called the domain of secondness or indexicality, illuminates the dimension of "clash" or "shock" that comes from the encounter with a work of art. Works of art *touch* us *so*. Gadamer writes in his essay, "Aesthetics and Hermeneutics," that "the intimacy with which the work of art touches us is at the same time, in enigmatic fashion, a shattering and a demolition of the familiar," indeed, it is a marking of *difference*. Clash, shock—"a joyous and frightening shock" ([1964] 1977, 104)—and challenge are on the one side, and affective, qualitative "definition" is on the other. The world of the artwork, which is not *as world* an object or thing but a referential whole of sense, is a horizon, a structured and qualitatively permeated matrix of felt significance, irreducible in its particularity and distinctive in its energetic effect. It is an instantiation of a unique, even if aesthetically slight, meaning-frame or form of sense, which elicits from us some action—even the action of nonaction or indifference. A work of art, ideally, interrupts, effecting to some degree a rupture in everydayness and its attendant habits of attending. The Peircean energetic interpretant can be assimilated to the demand (which clearly can be resisted) that Gadamer, echoing Rilke, insists every work of art makes on us: "Thou shalt change thy life." Being moved, or being touched, foregrounds, in Peircean terms, this dimension of a hermeneutical encounter. Qualitative definition and existential connection, which are the iconic and indexical dimensions of an artwork, are held inextricably together by the "urgent vital message" that the artwork, as a synthesized sign-configuration, the art symbol, presents.

The Peircean intellectual or logical interpretant foregrounds this articulated content of a work of art. In Langer's terms it is the "aesthetic idea" resident in the artwork as a structure, an idea or conception—not a concept—that is inseparable from the sensory garment of its presentational form. The logic of this form is not a discursive logic, but it is cognitive nonetheless. Murdoch's account of Harriet's response to the painting also charts the logical interpretant that the sign-complex has given rise to in Harriet as an existentially perplexed interpreter. The artwork, in this Peircean symbolic dimension, gives rise to thought, but it is not a thought that can exist independently of the symbolic structure itself. It is this structure that defines access to its content. As Dufrenne puts it, "The work's meaning is not exhausted in what it represents" ([1953] 1973, 65). Indeed, the logical interpretant in its aesthetic form is, as sense, "always immanent in the sensuous" (89), and what the artwork represents is conveyed only through what it expresses (65). Aesthetic signification, as immanent or embodied in the aesthetic object, does not "speak to me *about* its subject" (123) and does not preexist this object (124). Dufrenne's laconic remark bears on the complexity of this nondiscursive aboutness: "From Rembrandt to Rubens it is the same Christ, but it is not the same Christianity" (167). The projected atmosphere of a world as a matrix of significance is radically different in the two cases. As Wentworth puts it, "Representations illustrate a subject; expressions embody one" (2004, 204). The dialectical interplay between the plastic and the figurative elements, which constitute the pictorial meaning, entails a kind of dual apprehension that has parallels in other art genres, with their own formative logics. It means that as a consequence, Wentworth claims, paintings, as paintings, cannot ever have "a determinate stateable meaning." Pictorial meaning is "indeterminate, unstateable and intrinsically experiential" (215). Such meaning is not separable from the work itself or our encounters with it.

*Gadamer's Hermeneutic Distinctions*

Although it must be said that Gadamer (as opposed to Paul Ricoeur and Umberto Eco) keeps his distance from any formal semiotic approach to art, the differentiation of the three dimensionalities—the perceptual, the interpretive or hermeneutical, and the semiotic—is clearly and necessarily present in his work. In his essay "Intuition and Vividness" (1986c), Gadamer argues that an artwork is to be taken first of all as an invitation to intuition. Intuition is "processual" (161), time binding because it involves a "play of syntheses" (169), and it puts us in contact with an "affective whole" (162). But intuition is no unmediated state of sense perception or apprehension of an object. Rather, in his understanding, it intends a world—a referential matrix of meaning—and not just the objects in it (164). At times Gadamer connects the symbolic realm with conceptual understanding, and hence with signs, schemata, and conceptual expressions, which are in themselves, he contends, "abstract" (162), and hence not "vivid." Vividness certainly refers to a perceptual quality attendant on the work as an intuited whole or configuration. But Gadamer, for the most part, speaks of vividness as a property of the verbal arts, which for him, with his literary inclinations, have a perhaps fateful methodological priority. There is also a Hegelian background here: poetry is the most spiritual art form because of its embodiment in the least material medium, being comprised of puffs of "transparent" air or their transcriptions. At any rate, vividness, in this sense, belongs to what Gadamer calls "presentation as art" (167), which Langer assimilates quite generally to the creation of a prime symbol in the presentational mode, not the discursive.

Vividness potentiates the constructed perceptual form that carries the artwork, independent of medium, and is correlative to the insistence by Jakobson and the Moscow and Prague Schools on the "palpability of signs" as the mark of the "poetic" (that is, aesthetic) function of an utterance, no matter what its meaning or medium (see the classic collections Lucid 1977 and Matejka and Titunik 1976). Thus, the intuited whole is not "indicative" of something in the sense that it can be separated from what it points to. The intuited whole, Gadamer asserts, does not *point to*; it *points out*, and hence, as he puts it in his essay "Composition and Interpretation," "relates back to a kind of sign that interprets itself" (1986b, 68). The artwork, as vector, points us (indeed, carries us) "in a certain direction" (72). Both the poet and the interpreter "pursue a meaning that points toward an open realm" (72). The hermeneutical task is based on the fact that while "we have only to interpret that which has a multiplicity of meanings" (69), the symbolic nature of the artwork—understanding *symbol* now in Goethe's sense of a pregnant form that points to an inexhaustible system of connections and relevancies— entails, in the words of Friedrich Hölderlin, that in the last analysis, "we are a sign without interpretation" (in Gadamer 1986b, 73); that is, without what Peirce called a specifiable "final interpretant" of ourselves. There is no closure to the circle of interpretation and self-interpretation, which is rather a spiral or a widening gyre, as is experience itself. The unbounded, yet situated, nature of interpretation, that it makes up what Gadamer calls our historical-effective consciousness, is the hermeneutical correlative to Peircean unlimited semiosis, which is, indeed, its condition of possibility. Sheriff (1989, 1994), Johansen (2002, esp. 353–411), and Ibri (2009, 2010, 2017, 2020) give in both brief and extended formats indications of how to proceed here from a Peircean point of view.

In his essay "Art and Imitation" (1986a), Gadamer utilizes the analytical triad of *expression, imitation,* and *sign* to undertake an analysis of the significance of modern painting, with an eye to its general aesthetic relevance. Gadamer's first thesis is that the concept of imitation, understood as naturalistic resemblance or copy, "seems inadequate for the modern age," having been superseded since the end of the eighteenth century by that of expression, whose validity is itself challenged by the existence of kitsch (which Dufrenne would define as the substitution of emotion for feeling or affect). The classical concept of imitation, which aimed at the idealization of nature and held to a principle of resemblance, and the concept of expression, which aimed at the "display of inner feeling," lose their analytical and heuristic power when confronted with modern painting—which Murdoch's (and Harriet's) Giorgione definitely is not. We are accordingly led, so Gadamer claims, to the possible heuristic relevance of the concept of sign and a kind of sign-like language to explain, at least, the hermeneutical problems posed to us by modern painting. Gadamer admits, albeit in a most loose and elusive manner, that we "read" paintings. But modern paintings, he contends, present us with a severe problem: "We no longer see these paintings as copies of reality that present a unified view with an instantly recognizable meaning" (95).

Viewers of Piero della Francesca's or Caravaggio's radically dissimilar paintings titled *Flagellation* or of Johannes Vermeer's *Girl with a Pearl Earring* might question how, in the very heart of the high tradition, there could be an instantly recognizable meaning, which Gadamer strangely seems to identify with the subject of the painting. Be that as it may, in speaking of one of Kazimir Malevich's paintings of women, which I have not been able to confidently identify, Gadamer notes the extreme demand on the viewer to synthesize "the various different aspects and facets" of the painting, which, however, "no longer appears as a perceptible totality with an expressible pictorial meaning" (1986a, 95–96). There is a kind of refusal of meaning built into the painting's pictorial language, which functions as a type of shorthand. Gadamer concludes: "The concept of the sign [that is, a signifier with an assignable meaning] thus loses its proper significance and the modern language of painting increasingly tends to reject the demand for legibility in art" (96).

What does Gadamer think would constitute an "adequate response" to the art of the past (that is, the twentieth) century if the concepts of imitation, expression, and sign are unacceptable? Gadamer, in the end, stays true to Heidegger's deepest insight. He will not accept flat-out the Kantian repudiation of the conceptual or cognitive dimension of art and hence is hesitant to apply Kant's philosophy directly to modern art, as Paul Crowther (1989, 1993a, 1993b), among many others, has tried to do. But where is one, then, to look for the key overarching category? Gadamer wants to return to a universalization of Aristotle's fundamental concept of mimesis, which he insists has "an elementary validity" ( 1986a, 97). Aristotle, he claims, connected imitation with "the joy of recognition," and not with copying. "Recognition confirms and bears witness to the fact that mimetic behavior makes something present. However, this does not imply that when we recognize what is represented, we should try to determine the degree of similarity between the original and its mimetic representation" (98). Nevertheless, Gadamer goes on to assert that "the essence of imitation consists precisely in the recognition of the represented in the representation," without any advertence to a radical nonidentity between representation and the represented. They share, in Langer's sense, the same "logical form" that comes into existence with the created work. Imitation, in Gadamer's analysis, reveals "the real essence of the thing" (99): representation is intrinsically connected with recognition, that is, the cognizing of something *as* something. This process of cognizing *as* is part of a process of self-recognition, of developing familiarity with the world and hence with ourselves. This is Harriet's situation exactly. The self and the world are correlative—and neither one is a stable substance. Instead, they are meaning fields. The consequence for Gadamer is that without a binding tradition (perhaps dependent on substance metaphysics) and its demand for stability, modern art becomes incapable of being assimilated to a "purely objective pictorial representation of something" (100); hence, "the [traditional] concepts of imitation and recognition fail and we find ourselves at a loss" (101). Such a position is not restricted to painting or the other visual arts.


## Mimesis, Poiesis, and Semiosis

If that is our situation, then what, in short, is being imitated—or can be imitated—in the movement of mimesis in the fundamental sense? Here Gadamer makes a remarkable observation. For him, mimesis, quite generally and not restricted to imitation or copying in any traditional sense, "reveals the miracle of order that we call the *kosmos*" (1986a, 101). Modern art paradoxically bears witness to an essential task and achievement of all art: to reveal order as such and indeed reveal "a spiritual energy that generates order" (103) as well as capturing disorder in a paradoxically ordered form, a topic explored by Ehrenzweig (1965, 1971). Order—as ordering, including even the ordering of disorder—transcends the distinction between objective and nonobjective art. It is a manifestation of a generative energy (the theme of chapter 2). As for order and art, Gadamer writes, "Art is present whenever a work succeeds in elevating what it is or represents to a new configuration, a new world of its own in miniature, a new order of unity in tension. This can occur whether the work presents us with specific cultural content and familiar features of the world around us or are confronted by the mute, yet profoundly familiar, Pythagorean harmonies of form and color." From this remarkable observation Gadamer then draws a remarkable conclusion—remarkable in light of our discussion, that is. He writes: "If I had to propose a universal aesthetic category that would include those mentioned at the outset—namely expression, imitation, and sign—then I would adopt the concept of mimesis in its most original sense as the presentation of order." Mimesis, then, refers to "that spiritual ordering energy that makes our life what it is" (1986a, 103). The work of art exemplifies the "universal characteristic of human existence—the never-ending process of building a world" (104) through polyform acts of sign-constituted, perceptually embodied, interpretative mimeses. Semiosis as mimesis defines, even in Gadamer's reckoning, the unbounded and moving upper threshold of all productive and interpretative activity, just as it defines its lower perceptual threshold.

The parallelism between the receptive and productive dimensions of an aesthetic encounter overlaps the distinction between the perceptual, the hermeneutical or interpretive, and the semiotic dimensions. The work of art must have a material carrier of some sort, yet without being identical with it. The art *product*, as Dewey put it so as to mark the difference, is not the art *work*. And this necessary materiality, including semiotic materiality, of the art product gives it the character of being an artifact, a shaped or made thing, no matter what the medium. Dewey for his part, in *Art as Experience*, clearly affirms that the artist *perceives* the work at various stages of its realization, entailing a feedback relation as the work crystallizes the generative insight, which often only becomes concrete with the work's development, even if it is dictated, as in Henry James's late novels. The generative insight itself, however, is an interpretation, wedded to a possible expressive form, which, of course, is recognized as adequate only when the material medium in which the artwork is embodied is recognized to be fitting.

What is the generative insight an interpretation of? Langer would answer that it is the life of forms as embodying the logic of sentience. Works of art are expressive interpretations of the life of feeling, of the ways it feels to be in the world in every dimension and modality of human existence. But the matter of works of art is sign-bearing matter, not mere stuff. Its very perceptual reality is semiotically relevant, which presents us with an interpretative challenge. Choice of material configurations that embody the work of art is itself, then, a form of *poiesis* as a form of *ordering*. There is, consequently, a deep affinity, if not identity, between poiesis, mimesis, and ordering inasmuch as they are constitutive dimensions of semiosis. These dimensions—as well as the others we have been discussing—are not to be considered hierarchically. The aesthetic dimension, in spite of being rooted in the affective or emotive dimension—what Langer calls the dimension of feeling or felt life, which is a realm of affective tones—should not be schematized in such as way that we look for hierarchically ordered sequencing as some universal pattern. Works of art effect a partitioning of a complex continuum by structuring foreground and background relations in dynamic, even revolutionary, ways, just as language does. When Dewey writes that art "intercepts every shade of expressiveness found in objects and orders them to a new experience of life" ([1934a] 1989, 110), this interception is first and foremost a continuously creative and novel demarcation through an affective plenum, which it differentiates. In this sense all aesthetic reception and production are abductions, that is, discoveries or creative guesses, in which the perceptual, the hermeneutical or interpretive, and the semiotic are inextricably intertwined factors and dimensions, but not distinct types of abductive processes.

# CHAPTER 2

# Energies of Objects

## *Between Dewey and Langer*

### Framing the Issues

In his book *Art as Experience*, John Dewey developed a pragmatist approach to the flux of experience that took over and extended to the aesthetic domain central features of William James's and C. S. Peirce's analyses of consciousness, key elements and implications of which permeate Dewey's writings (Shusterman 2010, 2011). In his *Principles of Psychology* ([1890] 1983), which lurks throughout the background of Dewey's masterwork, James described the "free water of consciousness" (246) as a dynamic vortex of streams, eddies, and changing currents that encounter resistances that give it an ever-changing qualitative feel, manifested in what he called its "infinite iridescences" (229). These iridescences belong, not just to the felt qualities of the experiential flux itself, to the pulsing life of subjectivity, but also to the objective field of resistances itself, the stones, banks, and differential depths at which they are encountered. Peirce characterized in a related, though still aquatic, image this complex dynamic phenomenon as the "bottomless lake" of consciousness: "I think of consciousness as a bottomless lake, whose waters seem transparent, yet into which we can clearly see but a little way. But in this water there are countless objects at different depths; and certain influences will give certain kinds of those objects an upward impulse which may be intense enough and continue long enough to bring them into the upper visible layer. After the impulse ceases they commence to sink downwards" (1931–58, 7:457). Implicit in Peirce's only superficially static image is the idea that consciousness itself is a form or matrix of ordering. It is itself ordered, not just by its own immanent or autogenic impulses, but also by external or exogenic interruptions of its ongoing, fluctuating, underwater streams of experience. It is within this multileveled matrix that what Ernst Cassirer called the "form worlds" of meaning arise, often without explicit action on our part (1957, 448).

James saw this flux as marked or informed by a triadic structure. His triad is different from Peirce's triad of feeling, action and reaction, and thought, whose role in Dewey's work is more implicit; although important, its place is taken by Peirce's theory of "quality" (Innis 2011, 2019, 2020b). The stream of consciousness, in James's well-known description, is (a) oriented toward a *theme* or focal core, (b) which is located in a *field*, (c) which is itself surrounded by a *margin* or *fringe* that gives a distinctive "aura" to the forms of appearing. For Dewey, these forms make up, when certain conditions are fulfilled, the boundary-less realm of the aesthetic, a realm that, in his startling image, arises out of the lowland of experience the way a mountain arises out of a plain. The Jamesian theme-field-margin/fringe structure and Peirce's theory of quality must be seen as permanent background *frames* within which Dewey, both implicitly and explicitly, saw the experiential flux to be accessed and constituted and raised to a higher power in the realm of art and distinctively aesthetic experience.

Dewey follows James in his notion that experience grows at its edges. Consider this passage from Dewey's *Art as Experience*:

> We are accustomed to think of physical objects as having bounded edges; things like rocks, chairs, books, houses, trade, and science, with its efforts at precise measurement, have confirmed the belief. Then we unconsciously carry over this belief in the bounded character of all *objects* of experience (a belief founded ultimately in the practical exigencies of our dealings with things) into our conception of experience itself. We suppose the experience has the same definite limits as the things with which it is concerned. But any experience, the most ordinary, has an indefinite total setting. Things, objects, are only focal points of a here and now in a whole that stretches out indefinitely. This is the qualitative "background" which is defined and made definitely conscious in particular objects and specified properties and qualities. . . . This sense of the including whole implicit in ordinary experiences is rendered intense within the frame of a painting or poem. ([1934a] 1989, 197–198)

An art*work* for Dewey, as distinguished from the material art *product*, is, as he outlines in a pivotal chapter on the "organization of energies" ([1934a] 1989, 167–190), a framed, that is, organized, and *experientially realized* field of energies of various sorts encountered in particular objects, leading to our having an experience of it and not just noticing or dealing with it. In this sense it is a distinctive kind of form or thematic unity. For Dewey, the artwork is defined by, or constituted by, the work that the material art *product* (in whatever medium) brings about or induces in experience—by the types or dimensions of meaning-experiences it gives rise to or makes possible, including experiences of recollection and of stretching toward the future.

Although Dewey does not utilize semiotic terminology, we can say, avoiding technical terminological niceties, that an artwork is a sign-configuration with iconic, indexical, and symbolic dimensions, corresponding to Peirce's well-known triad of icons, indices, and symbols. Each artwork, when viewed as such a configuration, has (a) a defining felt quality, (b) embodied in differentially pertinent features in the artwork that elicit and control specific forms of resistances and forms of attending, which (c) carries or articulates a core import or "idea." Such an idea or core import enlivens and animates the artwork as its "spirit." As Susanne Langer has shown in her own semiotic aesthetic theory, such "import," embodied in presentational symbols, transcends discourse, which can gesture toward it in multiple ways yet never be adequate to what it is pointing to (Langer [1942] 1957, 1953, 1967, 1974, 1982). In Dewey's words, "there is no name to be given it" ([1934a] 1989, 197), since the meaning or idea of an artwork is present the way a pattern is present in, and inseparable from, a carpet. It can be talked about, gestured toward, but it cannot be said, as Langer powerfully argued.

Dewey clearly recognizes from the experiential side and without semiotic terminology that the energies of an artwork or "art object" give rise in the perceiver or interpreter engaging it to what Peirce called *interpretants* or *proper significate effects*, a terminology Dewey did not use in his aesthetics. Peirce schematized these interpretants in a number of ways, all of which are clearly derived from his system of categories and his well-known major triad of signs and semiotic dimensions. Briefly schematized, the iconic dimension, which is rooted in a shared quality of the sign and its object, gives rise to emotional or affective interpretants; the indexical dimension, which is grounded in an existential linkage between sign and object, gives rise to energetic interpretants, or modes of attending to and acting toward "the thing-meant"; and the symbolic dimension gives rise to logical interpretants, which comprise the unifying animating spirit of the aesthetic sign-configuration, its felt and fitting synthetic or unifying core. The Deweyan-Peircean point here, independent of terminology, is that the object—indeed for that matter, any object, and not just aesthetic objects—gives rise to, and is accessed through, different types of "proper significate effects." These effects, or powers to effect and affect, are resident in the object but are only activated in the experiential encounter in a self-reconstructing spiral of cumulation and conservation (Dewey 1896).

Nevertheless, for Dewey, notwithstanding the processes of experience-dependent activation, these powers themselves are objective and materially embodied as potencies. They are *real* even if, for us, they have to be *realized* in our experience, which they inform and, in their own way, activate. At both the experiential and semiotic poles, which ultimately are identical, experience itself is the emergence and creation of forms of various levels and types of complexity that are sources of differential degrees and kinds of semiotic energy.

It is this topic of energies of objects that is the focus of what follows, the dynamic properties of the *form worlds* emerging out of the protean nature of consciousness and the matrices of feeling or sentience. In one of Ernst Cassirer's seminar papers there is a passage, which was also cited in chapter 1, that captures the scope and import of art as one of these form worlds.

> The sphere of art is a sphere of pure forms. It is not a world of mere colors, sounds, tactile qualities—but of shapes and designs, of melodies and rhythms. In a certain sense all art may be said to be language, but it is language in a very specific sense. It is not a language of verbal symbols, but of intuitive symbols. He who does not understand these intuitive symbols, who can not feel the life of colors, of shapes, of spatial forms and patterns, harmony and melody, is secluded from the work of art—and by this he is not only deprived of aesthetic pleasure, but he loses the approach to one of the deepest aspects of reality. (1979, 186)

The references to rhythms—to nonlinguistic symbols, to feeling the life of the play of forms—encompass not just the deep structures of art but also those of nature itself and of its energies.

What provides, and how do they display, their energy, or types of energies? How, further, do the energies of art objects mirror the very energies of their originating and receptive matrices, the creative sensorium? I will take up these questions with conceptual tools from Dewey and from Langer, whose semiotic aesthetics has special relevance to these issues, and with subsidiary indications of Dewey's relation to Peirce, which is examined in detail in chapter 3.

## Giorgione's *The Tempest* and Hustvedt's Game of Glances

Dewey's primary thesis is that "an esthetic experience, the work of art in its actuality, is *perception*" ([1934a] 1989, 167). For Langer, what is perceived, the Deweyan art *product* on its way to becoming the art *work*, is a *presentational symbol* that mirrors and projects the "morphology of feeling" in processes of symbolic transformation. Such symbols must be both perceived and interpreted in an intertwined spiraling process. Dewey's nuanced investigations of the perceptual conditions effecting the transitions out of ordinary perception are complemented by Langer's remarkable exploration of the heuristic fertility of the art image to uncover the dynamics of minding and to present the infinite ways in which, in the broadest sense, we "feel" the world. Energies of objects can evoke in us deep resonances of self-recognition and inform our processes of self-interpretation. They enliven us in their givenness and in their creation, in the processes of undergoing and undertaking that make up the "swing and sway" of experiencing—the dialectic of passivity and activity, of undergoing and doing.

Following the example of chapter 1, I turn to another response of a quite different sort to a different Giorgione painting, *The Tempest*, recounted by the novelist and essayist Siri Hustvedt in *Mysteries of the Rectangle* (2005). Hustvedt's response, however, is not presented as one that a fictional character is undergoing. Her response is that of a dedicated looker at the "mysteries" to be encountered within the rectangle of a painting. The parallels between her real responses and those ascribed to the fictional character Harriet Gavender in Murdoch's novel support the indispensable notion of energies of objects.

Hustvedt's introduction to her book frames or foreshadows in a nontechnical way her discussions of the paintings that make up the book as a whole. It mirrors analytical elements at work in the discussion of Murdoch's presentation of a fictional encounter with a painting. Central categories of the introduction return in the essays on the individual paintings. The first general observation is the "immutable stillness" of painting, its mere presentness as a "wordless image" with an all-there-now quality that defines "what's inside its edges" (xv), which are bounded by a frame, whether virtual or real. Such a frame circumscribes the field of vision whose contents, as Dewey wrote in a passage cited earlier, are "rendered intense." At the same time, engagement with a painting is an intrinsically temporal process, involving "long viewing periods" and "periods of rest" in order for the image to, as Husvedt puts it, "settle" in the mind and come to "endure in memory," a process analogous to the flights and perchings that James ascribed to the dynamics of consciousness (xvi, xvii). What endures, and what is sought for, is felt insight into the "internal logic" of a painting, something that has to be "unlocked" and therefore requires a key of some sort. Such a key does not entail an ability to capture in discourse what the painting is about, as if it were, in principle, something outside the painting, which could be named. This point is clearly not restricted to painting alone. Indeed, it bears on what Cassirer called "intuitive symbols" as such.

A silent encounter with a painting, as well as clearly in the temporal arts, involves an "all over" apprehension, a marking of detail and relations, a synthesis or time-binding (xviii). Such a way of attending at the same time can be blocked or distorted by blind spots and tacit premises, such that "expectation prevents discovery" (xix). There is no purely objective apprehension of a painting—or of any work of art or text. The viewer, the reader of a text, the wanderer in a city, and so forth are "funded," just as the artwork as an embodied meaning-structure is itself funded. "No person," Hustvedt points out, "leaves himself behind in order to look at a painting" (xix). This is not an argument for subjectivism. Hustvedt remarks, perhaps too broadly or problematically, that in fact there is "remarkable uniformity of response" (xx) to such painters as Johannes Vermeer, Jean Siméon Chardin, and Francisco Goya on the part of Denis Diderot, Vincent van Gogh, Marcel Proust, and Charles Baudelaire. This is surely an unconventional and challenging combination of seemingly different receptive sensibilities.

Hustvedt proposes that we think of a painting first and foremost as a "material trace of another human consciousness." A painting is not just an abstract thought with an indifferent substrate, but rather "the marks left by a person's physical gestures—strokes, dabs, smudges" (xix). These traces must be attended to. They make up the inseparable energetic supports of a painting's Peircean material quality that conditions how a unique painting speaks to us and conveys its sense or vital message. These marks are not, however, the message itself, even if they are inseparable from it. For Hustvedt the vital message is accessed in and through the "feeling it gave me" (xx), in what is fundamentally a solitary experience informed by one's past experience, which in itself can never be solitary. Such a feeling is rooted in and configures the somatic and affective tone of the perceiver: "Visceral responses to an image … are inevitably avenues to meaning," although one cannot always name or be clear about the reasons for a picture affecting us in a certain way. Such a way of conceptualizing it is analogous to Peirce's notion of an affective interpretant as a modification of an essentially embodied consciousness. But such a felt response motivates us to pursue *why* we are affected in this way. The discovery of why is not automatic. It involves "mental peregrinations into the unknown" and recognition that the allure, the felt pull, of a painting—or any artwork, for that matter, and especially music—is not easily articulated. It involves "waiting for a while, to see what happens," a perceptual process that is an "adventure in an imaginary space" (xxi) but no arbitrary musing. Hustvedt charts the dimensions of this adventure and its energizing powers in her encounter with *The Tempest* (figure 2.1).

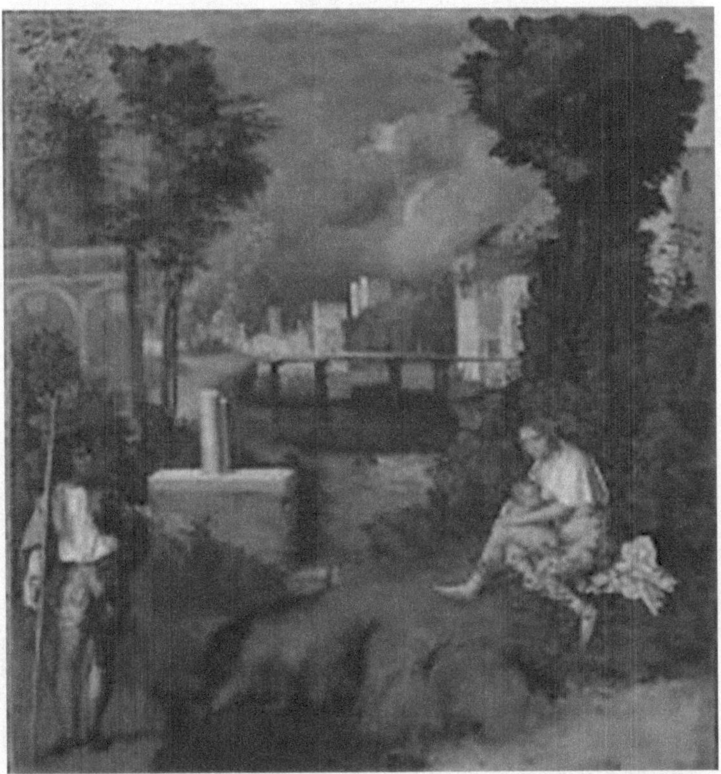

Fig. 2.1. Giorgione, *The Tempest*, 1506–1508. *Source*: Accademia, Venice.

Hustvedt wrote her essay "The Pleasures of Bewilderment" twenty-six years after her first encounter with *The Tempest* in a college art history course and after three visits to the Accademia in Venice, where the painting hangs. Looking back to the first encounter, she notes that it caused a "physical response . . . a genuine tremor of amazement." She "fell in love with it" and felt an "almost electrical connection to the painting." Indeed, the image "seemed to burn itself into my memory with an almost disturbing clarity," creating for her a "transcendent moment" (2). The disturbing clarity, however, paradoxically marks the "confounding" nature of *The Tempest*. The picture as a "dead thing," Dewey's art *product*, becomes "animated" in the experience of a "living person who enters into some kind of relation with it" (4); that is, the art *product* becomes the art *work*. This animation is not some form of deliberate or willful operative action performed on the art product, the material work of art, which is itself tensively passive, filled with potencies. There is rather a deep reciprocity in the encounter, a being saturated by the product that "radiates something," clearly an expression of energy. Hustvedt further remarks that *The Tempest* is small and forces closeness of vision, with a concomitant attention to detail and underlying relations. It resists, constrains, and lures the viewer's searching gaze.

Interpretation, however, is not just about noticing details, but also about grasping and being grasped by the artwork and its "idea," which is not a discursively accessible concept, as Langer has systematically established. At the same time, with respect to *The Tempest*, Hustvedt claims that "nobody knows what the painting is about" (4) and that it could be taken as a "painting without a subject" (5). Of course, this raises the question of how something could have a meaning but not be about something. But this something—the "thing-meant"—clearly does not have to be outside the sign-configuration. Hustvedt cites Kenneth Clark to the effect that the painting is a "free fantasy" (6) and not grounded in allegory or some determinate narrative.

Hustvedt's own approach to the painting is meant, in essential ways, to be independent of controversial art historical details and even, in fact, of an explicit or even systematic aesthetic theory. Her focus is on the schematic structure of the material configuration on the canvas and on processes of her being led to apprehend its internal relations and resonances as revealed in stages of diacritical apprehension. Remarking on her three visits to the Accademia, she characterizes them as repetitions of the "first rapture" *undergone* in first seeing the painting in the college course. This rapture is not something she evokes in herself. She also recounts how she had forgotten the figure of the man in the bottom left of the painting who is gazing at the woman across a divide. At the same time she argues that the man becomes, indeed is, her "vehicle of entry into an image I don't fully understand, but understand enough to be fascinated" (5). The gaze of the woman is outward, not toward the man, but our gaze is at what he is looking at, the woman. The figure of the man's role is indexical. But their presented gazes, which do not meet, bring to our attention the chasm between the figures who "will never approach each other" (6). The man and woman exist in separate realms.

The nudity of the woman, Hustvedt writes, signifies timelessness in "that enchanted landscape," where her face is "illuminated by light from a mysterious source" (1974, 6). Hustvedt makes much of *The Tempest* being about voyeurism itself in being an exemplification of a "game of glances in an imaginary place" marked by the "mysterious otherness of the nude woman" (7). The painting, for Hustvedt, initiates a reflective drama of looking that is rooted in the destabilizing presence of the man in the foreground whom the woman may not have seen. His visible body, looking at the woman, functions, she writes, as a pointer, not just to the woman, but also to the painter as a "hidden body or ghostly presence behind every canvas" (8).

*The Tempest*, Hustvedt argues, is marked by a deep ambiguity that is rooted in lack of codes, although she is right in claiming that we need, in some way, "known codes and precedents," even those that are unconscious, so that entry into an image is not blocked. Of course, culturally informed fore-structures of perceiving and feeling guide our approach to an artwork and encounter the constraining material configuration of the canvas or text or musical and choreographic scores and diagrams, which are themselves culturally saturated. In the case of this painting Hustvedt contends that its mysteriousness cannot be "solved" by "placing a narrative beside it" (9). The point is general, as is the sense that in the encounter with a pregnant artwork something always escapes us, not as something merely indefinite but, as Peirce argued, permeated by a rich "vagueness" marked by semiotic plenitude. In the case of those works to which we keep coming back, Hustvedt writes, we are confronted with a "quality of cryptic excess . . . as if an inanimate thing were endowed with an elusive, almost sacred power" (9). Of course, this is not the case with everything claiming to have an aesthetic import or value. But Hustvedt sees in Giorgione's painting an exemplification of what she calls the enigma of seeing, where there is a constant struggle to make sense of or do justice to what lies before us. Speaking clearly for herself, she admits that *The Tempest* will always "resist my understanding" (9) and thus demand from her a constant return. Such a constant return, willed and unwilled, is a mark of our own aesthetic engagements.

Hustvedt has given a revealing description of a deeply personal yet clearly self-analytical encounter with a remarkable painting, just as we saw in Murdoch's text in chapter 1. Her encounter with this painting is body-mediated, giving rise to a "physical response." The semiotic physicality of the painting itself is foregrounded in Hustvedt's case. She adverts to the strokes, dabs, and smudges of the painting as the product of a creative action that embodies or realizes Giorgione's vision in the art *product*, which becomes, in Hustvedt's deeply personal and memory-laden encounters and reencounters, the art *work*. As in Murdoch's text, we see the foregrounding of the painting's enigmatic significance, its animating spirit, escaping discursive formulation and translation.

What Langer calls the "vital import" of an artwork, however, has elicited in Hustvedt a decades-long work of existential engagement, and not just interpretation. The painting itself is a symbolic projection of a complex spiritual relationship. But, as in Murdoch's characterization of Harriet's encounter with "her" Giorgione, we see in Hustvedt's case that in spite of the manifest explicitness of *The Tempest*, indeed, its absurd precision of pattern, what it means evades the bounds of discourse, even though the configuration of marks on the canvas, its formed matter, was materially articulated and infused with a luring beauty. Hustvedt, just like Murdoch's Harriet, is drawn by a deep affective affinity between herself and the world projected in the painting, what Dewey called its "resonances" and James called its "aura." The affective quality or affective tone that structures the painting offers her a source both of self-recognition and of a kind of undefined, undefinable, and always receding self-completion. The painting speaks to her, energizes her, even though, by reason of the painting's nondiscursive semiotic logic, she is not able to say or fully comprehend what it is saying. Indeed, it is not saying anything at all. In this way, the perceptual, the affective, and the explicitly hermeneutical and semiotic dimensions are intertwined and reinforce one another in Hustvedt's encounter with *The Tempest*. They are put into rhythmic play in the aesthetic encounter with the art product, thus transforming it into the art work. This energetic rhythmic play of the dimensions of an aesthetic encounter belongs to experience as a process embedded in nature and to its expression in artworks with their constructed, as well as found, materio-semiotic supports.

## On Rhythms

We can engage once again informed by the theme of energies of objects the passage cited in chapter 1 from James Bunn, *Wave Forms: A Natural Syntax for Rhythmic Language*, which characterizes the deep structures of art and nature:

> Why should literary and artistic people interest themselves in the sometimes recondite theory of symmetry? In every art form one finds a rhythmic pattern as a base. These patterns, though formal, are everywhere evidence of material in action. Principles of symmetry provide a way of explaining how aesthetic patterns are enactments of the very principles that structure the universe in rhythmic patterns. Every artwork, whatever its nature, is constructed of materials that make the patterns develop at the same deep level as the laws of physics and biology. Perhaps the most important thesis is that the principles of symmetry can help explain the ways that nature distributes patterns as stabilizing structures. If symmetry conserves structures in rhythmic patterns of material, works of art also should enact those same kinds of harmonic principles but in wonderfully strange and sometimes discordant harmonies of form. So a fair answer to the question is, I believe, that symmetry theory can explain why the arts are not just an "add-on," but that they demonstrate in different media and by different enactments the ways that the world works, moves, and stabilizes itself in rhythms. What I have called natural syntax is a way of describing these physical transformations of pattern. (2002, xii–xiii)

Deweyan aesthetics sees the rhythmic energetic powers of a work of art as first and foremost found or encountered in perceptual experience. But the artwork's energetic powers depend, first of all, on the artist's felt awareness, rooted in the body, of the existence of rhythms in nature as a dynamic matrix of ordering, which are captured in presentational forms. Hustvedt's text adverts to these powers in numerous ways by delineating the qualities of her perceptual and affective foci. Distinctively aesthetic rhythm, though, goes beyond the play of natural rhythms displayed in vision and is rooted in the fundamental somatic tonus of our embodied engagement with the world. "Esthetic rhythm," Dewey writes, "is a matter of perception and therefore includes whatever is contributed by the self in the active process of perceiving" ([1934a] 1989, 167–168)—and in our attendant moving about in the world. This is certainly something we see both exemplified and described in Murdoch's text, which, as a presentational form in a linguistic medium, has its own rhythmic structure. Hustvedt's recounting of her engagement with the Tempest is not, however, fictional or written to have an artistic or aesthetic effect, as Murdoch's is. But both texts chart points of transition in the described active process of perceiving, guided by the pull of aspects of the painting and involving, what Dewey calls, "furtherance, through the energy of the elements, of a complete and consummatory experience" (168). Rhythm is "ordered variation of energy" and "variation is not only as important as order, but it is an indispensable coefficient of esthetic order" (169), as Bunn's text asserts.

Aesthetic order, in this view, is a process. It is an "ordering," a carrying forward, a cumulative progression, that is defined and measured, not in terms of static elements, but by what Dewey calls "functional and operative traits." The issue is not one of recurring units but rather of recurring *relationships*, which "serve to define and delimit parts, giving them individuality of their own" ([1934a] 1989, 170). It is precisely this individuality that initiates the new responses of Murdoch's character Harriet Gavender and Siri Hustvedt, *breaking as well as enriching* the familiarity stemming from their prior encounters with the paintings and *putting them into play*. They become conscious of a new effect—and of a new affect—and are thereby energized. Taking his lead from James's acknowledgment of the "ever, not quite" feature of our experiencing, Dewey writes: "Every movement of experience in completing itself recurs to its beginning, since it is a satisfaction of a prompting initial need. But the recurrence is with a difference; it is charged with all the differences the journey out and away from the beginning has made" (173).

Now, is this not precisely what is happening in Harriet's and Hustvedt's *reencounters* with their Giorgiones, with their differently weighted and motivated sense that it is charged with an ever-new, albeit enigmatic import? In their cases and in ours, in Dewey's words, "The need of life itself pushes us out into the unknown." The *life rhythms* of Murdoch's Harriet and of Hustvedt are marked by a dialectic of closure and awakening and, again quoting Dewey, "Every awakening settles something. This state of affairs defines organization of energy" (174). Harriet's and Hustvedt's experiences are a series of *reawakenings*, which were anticipated and sought after. The lesson for us, of which most of us are aware, is that the "sudden magic" of certain engagements with a work of art "gives us the sense of an inner revelation brought to us about something that we had supposed to be known through and through" (175). It is, as Dewey explains, the "variety and scope of factors, in being rhythmic each to each" that build up and inform our perceptual frames (176). Our prior frames have to be broken through or interrupted (an instance of Peircean secondness) in order for the requisite latent degree of energy to be evoked. But the energy also has to come from our own willingness to be put into play, to be caught up in and informed by the pregnant image. The willingness of Harriet and Hustvedt are not quite the same and are rooted in different existential situations. Such a willingness can clearly also surprise us, manifesting an openness or need we did not know we had prior to an encounter with an artwork, with a "fold," or with an event of "dynamic folding" in nature, an emergent wavelike breaking and overlapping of surfaces by depth forces (Corrington 2013, 2016; Deleuze 1993).

In an analysis of "an actual painting," albeit unnamed but apparently one of Renoir's bather paintings, *Bathers in the Forest* (figure 2.2), or one of Cézanne's *Bathers* from the Barnes Foundation collection, Dewey enumerates, with Albert Barnes's (1937) in the background, in schematic and illustrative mode,

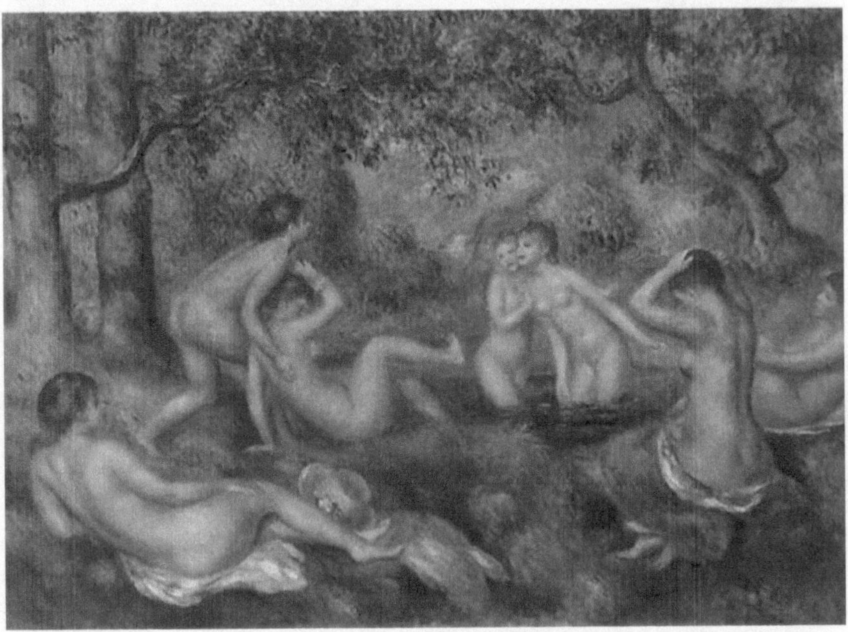

Fig. 2.2. Pierre-Auguste Renoir, *Bathers in the Forest*, about 1897. *Source*: Barnes Foundation.

five systems of rhythm or kinds of organic energy: (1) vertical and (2) horizontal rhythms controlling the movement of the eye across the painted surface that offer moments of halt or arrest (Jamesian perchings) in the visual engagement, (3) color rhythms associated with areas and masses, (4) spatial rhythms constituted by "spatial intervals determined by a series of receding and intertwined planes," giving rise to the impression of depth ([1934a] 1989, 179), and (5) rhythms of luminosity. It is clear that these are formal features of the artwork as a perceptual object (an art product, in Dewey's terminology), and their bald enumeration is not unique to a Deweyian aesthetic theory. This seriation of features, however, transcends the commonplace or obvious because it is clearly informed by James's differentiation of the transitive and substantive parts of consciousness and its assimilation into the image of the flights and perchings of a bird. But it is essential to note that the artwork that Dewey is using as his semianonymous illustration can manifest these formal features without necessarily having any aesthetic power, although the one he putatively is alluding to does.

It is the presence of tension and of stretched time, or the coordination of what Dewey called "various sensory-motor energies," that *moves* the perceiver, willy-nilly, beyond mere recognitions to engagement and maybe even self-transformation. The mark of an objective organization of energies, in this and cognate cases, is that the object "seems to move from within" ([1934a] 1989, 180), an aspect of engagement certainly found in Murdoch's linguistic presentation of the questioning movements of Harriet Gavender's perplexed consciousness and in Hustvedt's account of the dynamism or dynamics of glances in *The Tempest*. The livingness of the artwork instigates and controls the organization of our energies and, Dewey says, it is the factor of livingness that engenders in our engagement with the art product "the feeling of dealing with a *career*, a history, perceived at a particular point of its development" (181), in a process that is not closed, but rather is open. Hustvedt hesitantly foregrounds, or composes, a "soft" narrative frame for the state of affairs that is frozen in time in *The Tempest*, which culminates in the enigmatic, yet living, tone—a fusion of tension and stillness—of the silent image.


## On Livingness


Langer confirms that the sphere of art is where "diverse means and very subtle ways of projecting ideas *force* themselves on one's attention" (1967,

81; my emphasis). Of course, as Dewey remarks, in light of his transactional account of the organism-environment relation, lack of preparation in the perceiver can blunt or negate that force with deleterious consequences on multiple levels. The energies of the object or the art image have to be met by the energies of the perceiver. Hustvedt exemplifies the play of these energies and the willingness of viewers to submit to the image, in a different way than Murdoch's Harriet Gavender even though their deep motivations for doing so are similar. These creative energies of the perceiver both depend on and give rise to the perceived and felt object and also, as Langer shows, are mirrored in it.

Consider the following passage from Langer in light of the connection of energy with form or, more pertinently, living form:

> The artist's eye sees in nature, and even in human nature betraying itself in action, an inexhaustible wealth of tensions, rhythms, continuities and contrasts that can be rendered in line and color; and those are the "internal forms" which the "external forms"—paintings, musical or poetic compositions or any other works of art—express for us. Art . . . makes form expressive for us wherever we confront it, in actuality as well as in art. Natural forms become articulate and seem like projections of the "inner forms" of feeling, as people influenced (whether consciously or not) by all the art that surrounds them develop something of the artist's vision. Art is the objectification of feeling, and the subjectification of nature. (1967, 87)

In a later passage, Langer writes that in the artistic image there is an objective presentation of the "feeling of activities interplaying with the moments of envisagement" (99), a point consonant with Dewey's foregrounding of the rhythmic intertwining of undergoing and undertaking and with the long term pull of the "vital and urgent message" that Harriet Gavender experiences as addressed to her by the painting and just as Hustvedt feels herself so addressed.

For Langer, in line with her own construction of a naturalistic semiotic theory of mind, "all conscious experience is symbolically conceived experience; otherwise it passes 'unrealized'" (10), that is, unfelt. Langer's main thesis is that this symbolically conceived experience is realized paradigmatically in artworks which are images of feeling. The range of this notion is defined in the following passage:

> An image does not exemplify the same principles of construction as
> the object it symbolizes but abstracts its phenomenal character, its
> immediate effect on our sensibility or the way it presents itself as some-
> thing of importance, magnitude, strength or fragility, permanence
> or transience, etc. It organizes and enhances the impression directly
> received. And as most of our awareness of the world is a continual play
> of impressions, our primitive intellectual equipment is largely a fund
> of images, not necessarily visual, but often gestic, kinesthetic, verbal or
> what I can only call "situational." (59)

Moreover, in the case of artworks, Langer writes, "The image of feeling is
inseparable from its import; therefore, in contemplating how the image is constructed, we should gain at least a first insight into the life of feeling it projects,"
for "feeling is projected in art as quality" (106), which is the pivotal concept in
Dewey's aesthetics and the ultimate consequence of what he considered Peirce's
most important contribution to philosophy (Innis 2011). Moreover, it is the
distinctive *material quality* of a sign-configuration, such as the Giorgiones or
the Renoir or Cézanne *Bather* paintings, not what they are "about," that first
renders them interruptive, a *furtherance* for ongoing conscious engagement
and a *resistance* to habitual assimilation of experience, the sense of magical
accord or musical quality that breaks into the flow of experience.

For Langer, the formal structure of the art image animates sensibility in
the ways Dewey charts in his masterful chapter. Langer points out that the
organization of the experiential field involves "symmetry, or correlation of
counterparts, which creates the axis as a structural element" arising out of
the "resting tonus of the whole organism" (1967, 125). This is what Langer,
in agreement with Dewey, called the "whole vital substructure" of our lives
(99), which the engagement with works of art and aesthetic occasions in
nature aims to shape and sustain, as is evident in the cases of Murdoch's Harriet and of Hustvedt's own experience. In this way Langer confirms Dewey's
notion that "livingness" is the correlative distinguishing mark of the energetic
object or image, a mark that "turns" the dynamic field of attendings toward
it. The energetic object is a semiotic "attractor" (René Thom) and force field
of qualitative significance that lures us, drawing us in while enlivening and
guiding us. Dewey describes this process: "Even at the outset, the total and
massive quality has its uniqueness; even when vague and undefined, it is
just that which it is and not something else. If the perception continues, discrimination inevitably sets in. Attention must move, and, as it moves, parts,

members, emerge from the background. And if attention moves in a unified direction instead of wandering, it is controlled by the pervading qualitative unity; attention is controlled *by* it because it operates within it" ([1934a] 1989, 196). The inner process of art, Langer says, is "from felt activity to perceptible quality; so it is a 'quality of life' that is meant by 'livingness' in art" (1967, 152). Livingness is the prime mark of the expressive object and source of its energies as well as the energies of its perceivers.

Langer points out that livingness is presented by a *pattern of tensions*. This pattern "reflects feeling predominantly as subjective, originating within us, like the felt activity of muscles and the stirring of emotions" (164), precisely a characterization of Dewey's "live creature" and of what is happening to Harriet Gavender, but in a different register, as is also seen in Hustvedt's reflective engagement. The livingness of the image is rooted in what Langer calls a kind of "permanent tonicity" (175), which results from the dialectical fusion of structure and dynamism that exists in the image, as well as in the live organisms that we are, balanced between stability and instability, in what Dewey called the "moving unbalanced balance of things" in *Experience and Nature* ([1925] 1988, 314). Structure in the image is derivative from design, to be sure, but dynamism (or energy) arises through the *interactions* of diverse elements that are integrated into the image as a whole, just as the mind is itself, in Langer's conception, a spiraling process of integration—in fact, of self-integration—a continuous process of time-binding that holds our lives together. It is this mirroring of features of minding (and of existential perplexity) and the supporting of self-recognition that Murdoch's description foregrounds and that Hustvedt's reflective analysis manifests. Dewey's schematic description of the forms of rhythm indicate that it is the polyrhythmic structure and tensions of the image-configurations that lend the quality of livingness to what appears on the marked surface or in the shaped materials, including linguistic materials, as Murdoch's text so clearly reveals.

## On Experiential Forces

Langer and Dewey are interested in the ability, as well as the necessity, of an *Endgestalt*, the finished artwork or art image, to hold, as Langer remarks, "all the phases of the evolving vision" (1967, 179). In the realized form of the artwork we find retained all the experiential aspects "which an ordinary perceptual datum gives up as it reaches its full objective status; because the ordinary percept becomes a thing for the percipient, but the artist's creation becomes a symbol" (179), a presentational symbol or expressive form, which is a central notion or thread in Cassirer's project (Lauschke, 2007). It presents by means of its material configuration a complex physiognomy. Langer writes: "Everything that enters into a work has some physiognomy or at least the seed of physiognomic value. . . . There is a reflection of inner feeling in the most typically outward, objective data of sensation. . . . Their character is never as fixed and simple as the distillations our conventional store of qualifying adjectives has made from them" (179). Is it not the recognition of a reflection of inward feeling in the artworks that marks or grounds the engagements of Murdoch's character Harriet Gavender and of Hustvedt?

A work's ultimate character or import transcends discourse. Interpretive discourse offers only gestures toward decipherment, even if the work's matter is seemingly discursive, as in poetry or fiction. Not only do artworks, as pregnant images embodied in a medium, arise out of a rich reservoir of mental complexity, but Langer's thesis is that they also display, in their materially embodied inner logic, life and mind itself. For Langer, in short, the art symbol *projects a specific and distinctive image of mind*—or phase or dimension of *minding*. But it is not about the mind, even if it is permeated by features proper to minding. These features are what, for both Dewey and Langer, create in and by means of the artwork the *semblance* of being an organic whole and in this way, a dynamic unity of internal relations. Both Langer and Dewey make use of the notion of semblance, although in slightly different ways and with different emphases. But they share a strong sense of the living energetic wholeness of works of art, including even the "quiet energy" of miniatures.

Works of art and mental acts, Langer argues, have "characteristic dynamic forms" (200). Langer's chief, and eminently difficult and contentious, thesis is that the *logical form* of acts, their relational structure, is projected in the art symbol, although the projection does not entail that the artistic elements themselves appear as acts. Rather, the elements of the art symbol have formal properties "which, in nature, characterize acts" (204), such as inviolability, fusability, revivable retention of past phases, tension, gestalt-character, contrast, accent, and rhythm. All these properties are also delineated in so many terms by Dewey. When Langer says that the artwork, in its total qualitative dimension, gives the appearance of "springing out of a matrix or body of potentialities" (207), she is referring to a phenomenal feature or distinctive mode of appearing of the art object. All levels of feeling attendant on bodily existence are reflected, according to Langer, in the artwork: substantiality, depth, unity, individuality or "uniqueness." This last property is the source of the work's "aliveness" or "expressivity," its manifestation of energies. Mind as a *quickening* of nature in the rise of feeling is mirrored in the quickening of expressive media in the artwork, a key notion in Dewey's cognate organism-based aesthetics.

Langer further strengthens Dewey's notion of the energy of objects by introducing the very important concept of *gradients*. "Gradients of all sorts—of relative clarity, complexity, tempo, intensity of feeling, interest, not to mention geometric gradations (the concept of 'gradient' is a generalization from relations of height)—permeate all artistic structure" (211). It is these gradients that make up for Langer an artwork's "rhythmic quality" (212). Now, as Dewey remarked, rhythm is "rationality among qualities" ([1934a] 1989, 174). Langer confirms Dewey in her contention that the phenomenon of *phase beauty*, a notion clearly connected with gradients and transitions, is not only a mark of a work's completion but also the *result* of successive phases, both of its construction and of its perception. Thus, the organization of energies, to return to Dewey, is "cumulating and conserving" (179), analogous to the onward motion of the waves of the sea (177).

Indeed, in one sense, the wave structure of the flow of consciousness is an alternation of compressions and releases and of forms of resistance that prevent the immediate discharge of its energy. By means of this image of a wave structure, Dewey conceives of experience as "progressively enacted," thus extending James's image of consciousness as a series of flights and perchings, which is marked by dynamic balance and equilibrium. However, the "final measure of balance or symmetry is the capacity of the whole to hold together within itself the greatest variety and scope of opposed elements" ([1934a] 1989, 184), mirrored in our bodily existence and its feeling tone as a field of integrated tensions. This is a reformulation of the *unitas in varietate* principle of the classical tradition, a gesture toward the centrality of the "interworking of opposed forces" in a work of art, which entails that everything depends "upon the scale attempted" (185).

Dewey speaks of "reciprocal oppositions" that generate a tension that unfolds in "ordered extension" (186) and give a work of art "volume," which is by no means to be identified with bulk. As he puts it, the property of "extension, of related variety, is the kinetic phase which marks the release of energies that are restrained in ordered intervals of rest," in another echo of the flights and perchings of a bird image of James. As to this kinetic phase, consider the bearing of the following contentious and value-laden remark by Hans

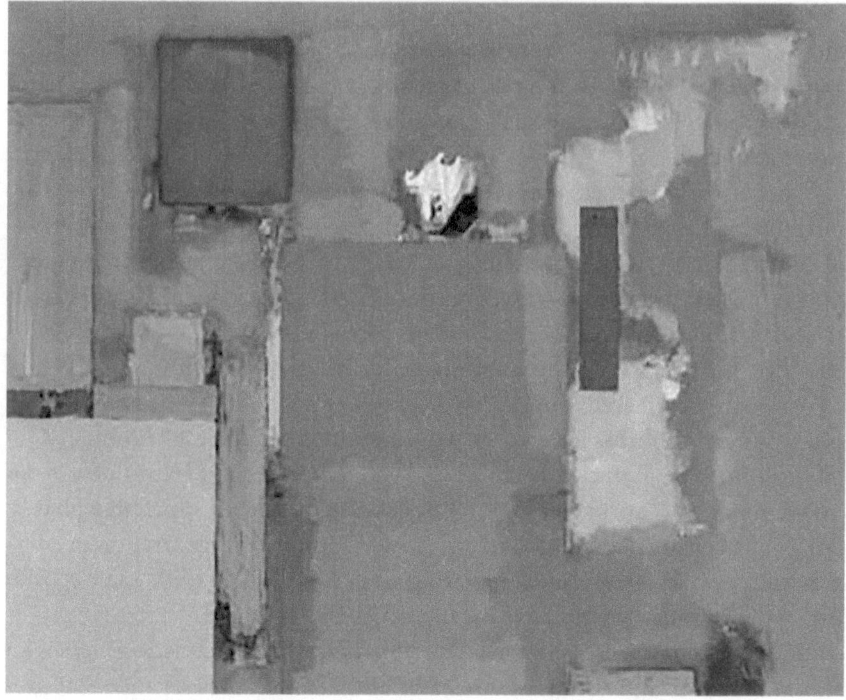

Fig. 2.3. Hans Hofmann, *The Golden Wall.* Source: Art Institute, Chicago.

Hofmann on such markedly different images as Hofmann's *The Golden Wall* (see figure 2.3) or Jackson Pollock's well-known *Autumn Rhythm* (Number 30). "A line concept cannot control pictorial space absolutely. A line may flow freely in and out of space, but cannot independently create the phenomenon of *push and pull* necessary to plastic creation. *Push and pull* are expanding and contracting forces which are activated by carriers in visual motion. Planes are the most important carriers, lines and points less so" (1967, 43). We do not have to accept the value judgment of this comment to acknowledge the analytical terms of flowing, push and pull, expanding and contracting, activation, and so forth.

Dewey recognizes that speaking of energy may seem to some to be out of place in dealing with art, but that one must acknowledge its centrality if we want to understand art's "power to move and stir, to calm and tranquil-lize" and to keep these aspects in some rhythmic balance. Aesthetic effect, as Dewey understands it, "is due to art's unique transcript of the energy of the things of the world." It is a transcript not of things alone, but rather of their energies or potencies. These transcripts, which are symbolic images of all sorts, connect aesthetic effect with "qualities of all experience as far as experience is unified." Art, as Dewey says, "operates by selecting those potencies in things by which an experience—any experience—has significance and value." The energies of objects are, or arise from, the potencies in things. Artworks strive to capture and make them manifest. Deweyan aesthetics demands a "commensurate perception" in order for the artwork—or *any object* that is engaged aesthetically—to be seen as having an "ideal quality," a kind of significance transcending and not reducible to mere factuality. Such a quality arises out of experience and, for Dewey, does not enter into it from some eternal realm of essences. "Order, rhythm and balance, simply means that energies significant for experience are acting at their best" ([1934a] 1989, 189).

For an artifact to be classified as having energy entails that it have a distinctive experiential force. Simply recognizing that it is an art *product* does not entail acknowledging it as having any worth or expressive power. It has value and force to the degree that it *emerges* as a striking figure out of labile grounds, the flat lands of common experience, and thus becomes, through experiential engagement, an art *work*. It is this sense of emergence, and its distinctive unique quality of embodied condensed and cumulative tensive rhythmic order(s), that attracts us and holds us in its grip. This is the point of Langer's claim, which is also Cassirer's, that the absence of a sense of uniqueness, of a distinguishing physiognomic quality, is the source of a work's deadness or lack of expressiveness. It does not give rise to an experiential field with "gradients of growth and development" (1967, 214) embodied or enfolded in it.

## Between Description and Prescription

Dewey's critique of the notion of a separate realm of "ethereal things" that ignores the universal structures and matrices of experiencing broadens the aesthetic field to encompass nature itself in all its forms of manifestation. Langer, for her part, remarks that the artistic image is "incomparably simpler than life" and that the "theory of art is really a prolegomenon to the much greater undertaking of constructing a concept of mind adequate to the living actuality" (1967, 244). The implication of these claims is twofold.

First, if life itself, in all its forms, is more complex than art, which mirrors it and is itself a distinctive form of natural processes rooted in human powers of symbolic transformation, then all of life, and all natural processes, can become objects of aesthetic experience or be looked at aesthetically. The universe itself becomes a realm of ramifying forms of the organization of energies. It is, in the last analysis, our perception and cognate activities that are slack, not the universe, which is itself a vortex of energies.

Second, one of the upshots of Dewey's *Art as Experience* is that it arrives at a position that is almost Zen-like in its prescription that we must learn to experience the suchness of things, to see them as embodiments of qualities in a mode of vision that simply lets them be in both their ordinariness and their extraordinariness. Both art and nature itself in its continuous upsurge of forms present to us objects, as Dewey puts it, "to the construction [and perception] of which the self has surrendered itself in devotion" ([1934a] 1989, 190). Langer writes, "Life is incoherent unless we give it form" (1953, 400). By practices of creative and constructive attending, we participate in the formative processes and energies of nature itself.

What Paul Celan said about poems applies to all art and to nature itself in its boundless creativity and ordered energies: they are "gifts, gifts to the attentive," to those ready to receive. Celan writes, "The attentiveness a poem . . . devotes to all it encounters, with its sharper sense of detail, outline, structure, color, but also of 'quiverings' and 'intimation' [is] a concentration that stays mindful" (1961, 409–410). Jean Daive, in *Under the Dome: Walks with Paul Celan*, characterizes Celan's approach to poetry as giving structure to an illegible world by a "vibration of sense used as energy" (2020, 31). For Celan, citing a remark by Nicolas Malebranche encountered in Walter Benjamin's "Reflections on Kafka," attending to these gifts in all their forms that poetry offers is "the natural prayer of the soul" (1961, 410). And Simone Weil ([1942] 1976), in a letter to Joë Bousquet, called attention "the rarest and purest form of generosity," which she elsewhere described as an attentive openness "ready to receive in its naked truth the object which is to penetrate it" (1951, 72).

Hermann Broch's great novel *The Death of Virgil* presents a striking image of the aesthetic scope of these processes, which, by its very form and material quality, as wedded to its linguistic medium, exemplifies what it is about.

> Certainly many instances of earthly *beauty*—a song, the twilit sea, the tone of the lyre, the voice of a boy, a verse, a statue, a column, a garden, a single flower—all possess the *divine* faculty of *making man hearken* unto the innermost and outermost *boundaries* of his existence, and therefore it is not to be wondered at that the lofty art of Orpheus was

esteemed to have the power of *diverting* the streams from their beds and *changing* their courses, or *luring* the wild beasts of the forest with tender dominance, of *arresting* the cattle a-browse upon the meadows and *moving them to listen,* caught in the dream and enchanted, the dream-wish of all art: the world *compelled* to listen, *ready to receive* the song and its salvation. (1945, 135; my emphases)

In a following passage of startling intensity, Broch ascribes to the dying Virgil (139–140) a fever-drenched dream that revealed an insight that the "duty of all art" was to be found in the process of "realizing the great equilibrium between the ego and the universe" wherein the soul "might recover herself in the universe, in the world, especially in humanity" in a "doubled growth" bound to the "symbolization of the beautiful" that even though "it were but a symbolic perception, it was precisely by this means that it was enabled to widen the inner and outer boundaries of existence to new reality" and reveal as well as effect its "deepest secret . . . the secret of correlation . . . the mutual relation existing between the realities of the self and the world, which lent the symbol the precision of rightness and exalted it to be the symbol of truth" and in its unfolding a "symbol of the human soul" (139–140). It is to considerations such as these that a reflection on the energies of objects leads.

# CHAPTER 3

# Quality and the Theory of Signs

## *Dewey's Peircean Aesthetics*

It is esthetic enjoyment which concerns us; and ignorant as I am of Art, I have a fair share of capacity for esthetic enjoyment, and it seems to me that while in esthetic enjoyment we attend to the totality of Feeling,—and especially to the total resultant Quality of Feeling presented in the work of art we are contemplating,—yet it is a sort of intellectual sympathy, a sense that here is a feeling that one can comprehend, a reasonable feeling. I do not succeed in saying exactly what it is, but it is a consciousness belonging to the category of Representation through representing something in the Category of Quality of Feeling.

—Peirce, "The Seven Systems of Metaphysics"

In light of the doctrine of categories I should say an object, to be esthetically good, must have multiple parts so related to one another as to impart a positive simple immediate quality to their totality; and whatever does this is, in so far, esthetically good, no matter what the particular quality of the total may be.

—Peirce, "The Three Normative Sciences"

## Centrality of the Theory of Quality

John Dewey developed a "Peircean" aesthetics without explicitly developing Peirce's aesthetic hints in the systematic ways interpreters of Peirce's work would like or have projected that Peirce would have done on the basis of the fragmentary hints strewn throughout his writings (see Jappy 2020). Dewey's aesthetics is not an alternative to the aesthetics of Peirce but rather one of its possible—indeed necessary—exemplifications and extensions. Dewey's *Art as Experience,* which makes no mention whatsoever of Peirce, is informed *operatively* by the unfolding of the aesthetic implications of what in his 1935 essay, "Peirce's Theory of Quality," Dewey considered Peirce's most important contribution to philosophy to be: his theory of quality (not his theory of signs or his speculative metaphysics). Toward Peirce's metaphysics and the theory of categories that informed it, he showed little sympathy. It is the notion of quality and the range of its application to, among other things, nondiscursive modes of thought that Dewey developed, again with no overt references to Peirce, in his essays "Qualitative Thought" (1930a) and "Affective Thought" (1931a), which were composed and published before *Art as Experience,* in the gestation period leading up to it. While Dewey does not exploit Peirce's theory of signs in the development of this aesthetic theory, his aesthetics mirrors its main lines. Thus, to speak of Dewey's "Peircean" aesthetics is to claim that there is a deep complementarity or congruence between them.

In "Peirce's Theory of Quality," which was ostensibly written to defend Peirce against a misunderstanding, Dewey sees Peirce's philosophical project as focused first and foremost on "the matter of experience as experienced." In this essay Dewey, while admitting that he was not confident of fully understanding Peirce's account of quality, writes, "I am quite sure that he [Peirce], above all modern philosophers, has opened the road which permits a truly experiential philosophy to be developed which does not, like traditional empirical philosophies, cut experience off from nature" (1935, 375). The intertwined connections between experience and nature were Dewey's lifelong philosophical concern. It is precisely a naturalistic *experiential* aesthetics, not an explicitly semiotic aesthetics, that Dewey wants to develop. Dewey, however, did not neglect the semiotic dimension. Indeed, he saw language and sign use as creative natural processes of specific sorts. When Dewey wrote in *Experience and Nature* that language is not like pipe conducting water and does not merely pass on "perceptions, sentiments, and thoughts which are complete prior to language" ([1925] 1988, 169), the same can be said for his approach to artworks and other cultural forms such as ritual. Artworks, like language, are "not 'expression' of something antecedent, much less expression of antecedent thought" (179). Language and art are "realizations" of thought and serve as indispensable supports and enabling conditions for constructing the shapes of meaning that guide our lives both individually and socially.

Within the descriptively rich matrix presented in detail in *Art as Experience*, one can see the *functional* role of the semiotic factors and their perceptual roots that define the types of significances of artworks as distinctive material sign-configurations, or meaning-bearing forms.

It is the *total felt significance* of such expressive forms that for Dewey induces an experienced aesthetic *threshold crossing* within the flux of experience and gives rise to the Deweyan equivalents of the Peircean "proper significate effects," or interpretants, of an artwork. Dewey calls this threshold crossing "having an experience," as opposed to merely passing through experience or restricting it to the perceptual-manipulative orientation that is the ground level of human-world interactions, a topic treated at length throughout Dewey's whole corpus of writings. Such a having of, or even being had by, an experience with its own individualizing quality is due to the semiotic power of precisely *this* artwork, which is marked by what Peirce calls its "material quality," referring to those characters that it has precisely as *this* sign-configuration and that are apprehended as intrinsic to the experience of it (1992, 43). This is the basis of Dewey's distinction between consummatory and instrumental experiences, for in consummatory experiences, "the meaning is as inherent in immediate experience as is that of a flower garden" ([1934a] 1989, 89). Consummatory experiences are had for their own sake: they are truly, in a Peircean sense, admirable in themselves, being their own end. They are wedded to an object or situation, whether artificial or natural, and it is the experienced quality of the object, event, or situation that, in the first instance, defines the experience.

Dewey characterized Peirce's discussion of quality as rooted in "a logical analysis of experience: an analysis based on what he calls Firstness, of sheer totality and pervading unity of quality in *every*thing experienced, whether it be odor, the drama of King Lear, or philosophic or scientific systems; Secondness, existentiality, or singular occurrence; and Thirdness, mediation, or continuity" (1935, 371). In a late essay (Dewey 1946, 91), Dewey says the metaphysical categories of Firstness, Secondness, and Thirdness have "perhaps not very happy" names and, already years before, confessed to being uncomfortable with Peirce's "panpsychic predilections." While Dewey was not interested in engaging Peirce's metaphysics, he nevertheless foregrounded Peirce's correlates of the categories in consciousness: feeling, existence as conative and involving effort and sense of resistance, and time-binding or synthesis. In sticking resolutely to the phenomenological side of the "logical analysis of a phenomenon, or any experience," Dewey, speaking in his own voice, asserts that "it is through feeling (including sensation as such) that qualities present themselves in *experience*." He then remarks, in a comment that parallels the three Peircean categories, that "existence itself is qualitative, not merely quantitative, is marked by stress and strain, and by continuities" (1935, 375).

If the qualities of things are *presented* or accessed through feeling, then feeling, on the experiential level, is a felt *sign* of quality, a significate effect of encountering a quality. Semiotics in its many forms sees the function of signs quite generally in making their objects known by giving us access to them. It does so by creating some unifying focus that introduces determination, continuity, or dynamic stability into experience. For Dewey, the point of artistic sign-production, as opposed to natural instrumentally oriented perception or the mapping of experience through discursive or formal systems, is to create novel objects that not only present, but in some way embody, the felt qualities of things. Dewey wrote that the purpose of artworks is to capture "every shade of expressiveness" in things, every Peircean tinge of sense, thus making them to be a "unique transcript of the energy of things of the world" ([1934a] 1989, 189).

Peirce, for his part, writes in "The Maxim of Pragmatism" (1998, 143) that aesthetics (esthetics) is concerned with "objects simply in their presentation." These objects are, or can be, material embodiments of new imagined qualities with distinctive feeling tones. They are not just those encountered already in experience, which clearly can induce consummatory experiences of the highest order, as Dewey so clearly showed. Artworks, as sign-configurations encountered in experience, make the presence of objects in their presentation and their generative matrices more intense. As Dewey puts it, glossing Peirce, "anything that is a feeling . . . is of some quality when that is present in *experience*" (1935, 375). Such a situation is epitomized in the intense or marked feeling attendant upon, and giving us access to, what artworks, in being experienced, bear on, rather than merely refer to. Artworks are sign-configurations of some sort, and as signs they must have an object, which can be internal to the sign itself that has created it as a possible object of the creative imagination. This is what Dewey calls the "sound doctrine" of Peirce's theory of quality, which is foregrounded in the "of" that binds feeling to its proper object, whether the feeling is mediated by an artwork or elicited by an existential situation, whether natural or social. And it is this sound doctrine of an intentional bond, of a realm of quality-defined *feeling-signs*, especially of constructed feeling-signs or affect-laden images, that Dewey explores and develops in *Art as Experience* as the phenomenological complement of his Peircean semiotic aesthetics.

Dewey's aesthetics starts low, in the accessible forms of elementary experience, as does, putatively, Peirce's *phaneroscopy*, with its commitment to the play of musement. The same is true of his version of pragmatism, And while Dewey does aim high toward an analysis of the general features of aesthetic experience and the structures and powers of expressive objects, he does not arrive at any putative ultimate formal scheme. Dewey is rather concerned with the "generic traits" of aesthetic experience (continuity, cumulation, conservation, tension, anticipation) that emerge and develop in the flux of our usual and ordinary encounters with objects and situations as experience stives toward wholeness and completion (see Jackson 1998). These generic traits are not to be taken in some a priori way. Rather, they are discovered by reflection on what happens in experience. New traits, as well as the sociocultural scaling of traits in the evolution of novel art forms, can emerge as experience itself evolves and is crystallized in forms, both natural and constructed, that arise in novel artistic practices and the spread of new aesthetic patterns of attending. A recognition of these traits leads to Dewey's central thesis that experience becomes aesthetic through the "clarified and intensified development of traits that belong to every normally complete experience" ([1934a] 1989, 53), a process in which there an "escape from convention to perception" (158) whereby the perceiver as a whole is brought into play. In such forms of experiencing, as Dewey put it in *Art as Experience*, "action, feeling, and meaning are one" (22), an echo, once again, of the Peircean categorial triad, although such a division is not by any means unique.

In one of Dewey's earlier essays, "Qualitative Thought" (1930a), we find a crucial connected observation that bears on his general pragmatist conception of philosophy and its role as rooted in and concerned with the various fields of experience in which we live our lives. It has a direct link to his aesthetics. Dewey writes, "The world in which we immediately live, that in which we strive, succeed, and are defeated is pre-eminently a qualitative world. What we act for, suffer, and enjoy are things in their qualitative determinations" (1930a, 195). Peirce and Dewey (following Peirce's lead) ascribe to everything encountered in experience a defining qualitative tone or tinge. In one of Peirce's enumerations, they include "the color of magenta, the odor of attar, the sound of a railway whistle, the taste of quinine, the quality of emotion upon contemplating a fine mathematical demonstration, the quality of feeling of love, etc." (1931–58, 1:304). Indeed, in another enumeration,

Peirce writes, "The *quale*-consciousness is not confined to simple sensations. There is a peculiar *quale* to purple, though it be only a mixture of red and blue. There is a distinctive *quale* to every combination of sensations so far as it is really synthesized—a distinctive *quale* to this moment as it is to me—a distinctive *quale* to every day and every week—a peculiar *quale* to my whole consciousness" (6:223). Such a notion cuts deep: "Every operation of the mind, however complex, has its absolutely simple feeling, the emotion of the *tout ensemble*" (1:311).

At the same time, Dewey holds that it is a grave mistake to take "qualitative determinations as fixed properties of objects" (1930a, 196). This is the very thing that artworks prevent us from doing. It is one of the main theses of *Art as Experience*. Dewey, of course, does not deny in any absolute sense fixed properties of objects, that is, real properties to which our language and other discursive instruments refer, and thus is not a nominalist in Peirce's accusatory charge. At any rate, fixed properties on the discursive level are intrinsically open to constrained development, in line with the evolutionary orientation shared by both Peirce and Dewey. A realist theory of knowing sees such temporally fixed properties as punctuations of a temporal process. While ideally such properties have a final determination or greatest upper bound, they are not accessible to us. The creativity of art, and of the artist, is oriented toward capturing in material forms, with different degrees of success, every emergent shade of expressiveness and qualitative determination of things in the world, a semiotic process that likewise has no upper limit. In somewhat different ways both Dewey and Peirce affirm an essential dynamic openness of experience on both its receptive and constructive sides, a widening gyre of significant forms, whether in discursive labors of theory construction and explanatory frameworks or in the material abductive leaps of artistic production.

Dewey clearly saw the universal aesthetic implications of Peircean Firstness, although he was not interested in such terminological novelties. Dewey had argued in his "Context and Thought" (1931b) and his *Logic* ([1938] 1986), which incorporated and developed central themes from earlier essays, that the discursive formations of propositions likewise arise out of a qualitative matrix of problematic situations, the originary and prepredicative "subject matter," what is being thought about or confronts one as needing to be dealt with in some form another. Thought in propositions, he writes, is "the integral development and reconstruction of subject matter." Such thought is controlled by this subject matter which, in the last analysis, is "totally and intimately" pervaded by a quality that makes the phenomenon encountered to be "just the one experience which it is." This quality, Dewey claims, is "ineffable" in the sense that it cannot be objectively denoted in such a way that it is not embedded in another experience with its own quality, in fact, a "totalizing unifying quality" (1935, 373).

This embedding quality, which frames every embedded quality, cannot be captured without residue in propositions, since these propositions would themselves be embedded in another total unifying quality. But what is most important for seeing a semiotic dimension in Dewey's aesthetics, when, as Dewey says, thought "goes out into symbolization," is that this does not mean exclusively propositional symbolization. Thinking so is a result of what Dewey called "that species of confirmed intellectual lockjaw" (1908, 133) exemplified in the epistemology industry, which would leave "thought in certain subjects without any logical status and control" (1930a, 196). Among these certain subjects, Dewey thinks, is aesthetics, along with morals and politics, for the analysis and judging of which aesthetics is of utmost importance because it supplies aesthetic norms, as Dewey discusses in the later chapters of *Art as Experience* ([1934a] 1989).[1]

## Going Out into Symbolization

Peircean semiotics clearly explodes the claims of uniqueness and exclusive power of propositional symbolization and the consequent linguocentrism attendant on it. Dewey's aesthetics, and indeed his operative semiotics, likewise opposes linguocentrism, even if Dewey rightly characterizes language as "the tool of tools . . . the cherishing mother of all significance" ([1925] 1988, 186; see also Innis 2018c). It is, after all, the language animal *qua tale* that produces art spontaneously and universally. Art as we know it, as well as ritual, sacrament, and myth, is produced by speaking beings who are aware of, or confronted by, the limits of language and turn, or are turned, to other authentic forms of meaning-making and expression systems in order to give sense to the world in an authentic and stable manner (Innis 2008). Dewey's aesthetics is oriented toward establishing or following the complex and diverse

---

1. I have discussed extensively some other aspects of this importance in "Pragmatist Aesthetics as Critique of Technology," chap. 5 in Innis 2002, and in Innis 1987.

experiential and constructive processes of how artworks are produced by a distinctive "going out into symbolization" that results in the creation of *objective forms* defined by, or embodying in a medium, a unified, even if complex, total quality. Such an objective form clearly belongs to the Peircean realm of iconicity and the different modalities of iconic signs. Dewey's general tendency throughout *Art as Experience* ([1934a] 1989) is to use *images* as a cover term. An art image functions as a frame for intensifying experience by bringing the defining quality and formal features of an occasion of experience to light and stabilizing it so that it can be returned to time and again. This form of symbolization is Langer's presentational symbolization ([1942] 1957, 1953, 1967–82; see also Innis 2009; Chaplin 2020). It involves a different type of abstraction than the generalizing abstraction that defines language and discursive systems and offers a key to exploring the whole realm of nondiscursive forms, such as ritual, sacrament, and myth, along with art in all its diverse forms.

Art images emerge out transformations of the primary matrices of experiencing, or what Peirce called the bottomless lake of consciousness and its forces operating below the surface (1931–1958, 7:457). These matrices are explored in different registers in the work of Anton Ehrenzweig (1965, 1971) and of Marion Milner (1957), where gestalt-free perception and the spontaneous and unplanned ordering of chaos are subjected to close examination. And while it is evident from the foregoing that Dewey was aware of, and alluded to, Peirce's inextricably linked triad of feeling, action-reaction, and thought, which models experience as a whole, the operative phenomenological basis and model of experience that permeates *Art as Experience* is the theme-field-margin schema of James's *Principles of Psychology* and the background flights and perchings image he uses to describe the transitive and substantive aspects of consciousness. The production of artworks is rooted in processes of seeing the constellations of experiencing themselves as pregnant with qualitative significances, the physiognomic valences that tinge and tone experience, and making a symbolic abstraction of their form. Langer, in *Feeling and Form*, characterizes this process in a fertile passage that is cited in different places in the differently focused analytical paths we are exploring in these chapters: "The comprehension of form itself, through its exemplification in formed perceptions or 'intuitions,' is spontaneous and natural *abstraction*, but the recognition of a metaphorical value of some intuitions, which springs from the perception of their forms, is spontaneous and natural *interpretation*. Both abstraction and interpretation are intuitive, and may deal with nondiscursive forms. They lie at the base of all human mentality, and are the roots from which both language and art take rise" (1953, 378).

This continuing experience of spontaneous abstraction growing by its edges and always haunted by what James called the "evermore" is a focal point of a text (also cited in other chapters), in which Dewey delineates the essential openness of experience and what artworks attempt to do: move us beyond the threshold of mere convention toward the grasp of the metaphorical value of some intuitions. Qualitatively infused images of the forms of the spiral of experience frame a significance beyond themselves, manifesting a fused as well as transferred sense of significance.

> We are accustomed to think of physical objects as having bounded edges; things like rocks, chairs, books, houses, trade, and science, with its efforts at precise measurement, have confirmed the belief. Then we unconsciously carry over this belief in the bounded character of all *objects* of experience (a belief founded ultimately in the practical exigencies of our dealings with things) into our conception of experience itself. We suppose the experience has the same definite limits as the things with which it is concerned. But any experience, the most ordinary, has an indefinite total setting. Things, objects, are only focal points of a here and now in a whole that stretches out indefinitely. This is the qualitative "background" which is defined and made definitely conscious in particular objects and specified properties and qualities. . . . This sense of the including whole that is implicit in ordinary experiences is rendered intense within the frame of a painting or poem. ([1934a] 1989, 197–198)

Speaking of the distinctive quality of pictures, Dewey writes: "It is something which externally demarcates it from other paintings, and which internally pervades, colors, tones, and weights every detail and every relation of the work of art" (1930a, 196; see also chapters 1 and 2). The picture, or indeed any artwork with its distinctive medium, emerges out of an engagement with a total subject matter to which the artist is attending by being *with and within it*. The artist captures, or aims to capture, a focal feature of the subject matter, in a unique, but by no means, exhaustive way by trying to find, with different degrees of difficulty, the appropriately fitting sign-configuration in which to embody it. The artwork can be seen as a hypothetical solution to a felt problem and, in this sense, is initially the result of an abduction, a generative idea, which in its material working out can also fail to present or be adequate to its object (a quality itself in its uniqueness because it lacks *expressiveness* or *livingness*, concepts that are discussed in chapter 2). This total subject matter, the complex internal object of the artwork, is not stated but rather is presented in the artwork—Langer's *presentational form*, as opposed to a *discursive form*.

This is a theoretical point that transcends art genres, as Dewey shows in several rich chapters in *Art as Experience* discussing the common and varied substances of the arts. The toned felt perplexity of the poet that Schiller described, the felt sense of a pregnant life episode as a kernel for elaboration and determination by the poet or fiction writer, the imagined space that guides the architect's eye and hand, the bodily feel of a gestural configuration in time of the dancer and choreographer, the striving toward the realization and development of the felt logical structure of a musical composition by the composer and the need to hold it in mind by the conductor and performer, all exemplify Dewey's general Peirce-confirming or Peirce-exemplifying analytical point.

Dewey's aesthetics complements and concretely illustrates Peirce's insight or claim that the artwork, as belonging to the iconic dimension, embodies in its material configuration or medium as a particular type of sign-configuration the defining quality of its subject matter. Engaging the artwork mediates a felt sense of significance, with attendant forms of directed attention to and grasp of a complex pattern of terms and relations. The "total resultant quality of feeling" that Peirce sees the artwork engendering incorporates the three Peircean dimensions of interpretants, the affective or emotional, the energetic, and the logical. When Dewey writes in a broad sense that "the existence of unifying qualitativeness in the subject-matter defines the meaning of 'feeling'" (1930a, 198), the subject matter is *felt life* in its inexhaustible variety that pragmatism takes as its field of concern and that "quickens" the live creature arising out of the aesthetic encounter. The artwork, which is embodied in the art product as a sign-configuration, furnishes the objective frame of the *form of feeling*, to use Susanne Langer's phrase, in which a subject matter, whatever it is, is presented in its immanent significance and not simply pointed to. Every feature of the artwork points to and is absorbed into the immanent intentionality and vectorial directionality of this form. The frame, or organized medium, and the subject matter, the thing-meant, share a distinctive felt quality: the framed totality exhibits the distinctive quality of what it is about, its object, which is a central notion in Buchler's theory of judgment (1966, 1974, 1979) and in Nelson Goodman's (1976, 1978) rather differently motivated approaches to art. This is why Dewey says in *Art as Experience* that the artist is skilled in thinking *in* qualities and not just *about* qualities. Such a remark is consonant with Peirce's own practices.

### Imaginal, Diagrammatical, and Metaphorical Dimensions

The artist thinking in qualities is thinking iconically. On the practically universally known Peircean semiotic principles, icons are defined by qualities shared between themselves and their objects. This is a logical relation. The iconic sign or sign-configuration, by reason of its materially embodied form, which results from a presentational abstraction of an object's felt significance, construes as well as constructs its object, to which it is inextricably linked. It is therefore both a means of interpretation and itself something to be interpreted. It is not a duplicate of the object but rather a presentation.

Just as Peirce divided signs into multiple classes, the most famous and fundamental being the universally known triad of icon, index, and symbol, he also divided icons into a triad of hypoicons of images, diagrams, and metaphors, depending on "the mode of Firstness of which they partake," a terminology that Dewey would no doubt hesitate to employ, but that allows Peirce to make the following triadic distinction concerning icons: "Those which partake of simple qualities, or First Firstnesses, are *images*; those which represent the relations, mainly dyadic, or so regarded, of the parts of one thing by analogous relations in their own parts, are *diagrams*; those which represent the representative character of a representamen by representing a parallelism in something else, are *metaphors*" (1931–58, 2:277). Dewey makes no explicit reference to or use of Peirce's triad of images, diagrams, and metaphors, nor of the icon, index, symbol triad, in his discussion of art. Nevertheless, it is possible to see Peirce's logical differentiation of hypoicons mirrored and applied in Dewey's pragmatist phenomenology as aspects or dimensions of an artwork—imaginal, diagrammatic, metaphorical—that bind it, and us, to its object or subject matter by differently weighted ways in which the artwork is internally iconically structured.

This division of hypoicons is another formulation in the category of Firstness of the iconic, indexical, symbolic triad of how signs relate us, through their interpretants, to their objects. There follows the consequent triad of affective or emotional, energetic, and logical interpretants and their psychological correlates as exemplified in the fundamental categories of consciousness: feeling, action-reaction, and thought. These three dimensions of our fundamental modes of engaging the world are all embodied in and brought into relation by artworks. As carrying an import, a synthetic unity, an artwork belongs to the symbolic dimension, exemplifying and arising out of the mediating synthesis of a manifold of experienced qualities and material particulars, and thereby supplying a principle of unity that controls our apprehension of something to be felt and understood, steered by attentional practices imposed by the artwork. These dimensions inform and structure the aesthetic going out into symbolization of the qualitative matrix of all experiencing, which is, as Dewey put it, "the background, the thread, and the directive clue in what we do expressly think of" (1930a, 198; Innis 2014)—in this case, "think of" in the way of art as a form of inquiry or, as Justus Buchler put it, "query" (1974).

Artworks as living *images* of a felt quality lie at the heart of Dewey's developed and Peirce's incipient and fragmentary aesthetics. But art images have a *diagrammatic* dimension involving relations of parts such that the quality the images make manifest is embodied in *material relational patterns*. These patterns "fit" their objects such that they condition or define the tone of the artwork, which clearly needs not be harmonious in any simple sense. What Langer called the morphology of feeling has to be embodied, as a pattern, in a presentational form. An artwork is clearly not an existential graph or a logical structure in the discursive sense, but when Dewey, in his discussion of intuition, speaks of the grasp of "terms and relations" governed by a defining quality, it is clear that these terms and relations have some indexical feature even though they do not necessarily have an existential connection with some everyday object. They are terms and relations that are immanent in a form. It is a pattern of internal relations correlated with and intrinsically linked to their object, a form of feeling. Still, as Dewey points out in a passage that would have pleased Peirce, while scientific thought in diagrammatic mode may not, but clearly could, have the *felt intensity* of artistic thought, it is nevertheless a "specialized form of art, with its qualitative control. The more formal and mathematical science becomes, the more it is controlled by sensitiveness to a special kind of qualitative considerations" (1930a, 200). Artworks have formal material features unique to themselves that uniquely define and enable access to their felt sense, just as the world of scientific objects is only accessed through complex symbol systems and experimental apparatus.

In this sense, the diagrammatic character of the artwork, in the ideal case, *constrains* our engagement with it, *resists* assimilation to a preconceived significance, and *furthers* our grasp of it. It is also one of the sources of the degree of energy in the artwork, which Dewey analyzed in the indispensable chapter in *Art as Experience* ([1934a] 1989) on the organization of energies (discussed in chapter 2). Such a phrase refers to the power of the artwork to connect the perceiver or interpreter to the artwork itself and to put them into motion and move them, thus inducing the Deweyan equivalent of the Peircean action-reaction characteristic of the energetic interpretant. Such an interpretant is felt, to lessor or greater degree, as a modification of the somatic tonus or attentional tension accompanying our embodied existence and conduct. The diagrammatic dimension of an artwork covers the double-faced indexical aspect of the artwork that binds the artwork to its internal object and binds the embodied subject or perceiver as a *felt force* to the artwork and to what the artwork is about.

As for the metaphorical aspect, Dewey's discussion of the association of ideas is of extreme importance. It continues to foreground the central role of quality in the aesthetic domain and indeed intersects with Peirce's characterization of the iconic nature of metaphor. Recall that Peirce thinks of metaphor as based on or informed by a parallelism. A parallelism is fundamentally a kind of linkage. Now, on Deweyan grounds, metaphors are another way in which a quality is captured by the process of going out into symbolization that embodies qualities in forms and sign-configurations, whether discursive or not. Iconicity in the metaphorical mode, independently of form of material embodiment, is based on a link or binding that articulates what Langer, as opposed to Peirce, was not afraid to call an "idea"—or an "import," to distinguish it from a discursive idea or instrumental concept.

What does Dewey offer for determining the status of this metaphorical link or linking dimension in the aesthetic realm? And what does it have to do with association? Dewey's main general thesis is that "existentially, thinking *is* association as far as the latter is controlled." Association means "connection of objects or their elements in the total situation having a qualitative unity" (1930a, 202): the blotting-paper voice, the dark night of the soul, the balance of powers, the flash of insight. The Peircean point here, with another echo of the Peircean categorial triad, is to be found in Dewey's use of the word "connection," which is his term for *synthesis*, whether operatively performed or elicited spontaneously in a process of undergoing.[2] It is association in this sense that binds elements together. This binding, as Dewey analyzes it, is rooted in a

---

2. These topics are taken up with nuance and aesthetic sensitivity by Hausman (1984, 1989).

sense of mutual belongingness, exemplified, in Dewey's homey example of the difference between a bird in a nest as a "single total object" and a nest and the branches of a tree. Mutual belongingness points to an affinity rooted in a shared quality. The bird in a nest has a unique feel, while a nest on a branch does not, just as the "flash" of insight has a different feel from the "burp" of invention.[3]

Dewey's idea, apart from the topic of metaphor, is that a "situational object" is connected by a felt sense of pertinency and relevance of elements that belong together in ways that cannot be said, but which inform our saying. While the analysis of the situational object—for example, a painting—can devolve into a differentiation of separate objects or formal features, these are held together by the unitary quality exemplified in the objects, forces, or features appearing in the painting *if they fit*. The painting can fail, as all artworks can, by lack of fit, as words can fail to fit in a poem, or gestures and movements in a dance, and so forth. It is this sense of an *achieved unifying* quality that produces the connections between presented objects and their features. Artists are dedicated to constructing such situational objects—artworks—with their webs of felt connections or connecting elements. For Dewey, a felt quality, which is grasped by the artist and indeed is grasping the artist, induces a search for material configurations that will embody it. Such a quality is what is first apprehended in an aesthetic encounter with these configurations which must be found or discovered by the artist in an abductive process. The flash of insight leads to immense labor, but the flash comes, not by the deliberate striking of a match, but rather by being caught up in a play of forms and ideas over which one has no control. In this way Dewey extends Peirce's account of abduction, and indeed echoes Schiller's reflections, which so influenced Peirce, and points toward the model of play exploited by Gadamer in his own treatment of the domain of art (discussed in chapter 1).

## Deweyan Interpretants and the Artwork

Dewey's pivotal and well-known distinction between the art *product* and the art *work* has hermeneutical importance and foregrounds different aspects of the nature of interpretants. Dewey's art product, when looked at within a

---

3. See M. Johnson 2007, which treats the themes engaged in this book in complementary ways and with fine examples.

Peircean framework, is the material or individual iconic sign-configuration. The art work is the experiencer's realization of the art product, making it come alive in the perception and imagination of the experiencer—and of the producer, too. Dewey admits that the producer or artist also stands in relation to the artwork as an interpreter, able to be surprised by the novel meanings expressed in it, including those meanings arising in the complex processes of creation of the work. Realization, in Deweyan terms, is described as a kind of intuition, but it is not immediate; rather, it is a form of mediation, which is both constructive and interpretive. Dewey writes: "Intuition . . . signifies the realization of a pervasive quality such that it regulates the determination of relevant distinctions or of whatever, whether in the way of terms or relations, becomes the accepted object of thought" (1930a, 199).

For Dewey, intuition in this sense is an outcome of complex processes of inquiry—aesthetic inquiry. Such an outcome, whether productive or receptive, underlies our laconic characterizations of what it is that we have grasped, or been grasped by. An intuition, in Dewey's account, aims to "sum up and integrate prolonged previous experience and training, and bring to a unified head the results of severe and consecutive reflection" (1930a, 199). This bringing to a "unified head" is the work of synthesis, or time-binding: Peirce's category of Thirdness in the categories of consciousness. It is interpretation in the deepest and widest sense as interpretive synthesis. Such a synthesis is dependent both on the receptivity and activity of the interpreter or perceiver and on the artwork's semiotic or perceptual agency or energy, which engenders, in the ideal case, the range of significate effects that it is fit to produce.

Peirce offered two schemas of interpretants that are important for this discussion. One schema distinguishes between emotional or affective, energetic, and logical interpretants. This schema follows the distinctions between the three categories of consciousness. Peirce never repudiated his claim that "every kind of consciousness enters into cognition" (1931–58, 1:381). Such a claim also encompasses the experience of artworks, which is rooted, to be sure, in the semiotic structure of experience itself as a play of signs all the way down and all the way up, a theme I have explored elsewhere (Innis 1994). Although feelings, in Peirce's words, "form the warp and woof of cognition," and while "the will, in the form of attention [to the other], constantly enters," cognition is neither feeling nor the polar sense. It is, as Peirce says, "consciousness of process, and this in the form of the sense of learning, of acquiring, of mental growth." It cannot be immediate for it cannot be "contracted into an instant." It is "the consciousness that binds our life together. It is the consciousness of synthesis" (1931–58, 1:381). So, as Peirce says, we have "three radically different elements of consciousness, these and no more" (1:382). All of these elements or dimensions of consciousness—feeling, steered attention, synthetic processes of unification—are put into play in engaging artworks.

The second schema classifies interpretants as immediate, dynamical, and final. Peirce characterizes the immediate interpretant in a number of ways as "the *Quality* of the impression that a sign is fit to produce, not any actual reaction" (1931–58, 8:315), "the total unanalyzed effect that the Sign is calculated to produce, or naturally might be expected to produce . . . the effect the sign first produces or may produce upon a mind, without any reflection upon it . . . the peculiar interpretability" of the sign "before it gets any Interpreter." As to the dynamical interpretant, it is the "direct effect actually produced by a Sign upon an Interpreter of it, . . . that which is experienced in each act of Interpretation and is different in each from that of any other" (1977, 110–111). The final interpretant, which plays a role in Peirce's realist theory of knowledge, is "that which *would finally* be decided to be the true interpretation if consideration of the matter were carried so far that an ultimate opinion were reached" (1931–58, 8:184) or "the one Interpretative result to which every Interpreter is destined to come if the Sign is sufficiently considered" (1977, 111), which is clearly a problematic notion for the interpretation of artworks.

Each of these schemas has a certain analytical value, and one need not try to determine their ultimacies. The pragmatist phenomenological perspective that Dewey operates with, as opposed to a semio-epistemological approach, foregrounds and makes concrete principally the intertwining of the perceiver-centered dynamic interpretant whose dimensions are precisely the affective, energetic, and logical interpretants that follow the triadic schema of consciousness. In the aesthetic domain especially, the response of the self to artworks and to all objects of aesthetic interest is an interwoven and differentially weighted complex of factors, which can be described in multiple ways depending on the vast continuum of differences in the affective, actional, and conceptual systems of the perceiver. Peirce's "total resultant Quality of Feeling" brings the whole self *as an embodied being* into play. Dewey gestures toward this complex of factors by foregrounding, first and foremost, its bodily rootedness in the passage from *Art as Experience*, where he delineates essential features of the interaction between perceivers and the environment that clearly are applicable, not just to the perception of a painting, as has been pointed out, but, mutatis mutandis, to other art forms, such as sculpture, music, dance, or even walking about in a city.

It is not just the visual apparatus but the whole organism that inter-acts with the environment in all but routine action. The eye, ear, or whatever, is only the channel *through* which the total response takes place. A color as seen is always qualified by implicit reactions of many organs, those of the sympathetic system as well as touch. It is a funnel for the total energy put forth, not its well-spring. Colors are sumptu-ous and rich just because a total organic response is deeply implicated in them. ([1934a] 1989, 127)

This total organic response involves a form of engaged criticism that we could call *diacritical judgment*. Such judgment aims to be adequate—in the deepest sense of *adequatio*—to the significant differences of and in its objects. The use of the term diacritical judgment can be taken as referring to the self-reflective and self-analytical nature of our becoming aware of how the significate effects of an artwork are grounded and what they are. Dewey writes:

Criticism is judgment. The material out of which judgment grows is the work, the object, but it is this object as it enters into the experience of the critic by interaction with his own sensitivity and his knowledge and funded store from past experiences. . . . [J]udgments have a com-mon form because they all have certain functions to perform. These functions are discrimination and unification. Judgment has to evoke a clearer consciousness of constituent parts and to discover how consis-tently these parts are related to form a whole. Theory gives the names of analysis and synthesis to the execution of these functions.

They cannot be separated from each other because analysis is dis-closure of part as parts of a whole; of details and particulars as belong-ing to a total situation, a universe of discourse. This operation is the opposite of picking to pieces or dissection, even when something of the latter sort is required in order to make judgment possible. No rules can be laid for the performance of so delicate an act as determination of the significant parts of a whole, and of their respective places and weights in the whole ([1934a] 1989, 313–314).

Dewey does not assume that interpretation as realization is the work of some-one, or on someone, without a body. And neither does Peirce: "Each man has his own peculiar character. It enters into all he does. It is in his consciousness and not a mere mechanical trick. . . . [A]s it enters into all his cognition, it is a cognition of things in general. It is therefore the man's philosophy, his way of regarding things; not a philosophy of the head alone—but one which pervades the whole man. This idiosyncrasy is the idea of the man" (1931–58, 7:595). Peirce proposed in laconic fashion that the idiosyncratic "idea" of a person that pervades the whole man and not the head alone is the felt unity—or disunity—of the affective, actional, and thought fields, embodied in habits, that make up a person's life and make up their fore-structures of existence. It marks the felt pervasive quality of a person's life. The body, with its in-dwelt, complex field of resonances, is fully implicated in the work of interpretation in all forms and at all levels, resulting in *the total organic response*, in a continuum stretching from the lowest to the highest thresholds. The artwork, according to Dewey's principles, is the living image of an ultimately ineffable affective tone that grasps us and to which we respond in ways that are dependent on the dynamic tensions between our affective, actional, and intellectual commitments.

## An Exemplification: Engaging Michelangelo's *Moses*

### *Robert Browning*

In the church of St. Peter in Chains, in Rome, there is a remarkable sculpture of Moses, by Michelangelo (see figure 3.1). Here is how the poet Robert Browning engaged it in sonnet form, even as it engaged him, in his attempt to capture or respond to its distinctive or defining quality.[4]

The "Moses" of Michael Angelo

And who is He that, sculptured in huge stone,
Sitteth a giant, where no works arrive
Of straining Art, and hath so prompt and live
The lips, I listen to their very tone?
Moses is He—Ay, that, makes clearly known
The chin's thick boast, and brow's prerogative
Of double ray: so did the mountain give

---

4. http://www.bartleby.com/98/76.html; cited in Hollander 1995, 163.

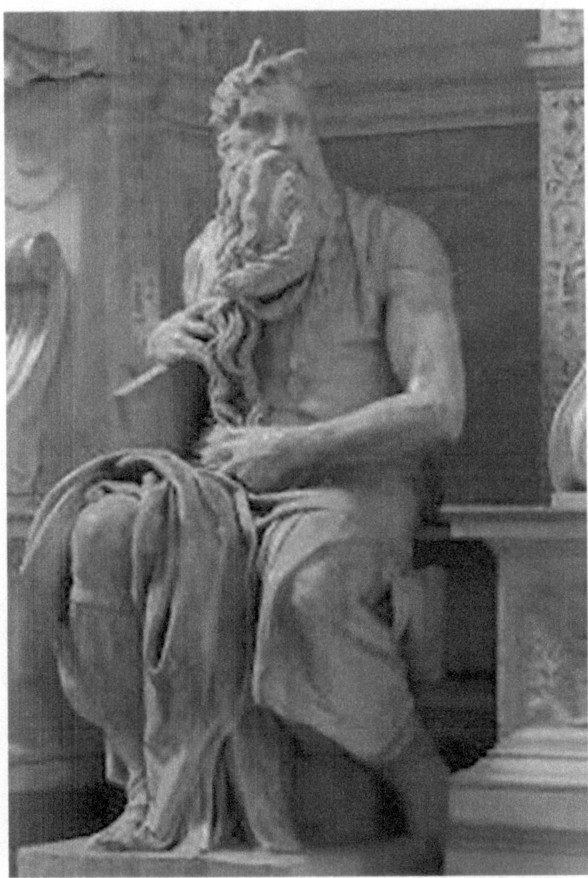

Fig. 3.1. Michelangelo, *Moses*. Source: Saint Peter in Chains, Rome.

Back to the world that visage, God was grown
Great part of! Such was he when he suspended
Round him the sounding and vast waters; such
When he shut sea on sea o'er Mizraïm.
And ye, his hordes, a vile calf raised, and bended
The knee? This Image had ye raised, not much
Had been your error in adoring Him.

The paradoxical tension of this poem is the double ascription, by a kind of metaphorical apprehension, of a divine aura both to the visage of Moses, a visage of someone who has been face to face with the divine visage, and to

Michelangelo's image of the visage of Moses. Art and divinity appear conjointly in the statue. Browning's poem is itself a complex interpretant, a critical judgment of value and a detailing reenactment of a perceptual engagement. It points to the overpowering *quality* of the stone image, which, in a sense, moves it to a place that intimates through association the divine nature of artistic creativity. It is a judgment grounded in details appearing in or on the form: (a) a huge stone (which foregrounds the medium), (b) a giant (in every sense of the word, both physical and spiritual), (c) the appearance of lack of effort, no straining art—God's effortless creation by word is assimilated to or associated with the effortless freeing of such an image from a huge stone by Michelangelo, (d) lips from which the announcement or enforcement of the divine message is to emerge, even if the Tablets of the Law are the real locus of the message, (e) our participation of or in divinity shown in his visage from Moses's vision on the mountain and the consequent miraculous power the image has, the perception of which puts us in contact with a divinity who worked, not with words, but with hammer and chisel.

The unfolding of Peirce's emotion of the *tout ensemble* or Dewey's defining quality in Browning's poem involves, not just the *feeling* of being grasped by a determining quality, but also that of being overwhelmed, of undergoing what, in another context, Peirce categorized as a "percussive" *forcing* of attention on and by the visage of Moses, just as Moses's attention was forced by the power of the unnamed source that transformed him. And, of course, on another plane, the seeming rhetorically structured *ironic argument* of the poem is that we, too, could be justified and not reproached for adoring it and dancing before it. It is no "vile calf." Indeed, it is itself, in one sense, "golden."

*John Dewey*

Closer to home, in *Art as Experience*, when speaking of sculpture and its medium, Dewey wrote:

> The emotions aroused by sculpture are of necessity those belonging to what is defined and enduring.... Sentiments of the vague, transient, and uncertain do not go well with the medium. Akin to the architectural in this respect, it differs from it as ... the singular differs from the collective. What is said about art as union of the universal and individual is peculiarly true of sculpture; so much so that the idea that this

union provides a formula for all works of art probably had its source in Greek statuary. Michelangelo's "Moses" is highly individualized, but it is no more generic than it is episodic, for the "universal" is something quite different from the general. The attitude of the sculptured figure with its energetic but restrained forward impulsion expresses the leader who sees from afar the promised land he knows he will not enter. But it conveys, in a highly individualized value and feeling, the eternal disparity of aspiration and achievement. ([1934a] 1989, 237–238)

In the following paragraph Dewey writes that "emotions to which the medium is best suited are finish, gravity, repose, balance, peace" and a little later adds, "To portray the human form in the guise of the gods and semi-divine heroes is not an enterprise to be lightly undertaken" (238).

Key themes of Dewey's aesthetics, with their Peircean echoes, are put into play in this paragraph: (a) the expressive power of a medium, with the significance of an artwork growing out of the medium, not imposed upon it, (b) the artwork as the union of the universal and the singular, which the figure of Moses represents, (c) the ascription of a "restrained impulsion" to the figure of Moses, due not to an episode, which clearly lies behind the statue, but to the eternal tension between aspiration and achievement, not just in the physical sense but also in the deepest spiritual sense; indeed, the promised land is not a physical place that we can occupy. The Tablets of the Law, the symbolic order, also rest uncomfortably, not just in Moses's hands but also in our own, always on the verge of slipping out of our grip, which is certainly a metaphorical aspect of the visual image. Moses is possessed, not just by an idea, but also by a presence that does not so much console as trouble him, challenging him with the sense of a mission he knows he cannot bring to completion. These features are read off the statue and are Peircean indexical features of the form that constrain our engagement with the *Moses*.

It must be admitted, however, that Dewey's own comments are, in fact, rather prosaic, as if he does not grasp the auratic nature of Michelangelo's figure or the significance of the tenuousness of the grasp on the Tablets of the Law, which could be shattered if not kept in Moses's hands and which in fact had almost slipped or been cast away. Not all interpretations are complete or completely adequate. But it is inarguable that there is also a conceptual or philosophical point to Dewey's engagement that brings into focus a different aspect of the object or thing-meant by the sculpture as a multidimensional sign-configuration. Dewey's remarks also bear unwitting witness to the ultimate failure of words to replace the artwork itself, which is governed by another syntax and semantic structure—even if it is embodied in a linguistic form that, as Browning's poem itself illustrates, can only gesture to both perceptual foreground and historical background of the sculpture.

*Sigmund Freud*

In 1914 Sigmund Freud published an essay anonymously in *Imago* titled, "The Moses of Michelangelo." Here is a passage from that essay in which Freud, starting from the head and focusing on the body as a locus of expressivity, interprets the statue as exhibiting different levels of energies and emotional strata. The statue, Freud writes, displays "three distinct emotional strata. The lines of the face reflect the feelings which become predominant: the middle of the figure shows suppressed movement; and the foot still retains the attitude of projected action. It is as though the controlling influence had proceeded downward from above. . . . The [left] hand is laid on his lap in a mild gesture and holds as though in a caress the end of the flowing beard. It seems as if it is meant to counteract the violence with which the other hand had misused the beard a few moments ago."[5] What are those lines of the face whose manifested feelings become predominant? What are those feelings? For Freud, the face of Moses does not show divinization, or the glory of the Lord. Rather, it belongs to the world of stress and strain, of Peircean secondness, a world of resistances in every sense of that term. As to the suppressed movement of the middle of the figure and the attitude of projected action, which Dewey alluded to, what was that action that was aborted? Throwing the Tablets of the Law to the ground? And what is the connection between the mild gesture of the left hand and the violence immanent in the right hand, which appears on the verge of tearing Moses's beard out in anger and disappointment? Has Freud not adverted to the precarious safety of the Tablets, which could easily slip from our grip, and not just that of Moses?

---

5. This text, which is cited in Hollander 1995, is to be found in Freud (1913–14) 1955, 13:230. In the course of his essay, Freud reviews many other interpretations of this sculpture, a topic that has itself become an issue of contentious discussion. The present task has a different goal.

How do we know this? It is because our experience of this statue is, as Dewey would say, *funded*, or because of Peircean *collateral knowledge*. We know the story and the demands it makes on us. Freud engages the *Moses* as an enfolded psychic or somatic history, a presented progression of inner and outer movements. The movements, both past and dynamical and now presented as on the verge of being carried out, make manifest the livingness of an organism despite the hardness of stone. But its inner dynamism is not the type of dynamism of divinization ascribed to the statue by Browning or the type of laconic reflection of Dewey on the appropriateness of a medium. Freud intimates but does not state that the *Moses* is about our relation to the Law. His reflections are more about Moses than about the *Moses*. But, of course, this cannot be described as wrong.

For Freud, the divinity manifested in the *Moses* is not an aura that possesses us. It is duty. The *Moses* gives rise to thought for Freud. Working with the "loaded dice" of language and his ambiguous relation to his cultural tradition, Freud tries to develop or formulate a kind of language-based response to it, perhaps a weakened intellectual interpretant that the artwork gives rise to or effects in him. Freud, with his fore-structures, brings a distinct set of problems to the *Moses*, whose aesthetic features are shunted to the side while physiognomic features, with which Freud as a physician was familiar, are foregrounded. At the same time, Freud's existential relation to the sculpture involves affective and energetic interpretants. It is a charged work even for him. Dewey is right that artworks themselves are not discursive arguments, although they can clearly be argumentative, giving rise to further discursive arguments and reflections. At any rate, we can safely say that Freud simply does not see what Browning and Dewey see even though he does see something: but it is not the promised land and not a divine aura on Moses's face. Here we are on the borderlands of the psychoanalytic approach to art. We are reminded of the Scholastic axiom: *Quidquid recipitur, recipitur secundum modum recipientis*—Whatever is received is received according to the mode of the receiver.

*Giorgio Vasari*

Finally, in Giorgio Vasari's *Life of Michelangelo*, we find another angle of approach to this remarkable statue. Vasari writes:

Michelangelo finished the Moses in marble, a statue of five braccia, unequalled by any modern or ancient work. Seated in a serious attitude, he rests with one arm on the tables, and with the other holds his long glossy beard, the hairs, so difficult to render in sculpture, being so soft and downy that it seems as if the iron chisel must have become a brush. The beautiful face, like that of a saint and mighty prince, seems as one regards it to need the veil to cover it, so splendid and shining does it appear, and so well has the artist presented in the marble the divinity with which God had endowed that holy countenance. The draperies fall in graceful folds, the muscles of the arms and bones of the hands are of such beauty and perfection, as are the legs and knees, the feet being adorned with excellent shoes, that Moses may now be called the friend of God more than ever, since God has permitted his body to be prepared for the resurrection before the others by the hand of Michelangelo. The Jews still go every Saturday in troops to visit and adore it as a divine, not a human thing. (cited in Hollander 1995, 163, 165)

So, we are back to Browning, who apparently in his last line is alluding to Vasari's association of the statue to the Golden Calf that the Jews once again adore. As to Peirce's contention that aesthetic perception is concerned with objects simply in their presentation, Vasari's take is "superficial." It remains on the surface of the body and speaks, out of a theological or biblical frame, of the perceptual properties of the statue, the multisensory "soft" and "downy" hairs of Moses's beard, as a transfiguration or even transubstantiation of stone, as Browning foregrounds. The transfiguration of stone is analogous to, indeed a metaphor of, the transfiguration of Moses, something that he did not do but rather something that he underwent. So, as our rotation of engagements with the *Moses* shows, there is nothing simple about engaging "objects in their presentation."

## Beyond the Propositional

Thinking of artworks as unique transcriptions of the energies of things involves both productive and interpretive abductions. On the productive side, the artwork has to be "materialized," just as it has to be "realized" in the perceiver or interpreter. It is a material process of concrete activity of painting, chiseling, moving strings or hitting keys, writing words, constructing sounds, or moving the body in dance or ritual within the frame of a gestural logic. Such a process unfolds the implications of the generating insight. But a material unfolding of an insight can fail to capture the solution to the problematic situation in which the artist is found or to foresee its implications for bringing it to a stable form. If the initial lure or the resultant felt insight is trivial or not rich enough, no amount of material embodiment will compensate. In addition, the artist can fail for a number of reasons, such as lack of talent or insincerity, to produce an art product that can mediate the insight or idea that informs the projected work. Its semiotic embodiment may be weak and devoid of energy.

Peirce's notion of the emotion of the *tout ensemble* (1931–58, 1:311) is paradoxically the source of the failure of any sign-configuration to capture totally the sense that is intended. It is especially true of artworks that are constructed with quality (Firstness) at their core and are therefore explicitly and thematically aesthetic, that is, they are sign-configurations oriented toward augmented perception in its own right, including imaginative perception. Dewey was extremely forthright concerning the implications of the "failure of words" to say all that is meant in a work of art, which itself exhibits its meaning but does not state it. This is the central message of his two important chapters on expression in *Art as Experience*. In his pregnant essay "Qualitative Thought," Dewey writes: "Language fails not because thought fails, but because no verbal symbols can do justice to the fullness and richness of thought. If we are to continue talking about 'data' in any other sense than reflective distinctions, the original datum is always such a qualitative whole" (1930a, 199).

That the original datum in the case of artworks, even verbal art, is not embodied in a statement and that its significance cannot be captured in a network of statements is clearly a consequence of the artwork's unique multileveled semiotic structure. It is not propositional, but rather, in Dewey's words, superpropositional, even if it is constructed in a way that looks discursive, as in, for example, a poem or a novel. As Dewey says, "There are other meanings that present themselves directly as possessions of objects which are experienced" ([1934a] 1989, 83). Such objects are distinctively, if not exclusively, aesthetic objects, since ritual actions, among other things, also belong in this category. They do not have meaning by merely opaquely pointing away from themselves to the thing-meant. A sign-configuration that points, Dewey writes, "indicates rather than contains meaning" (90).

Inasmuch as an artwork is for Dewey first and foremost an expressive object, whose meaning is individualized, it does not have the generality of a diagram. Its relational pattern, however, does have an intrinsic connection with what it is expressing. As an expressive form it is marked by a defining quality that it shares with its object. It is bound to its object by a unique configuration of material supports, and bears on an "ineffable" core of significance, which we insightfully *feel*, but cannot say, even if such an expressive form could only be produced by the "language animal" that we are. Dewey writes, "The diagrammatic drawing that suggests grief does not convey the grief of an individual person; it exhibits the *kind* of facial 'expression' persons in general manifest when suffering grief. The esthetic portrayal of grief manifests the grief of a particular individual in connection with a particular event. It is *that* state of sorrow that is depicted, not depression unattached. It has a *local* habitation" ([1934a] 1989, 96). But it has no *name*. Still, the diagrammatic dimension of artworks for Dewey has a fundamental, nondiscursive, "rightness," which belongs to the qualitative dimension of a distinctive form of mediating structure and its underlying medium. Peirce and Dewey are in deep agreement here on the substantive plane, although the terminology is not always, or even frequently, the same.

An artwork such as a picture or a poem is, in Dewey's words, "a new object experienced as having its own unique meaning" (92), involving paradigmatically a *fusion* of an emotional tone and a thing-meant. So, when viewed in Peircean semiotic terms, an artwork is a constructed object, an iconic sign with a distinctive feel by reason of being an embodiment of the morphology of feeling. It has, moreover, a distinctive type of indexical binding of perceptual vectors to the thing-meant, whose expressiveness it captures and constitutes, as Hustvedt's experience of Giorgione's *The Tempest* (discussed in chapter 2) foregrounded. Expressiveness for Dewey is the palpable qualitative *how* of an artwork's mode of appearing. It is *the* mark of an iconic sign functioning aesthetically. It foregrounds the material quality of the aesthetic medium, whether the external medium of paint, sounds, bodily movements, and so forth, that is linked to and dependent on the *internal medium* of affect-laden images that shape and realize our awareness at all levels.

The going out into symbolization in the form of the creation of artworks is rooted in semiotic processes at the most fundamental stages of our encounter with the world. Langer, writing independently of Dewey and Peirce and from a perspective that fuses the perceptual with the semiotic, has foregrounded, through rich sets of studies, that "all conscious experience is symbolically conceived experience; otherwise it passes 'unrealized'" (Langer 1967, 100).

To explain it more fully, "as most of our awareness of the world is a continual play of impressions, our primitive intellectual equipment is largely a fund of images, not necessarily visual, but often gestic, kinesthetic, verbal or what I can only call 'situational.' . . . [W]e apprehend everything which comes to us as impact from the world by imposing some image on it that stresses its salient features and shapes it for recognition and memory" (59). This shaping of salient affect-laden features of experiencing through images is materialized in the complex processes by which an artwork, as a constructed image or image-field, comes into being. Its principal function, as I have been detailing, is to generate a *felt insight* or *insight through feeling* into a "toned idea," and so in this way as a concomitant of experience to affect us and give rise to the total resultant quality of feeling or felt life. Artworks move us out of the ordinary into a perceived and imagined world of infinite qualitative gradations of felt sense that penetrate us at all levels of our being.

## Conclusion

A Deweyan aesthetics can agree, and can functionally show, that on Peircean principles, the artwork is a union of iconic, indexical, and symbolic *factors*. Dewey does not argue for, nor feel, the need to argue for this thematic semiotic schematization, which at any rate, it must be admitted, is not unique to Peircean semiotics. We have seen equivalents of the Peircean psychological and semiotic categories and their aesthetic exemplifications functioning operatively in Dewey's rich rotations of the experiential matrices and formal frames of art. Working from the heart of the pragmatist project, Dewey took up and developed in the aesthetic domain Peirce's fundamental insight into the role of quality, the *experienced quality* of all the factors that give art the power to inform and control the *conduct of life* and the *course of experience*. This is the goal and the upshot of pragmatism's deepest principle for living, which is fundamentally to be guided by an aesthetic rationality.

The experienced quality of artworks is informed by an "esthetic rhythm," which is a core theme of chapter 2. Such rhythm is marked by an "ordered variation of manifestation of energy." This kind of variation is not only as important as order, but, in Dewey's words, it is "an indispensable coefficient of esthetic order" (169). "Esthetic rhythm," Dewey writes, "is a matter of perception and therefore includes whatever is contributed by the self in the active process of perceiving" (167). What is contributed by the self is a *funded* response, and such a response is a complex interpretant, with each type, or dimensional aspect, of a total interpretant—affective, energetic, logical—intensified, gradated, and made palpable. Dewey presents the Peircean proper significate effect of a work of art as precisely the felt organization of complex, multileveled energies of the flux of consciousness, as a development of subjectivity and its powers to engage the world in ways not supplantable by discursive instruments, which nevertheless enable us to attend to them in heightened ways. Art allows us to learn what it means to feel the world and what it means to feel the feel of the world. This is the point and teleology of the "going out into symbolization" in the aesthetic dimension. Participation in this going out puts in play experiences of receptive creativity and creative receptivity that potentiate the felt quality of our lives, enable and steer our paths of action and perception, and enrich our understanding in ways beyond words. In short, as I proposed at the outset of this chapter, Dewey's aesthetics is not an alternative to Peirce's but rather one of its possible, indeed necessary, exemplifications and extensions.

# CHAPTER 4

# Aesthetic Naturalism and the "Ways of Art"

## Linking Dewey and Samuel Alexander

### Dewey Reads Samuel Alexander

In a letter to Sidney Hook of May 16, 1930, John Dewey wrote: "Ive [*sic*] just got hold of some things of S. Alexander on artistic production that seem to be very significant metaphysically" (Dewey 1930b). He gave no indication in the letter, which dealt with another issue, of just what these materials were. The year before, while in Great Britain to deliver the Gifford Lectures before traveling on to Europe, he had received an invitation to attend a meeting and to have dinner with Alexander. In a letter of May 5, 1929, Dewey had written that he would especially enjoy the chance "to meet you personally—whom I have often met so instructively to myself in writings—and be honored to be your guest" (Dewey 1929). However, there is no evidence such a meeting occurred.

Alexander was known for his *Space, Time, and Deity* (1920), which was based on his deeply metaphysical 1916–1918 Gifford Lectures. Book 3 of this work includes an eighty-page chapter devoted to values, with a section on "beauty and ugliness." There is no indication in Dewey's work that he had read this book. Over a long period of time after the publication of *Space, Time, and Deity*, Alexander had further engaged with aesthetic and value issues in a variety of contexts and modes. Texts dealing with these topics were integrated and collected in two volumes: *Beauty and Other Forms of Value* (1933) and *Philosophical and Literary Pieces* (1939).

On May 15, 1930, the day before he wrote the letter to Hook, Dewey wrote to Corinne Chisholm Frost, with whom he had corresponded previously, sending her a number of extracts from several pages of a central part of Alexander's essay "Artistic Creation and Cosmic Creation," which clearly is one of the "things" referred to in the letter to Hook. Here is the letter in full, with page numbers to Alexander's essay as found in *Philosophical and Literary Pieces* (Alexander [1927a] 1939). The words that have been struck through are mistakes in transcription on Dewey's part and those in brackets are the correct words in Alexander's text.

Dear Corinne Chisholm,

I just ran across the following in the English philosopher Samuel Alexander. "It has been suggested that the stuff of the world is space-time itself, which physicists hold to be no mere receptacle of things but something quasi-physical . . . [271]. Within this space-time which is below ~~fission~~ [fusion] there is an element which corresponds to spirit and one which corresponds to [~~time~~] [matter], and these are respectively time and space. . . . They are indissoluble ingredients and neither has an existence independent of the other. . . . It follows that all stable things. . . are but groups of motions or changes . . . which preserve their form . . . [272]. The primordial world . . . germinates into the infinite variety of things in all their grades of development. This impulse of creativeness I call the nisus of the universe . . . this nisus is the element of time ~~its~~ in the primordial world, its principle of mobility and restlessness. Yet . . . time could do nothing, could not even be, except for space; which is thus also creative . . . space by itself is but the totality of *events* considered without their movement [273]. The mechanical is penetrated with time which is the predecessor of mind and the mechanical is not opposed to ~~mind,~~ [life] so much as that it is simpler, more uniform, and of more routine a character; so that the functions of life when they harden into custom recede into the material order . . . [275; note especially Dewey's substitution of "mind" for "life"]. So far is natural selection from being incompatible with value that value is rather one way of describing an essential factor of natural selection. For value always rejects unvalue and is established by that process. . . . Natural selection is [in fact] the history of value in the organic world [276]."

Sincerely yours, | John Dewey. (1930c)

These passages reformulate and extend key ideas developed in *Space, Time, and Deity*. Dewey, so far as I have been able to determine, never again referred explicitly to this lecture. The passages he cited, however, are surrounded by, or embedded in, rich treatments of the nature of artistic production and aesthetic experience, which is the central theme in Dewey's *Art as Experience* ([1934a] 1989) and of a central chapter of *Experience and Nature* ([1925] 1988). It is safe to say, in light of his critique of theism, that Dewey would agree with Alexander that it is a mistake to use the analogy of artistic or other finite creation as an explanation for the "ways of the universe," which for Alexander "may be past finding out, but the ways of art need not be" ([1927a] 1939, 258). Alexander's speculative metaphysics and Dewey's descriptive metaphysics, while quite different, agree on this: the origin of the world is not thinkable using the analogy of artistic creation, which is clearly not *creatio ex nihilo*. Accordingly, the line we will follow here to link Dewey and Alexander will be "the ways of art."

In the letter to Hook, Dewey writes of "some things" and not just of one thing. As it turns out, in the chapter on "The Act of Expression" in *Art as Experience* ([1934a] 1989, 70), Dewey cited a passage from another lecture of Alexander, "Art and the Material" from 1925 ([1925],1939), which, while ostensibly dealing with the production of poetry, is meant to be of general aesthetic relevance and application. Alexander writes (given here as cited by Dewey with elisions): "the artist's work proceeds not from a finished imaginative experience to which the work corresponds, but from passionate excitement about the subject matter. . . . The poet's poem is wrung from him by the subject which excites him" ([1925],1939), 213). This passage motivated Dewey to "hang four comments."

- The real work of art is the building up of an integral experience out of the interaction of organic and environmental conditions and energies. (70)
- The thing expressed is wrung from the producer by the pressure exercised by objective things upon the natural impulses and tendencies—so far is expression from being the direct and immaculate issue of the latter. (70)
- The act of expression that constitutes a work of art is a construction in time, not an instantaneous emission . . . the expression of the self in and through a medium, constituting the work of art,

> is *itself* a prolonged interaction of something issuing from the
> self with objective conditions, a process in which both of them
> acquire a form and order they did not at first possess. (71)
>
> - When excitement about subject matter goes deep, it stirs up
>   a store of attitudes and meanings derived from prior experi-
>   ence. As they are aroused into activity they become conscious
>   thoughts and emotions, emotionalized images. (71)

We must assume, notwithstanding only one explicit reference to Alexander in Dewey's writings, that Dewey read in their entirety the essays "Art and the Material" (Alexander [1925] 1939) and "Artistic Creation and Cosmic Creation" (Alexander [1927a] 1939). The hanging comments show that many of their ideas and theses intersect or overlap. The expansion in *Art as Experience* of the themes of Dewey's chapter "Experience, Nature and Art" from *Experience and Nature* developed some key lines of analysis that were drawn, in important respects, by Alexander.

In spite of their different positions on the question of theism, the texts extracted in the letter to Corinne Chisholm point to a deep connection that bears on the contours of an aesthetics rooted in a naturalist philosophical vision: a fundamental metaphysical naturalism marked by processes of emergence, including paradigmatically aesthetic emergences, what Dewey called, in *Experience and Nature*, "emergent growths" ([1925] 1988, 291). Several passages included in that letter bear upon this theme in *Experience and Nature*: "It follows that all stable things . . . are but groups of motions or changes . . . which preserve their form. . . . The primordial world . . . germinates into the infinite variety of things in all their grades of development. This impulse of creativeness I call the nisus of the universe." For Alexander and for Dewey, artworks are created things, multifactored artifacts that embody envisioned forms marked, as we have seen, by what Dewey called the "organization of energies" held in rhythmic balance. Their germination in the dynamic impulse of creativeness generates an infinite variety of things of aesthetic value in all grades of development. The effective locus of their germination, what Dewey called "the live creature," manifests in a special way this universal nisus, striving to express the experienced qualities of the world in novel objects created out of the manifold substances of the world itself.

What can we see in Alexander's two essays that link their two projects? In what ways does Dewey's explicitly pragmatist aesthetics both appropriate and go beyond these links? How do their shared insights further our attempts to locate the place of art and aesthetic experience in a world in process? These questions will guide us in the following discussion.

## Embodiment in a Medium

To begin with what functions almost as ultimate premise for both Dewey and Alexander: the external work of art is not to be thought of as "a kind of translation into material form of something purely mental" (Alexander [1925] 1939, 211). It is not a transferal or externalization of something already essentially complete, as Benedetto Croce, for example, putatively proposed. Although, as Alexander put it, "a poem is not marks on paper, but words spoken or heard," and even if in some modern poetry the visual design of the marks on paper do in fact condition and are fused in a multisensory way with what the poem expresses, the poem itself for Dewey and Alexander is nevertheless a thoroughly material creation, what Dewey called the art product, to be distinguished from the art work, which is "realized" in the body-based interpretive encounter with the art product. And clearly poems can fail just as the chisel and brush of the sculptor or painter can fail to "realize" the art work embodied in the art product, and just as the finishing of a piece handed over to a pupil can also "rob the conception of its vitality" (212), what Dewey thought of as its *livingness* or organic quality, such that the work "seems to move from within" ([1934a] 1989, 180), giving "the impression of life" (181).

Alexander writes that with regard to "the practice of the artist—the condition of mind in which he works," and to the question of what the artistic expression is, the answer is that it is not "the embodiment of imagery or thought in the artist's mind" that is already complete. The poet's thoughts are not "already words," any more than the painter's actions are already complete prior to their mere execution. Using Shakespeare's line, "Wash me in steep-down gulfs of liquid fire" (from *Othello*), Alexander argues that Shakespeare did not have these exact words in mind when he wrote. Rather, they are an "overflow" of his excitement into these words, which are elicited by his drive toward constructing a meaningful expression. Shakespeare was, in Alexander's conception, passionately excited about what he calls the "subject matter," a phrase that Dewey often used. A poem is "wrung" from the poet "by the subject which excites him, and . . . he possesses the imaginative experience embodied in his words just in so far as he has spoken them" ([1925] 1939, 213) or as, in the case of a painter, just insofar as he has marked the surface with his strokes applying pigment. The poem, or the painting, is not a translation of a preexistent content. The poet does not know beforehand just what he wants to say or how he will say it. As for Dewey, both scientists and artists "press forward toward some end dimly and imprecisely prefigured, groping their way as they are lured on by the identity of an aura in which their observations and reflections swim" ([1934a] 1989, 80).

So, what exists for an artist prior to the execution? Alexander answers in words that easily could be ascribed to Dewey: "What does exist is the subject matter which detains him and fixes his thoughts and feeds his interest, giving colour to his excitement which would be different with a different subject matter. Excitement caused and detained by this subject, and at once enlarged, enlightened, and inflamed by insights into it bubbles over into words or the movements of the brush or burin or chisel" ([1925] 1939, 214). The key, for Alexander and for Dewey, is *excitement*: being grasped by a subject matter that *interests* one, pulls one in and toward—an expressive product emerging from one's material-semiotic labor and, indeed, for the perceiver or interpreter, from one's encounter with a work of art that, as Rita Felski (2020) characterized it, "hooks" one. As to excitement, Alexander says: "It is, I suppose, the nervous excitement set going by an object seen or thought of, but it is felt in secondary excitement of the organic system, and may extend all over the body around the heart and down the spine and in the secretory and excretory parts. It is, at any rate, a mass of feeling with a dominant feature of pleasurable tension" (Alexander [1925] 1939, 215–216). Such excitement in art, Dewey remarks, is "excitement-about-something" ([1934a] 1989, 72), not something merely subjective or inner. The emotion of 'being excited' is "*to or from or about* something objective, whether in fact or idea" and involves the "interpenetration of self with objective conditions" (73).

For Dewey, the artist, in realizing an artwork, and the perceiver, in encountering an artwork, are not radically different. The artist, in whatever medium, responds to the progressively developing material production of the artwork: "The real work of an artist is to build up an experience that is coherent in perception while moving with constant change in its development" ([1934a] 1989, 57). Such work exploits a complex medium of supports which, to allude to Gibson's ecological approach to psychology, *afford* the artist's activities. This is Alexander's material in which the artwork is embodied.

The perceiver engages the artwork by not merely recognizing it so as to label it with a glance but, as Dewey writes, in an act of perception that "proceeds by waves that extend serially throughout the entire organism." For Dewey, in the aesthetic dimension "the perceived object or scene is emotionally pervaded throughout," such that it touches us, and we become receptive to it, surrendering ourselves to it by reason of its affective power. Each artwork demands of us an "adequate yielding of self" (59), which is not something purely passive, even if it involves the radical passivity of openness to novelty. Perception is "an act of going-out of energy in order to receive, not a withholding of energy. . . . We must summon energy and pitch it at a responsive key in order to *take* in." Such perceptual taking in is re-creative. Just as the artist selects, simplifies, clarifies, abridges, and condenses, so the perceiver follows in the same way, performing or being caught up in a spiral of acts of abstraction and detailed perception that progressively extract what is significant. These are factors entering into comprehension in the literal sense of the word: "a gathering together of details and particulars physically scattered into an experienced whole" (60).

Alexander foregrounds often as exemplars the sense of fitness of words to situations in the case of poems. This sense is general: it is guided by "the excitement of the proper creative tendency," a tendency in "the ways of speech or movements of the hand directing brush or chisel" ([1925] 1939, 216). The excitement of the artist is a "*directed* one" (217). It is "detained and fixed by the subject matter, and again, because of the specific character of the excitement, it is always on the point of expressing itself in the medium." There is a play of ideas and images in the imagination, but they are not fully formed "anticipations of the expression contained in the work of art." There are "inchoate tendencies to such outward expression. . . . Such inchoate tendencies *are* anticipatory of the ideas embodied hereafter when the labor is complete in the work of art, but are for the most part vague directions or aspirations of the mind which receive definition in the finished work." It is the omnipresence of the vague that overshadows the claim of definite images or words that are merely translated into the finished artwork. The work of art is generated by excitement, a kind of fertile and dynamic vagueness, marked by felt tendencies or vectors, and not by "any imaginative artistic experience" that is prior to the processes of embodiment. The imaginative artistic experience "is generated in and through the expression itself" (217–218). Determining the relations between expression and experience is an ever-present shared concern for Alexander and Dewey.

## Understanding Quality

Alexander, in another link with Dewey, wants to "trace the connection of the experience of beauty with the experience of external things in general . . . while art introduces a creative act, the specific artistic experience, like the cognitive one, is a discovery or revelation." Alexander's position—"we know in and through acting"—is very close to Dewey's core argument in his masterful article "The Unit of Behavior" from 1896. Knowledge, in all its levels, Alexander asserts, "is revealed to our apprehensions and revealed through action" ((([1925] 1939, 220). Alexander claims, using the term *quality* in a way almost identical to Dewey's, that "the point is that an external quality extorts from us through our susceptibility to it an expressive response, and in that response reveals itself." In short, while innocent of any extensive familiarity with pragmatism, Alexander follows James and Dewey in holding that the response determines what the stimulus itself really is, *into* which we respond and not *to* which. In shrinking we realize something *as* repulsive, in fleeing we recognize something *as* dangerous, grasping and eating determines something *as* eatable. Alexander speaks, as Dewey does, of "the discriminating reactions through which differences of sense qualities are revealed to us" (221). The afferent and the efferent, in dialectical continuity, determine the processes of apprehension. Experiencing is a circuit or spiral of self-reconstruction, of action-based perceivings, responding into, segmenting, and constituting experience. Through those responses the objects are revealed to us in selective, and not full, form.

In a characterization of the encounter with a painting, a text cited in other chapters, Dewey fleshes out and exemplifies in a way consonant with Peirce the idea of the apprehension and discrimination of a luring and defining *quality*. "Even at the outset, the total and massive quality has its uniqueness; even when vague and undefined, it is just that which it is and not something else. If the perception continues, discrimination inevitably sets in. Attention must move, and, as it moves, parts, members, emerge from the background. And if attention moves in a unified direction instead of wandering, it is controlled by the pervading qualitative unity; attention is controlled *by* it because it operates within it" ([1934a] 1989, 196). For Alexander, images and ideas, as mental products rooted in the body as matrix of tendencies, are, to be sure, "initiated from within," but they are, in his estimation, best understood "by reference to preparatory or anticipatory movements in a complex experience. . . . Images may be described as expectations . . . in expecting we have ideas," and not vice versa. In our adopting an appropriate behavioral response "the object is presented or revealed in idea" ([1925] 1939, 222), rooted in "anticipation by way of ideas" (223). Indeed, as Dewey writes in *Experience and Nature*, "to be conscious of meanings or to have an idea, marks a fruition, an enjoyed or suffered arrest of the flux of events. But there are all kinds of ways of perceiving meanings, all kinds of ideas. . . . The idea . . . directly liberates subsequent action and makes it more fruitful in a creation of more meanings and more perceptions" ([1925] 1988, 278). When Alexander writes that our perception of an artwork is "always colored by our imputations, so that Hermes in the marble block is for the aesthetic appreciation alive and divine," this notion of imputation is guided by an idea in Dewey's sense as enriching perception, involving the creation of a new meaning ([1925] 1939, 223), or as Dewey puts it, "responding to things in their meanings" ([1925] 1988, 278).

For Alexander, speaking almost as a pragmatist, "fundamentally . . . and originally, things are known to us as they reveal themselves through practice" ([1925] 1939, 223). But as we transition to the aesthetic order we are emancipated from practical interests for the sake of contemplation, which for Dewey constitutes a "consummatory experience." In artistic production a "fresh," "physical" object is created for the sake of appreciative contemplation—or at least, as Alexander puts it, "arrangements of them, words or sound or drawings or pictures or even sculptured stones, external things independent when once created of the creative art. It is these physical creations which become in the end the material of art" (223–224), art *products*, as Dewey says, on the way to becoming art*works* in being "realized" in perceptual-interpretive processes. These are processes of "appropriative enjoyment . . . appreciative possession" ([1925] 1988, 281). Art products, in being perceived, become more than strangely configured material things; they become as Dewey puts it new types of objects, "things-with-meanings" (278) which fulfill "the characteristic human need . . . for possession and appreciation of the meaning of things" (272).

Alexander, in deepest agreement with Dewey, affirmed that these formed objects do not function as mere "signs," pointing away from themselves to something else in the mode of indication. With regard especially to poetry, the type of artwork he is most comfortable with, Alexander writes: "Words or other expressive products become the material of art [when] they are used . . . in themselves for their own sake. . . . Language becomes aesthetic only when it in turn becomes an object, and as such is revealed to the speaker charged with its meaning . . . or fused with it" ([1925] 1939, 224). This fusion of language and meaning is the foundation of the literary work's expressive power just as the material strokes and paint textures are fused with a painting's meaning. Language itself becomes material and not a transparent lattice that is external to the material it is laid over to segment and order, a theme explored in great detail by Roman Jakobson's classic writings (1988). It has a material quality of its own. Neither Alexander nor Dewey avails themselves of a systematic semiotic conceptual scheme such as Peirce's where (as is noted in other chapters) the notion of the material quality of a sign plays an essential role. But such a focus on the material or the medium foregrounds it in a nonmystifying way. As Dewey puts it, art effects "a connection of means-consequence into meanings . . . in art everything is common between means and ends" ([1925] 1988, 277).

Alexander's general point about language as a medium is that the material quality of word, marble, or drawing has "welded into its being the things which it means" ([1925] 1939, 224). Returning to his recurring Hermes example, he writes that it does not "merely mean life and divinity but is divine and alive, in so far as we appreciate it as a work of art," a point made by Vasari and others about Michelangelo's *Moses*, which was discussed in chapter 3. While in the case of poetry the words are "alive with the qualities they mean," in the case of the Hermes, "the dead marble is alive." In a poem words are "new things" (225), just as stone in sculpture becomes flowing drapery or soft, downy skin or supple muscle.

In foregrounding the expressive character of the material, that it is not merely indicative or an indifferent support, Alexander anticipates, with remarkable closeness to Dewey's later form of expression, one of Dewey's main theses. Alexander writes, "Every work of art exhibits unification into an expressive whole" ([1925] 1939, 226), such unification being elicited by the "dominant interest of the subject matter which detains and guides creation." In the "organization of the product" we have a "spontaneous overflow of unified feeling into expressive gestures." These expressive gestures are rooted in a "bodily life . . . rhythmical in its nature," which gives order and stability to the product and "fit it as once to express and knit together the dominant passion excited by the subject matter" (227).

Dewey, for his part, develops this idea in the following way. An artist, working in whatever medium, is not the arbiter of the development of an artwork. It is the subject matter defined by a specific tone or quality, which is not foisted as an external emotion on the material. The emotion emerges progressively from the material, from "the movement of the subject matter portrayed" or in process of being portrayed. In as much as "a sincere emotion . . . controls the material," the artist, in being led by this emerging quality, heavy with its antecedent phases, is able to "fuse everything assembled into a vital whole." Dewey is right to foreground the important phenomenon that "emotion leads one to gather material that is affiliated to the mood which is aroused" ([1934a] 1989, 74). Working with materials becoming the medium for creating an expressive object entails being led by tendencies and felt vectors, a way of thinking that Dewey derived from James's notion of the transitive parts of consciousness, a concept that is absent from Alexander's reflections. In Dewey we sense more than with Alexander the excitement and immediacy of working with stuff, although their positions are substantially identical.

Both Alexander and Dewey emphasize this sense of affiliation or affinity between mood or emotion and material. For Dewey, emotion "operates like a magnet drawing to itself appropriate material: appropriate because it has an experienced emotional affinity for the state of mind already moving. . . . Selection and organization of material are at once a function and test of the quality of the emotion experienced" (75). Order and stability belong to form, and form involves selection of elements as well as their combination. Such a felicitous fitting together of elements engenders what Alexander calls "magic" and Dewey, following James, an "aura." But this aura is correlative, if we follow up Alexander's notion of imputation, to action on our part, creative action on the side of the producer and appreciation on the side of the perceiver. Imputation is something we do along with undergoing. Imputation, in Alexander's reckoning, gives an object its aesthetic character generating appreciation of beauty ([1925] 1939, 227) in both nature and in art. Such imputation "involves a coalescence of the material and the mind" (228) and thus mediates a kind of nonconceptual knowledge involving the play of faculties in the harmonious combination of imagination and understanding limned in Kant's aesthetic theory.

Dewey would certainly agree with Alexander's assertion that "all cognition is discovery in which the object is revealed to the mind" and that it "reveals to [the artist as well as the perceiver] his own meaning, . . . the artistic experience [being] not so much invention as discovery." The artwork can surprise the artist "with the definition of his own mood of mind" ([1925] 1939, 228), just as the scientist is or can be surprised. For Alexander, the public object of art is the instrument by which the artist "acquires that very private experience which is embodied in the work" (229), as we saw Dewey recognizing in his four comments.

It is well known that great artists, and great scientists, have the feeling of being "inspired from something outside themselves." But as to the artist's creativeness, Alexander makes the remarkable comment that would resonate with Dewey's own concerns: namely, that it "conceals from us his real passivity. Every artist is in his degree like Shakespeare, who was a reed through which every wind from nature or human affairs blew music" ([1925] 1939, 229). And we, the perceivers and interpreters of their products, find the wind blowing through us, too, in our open creative appropriation of their contents.


## More on the Medium


In the chapter on "The Varied Substance of the Arts" in *Art as Experience* ([1934a] 1989), Dewey classified the arts not according to sense modalities, but rather according to their mediums, Alexander's "material." Dewey must have seen, in his reading of "Art and the Material," Alexander's contention that "in virtue of the material one art may be more suitable than another to express a given subject, and a particular art wholly unsuitable" ([1925] 1939, 230). Speaking of sculpture in *Art as Experience*, Dewey wrote, in a passage dealing with Michelangelo's *Moses* (cited and discussed in chapter 3), that "the emotions aroused by sculpture are of necessity those belonging to what is defined and enduring. . . . Sentiments of the vague, transient, and uncertain do not go well with the medium. Akin to the architectural in this respect, it differs from it as . . . the singular differs from the collective" ([1934a] 1989, 237). In the following paragraph Dewey writes that "emotions to which the medium is best suited are finish, gravity, repose, balance, peace" and a little later adds: "To portray the human form in the guise of the gods and semidivine heroes is not an enterprise to be lightly undertaken" (238). Of course, Gian Lorenzo Bernini's *St. Teresa in Ecstasy* is not exactly an exemplar of these emotions, nor is the Laocoön statue in the Vatican Museums. But the point is not an individual ascription of appropriateness but rather that of the centrality of the creative fusion of material or medium and subject matter. Alexander claims that the subject matter in one sense chooses by an inner affinity its form of material embodiment and "chooses and modifies the images" such that "the artist finds himself compelled by his material to fresh or altered imagination," and by the "reciprocal moulding of material and images upon each other" ([1925] 1939, 230). Included in the material is the writer's physical pen or, to refer to a famous example, Peirce's inkstand, without which, he claimed, he would not be able to think.

For Dewey, "the selection of materials . . . extracts matter from a multitude of objects, numerically and spatially separated, and condenses what is abstracted in an object that is an epitome of values belonging to them all" ([1934a] 1989, 73). Physical material undergoes change quite generally by being made into media of expression, rooted indeed in the body whose transformation in dance, in what Dewey called the automatic arts, is paradigmatic of the transformation of physical movement into gesture.[1] Inner materials such as images, observations, memories, and emotion are likewise transformed or "progressively reformed." Indeed, "as the painter places pigment upon the canvas, or imagines it placed there, his ideas and feelings are also ordered. As the writer composes in his medium of words what he wants to say, his idea takes on for himself perceptible form" (81). The progressive organization of inner and outer material is "in organic connection with each other." This sense of progression proceeds from "an emotion comparatively gross and undefined" that must be worked through by a "series of changes in imagined material." Long periods of gestation mark the production of the artwork, whose generated idea, to be sure, could emerge in a flash, but only for very few. Most of us lack the "capacity to work a vague idea and emotion over into terms of some definite medium" (82). But in a work of art emotion must be informed by material: "Emotion is informed and carried forward when it is spent indirectly in search for material and in giving it order, not when it is directly expended" (76). Artistic expression is not self-expression, even if the expression originates from a self and the self identifies with it. As Dewey says, in a comment of general relevance, "objective material becomes the content and matter of the emotion, not just its evocative occasion" (74–75). The artwork is not the mere effect of an emotion but rather its formed outcome and embodiment.

## The Materiality of Inspiration

In Alexander's essay "Artistic Creation and Cosmic Creation" ([1927a] 1939), which was written after "Art and the Material," we find the same topics taken up within the context of a deep reflection on emergent theism, not a metaphysical concern for Dewey, although there are aesthetic aspects in Dewey's nontheistic reflections in his *A Common Faith*, as the following passage illustrates: "The idea of a whole, whether of the whole personal being or of

---

1. Langer treats dance in two powerful chapters in *Feeling and Form* (1953), chaps. 11 and 12, pp. 169–208, dealing with "virtual powers" and the "magic circle."

the world, is an imaginative and not a literal idea. The limited world of our observation and reflection becomes the Universe only through imaginative extension. It cannot be apprehended in knowledge nor realized in reflection" (1934b, 18–19). In a passage, cited before, in *Art as Experience*, Dewey had written, with echoes of James, of the feeling that accompanies intense aesthetic perception, that "however broad the field, it is still felt as not the whole; the margins shade into that indefinite expanse beyond which imagination calls the universe" ([1934a] 1989, 198).

Alexander writes that in the artwork "spirit and matter are blended and at one" ([1925] 1939, 259), a more metaphysical way of speaking, which Dewey did not take up in his own account but did cite in the passages sent to Corinne Chisholm. We must assume he found the idea not only interesting but acceptable. For Alexander, in the work of art "form and significance are blended into one" (260) and the "physical material is organic to artistic creation" (261). The subject matter is expressed in a significant form and the artist finds out what he wants to express by expressing it, although aesthetically significant form is also created in the universe's continuous upsurge into novelty, in a kind of burning fountain of forms. What results, in both art and in natural processes, comes as a revelation, a surprise, not able to be anticipated in detail and in its concrete reality (262). The continuous correction of subsequent versions by poets and painters, a process of progressively finding how to realize the subject matter under the constraints of the embodying material or medium, exemplify constraints in natural processes.

The artist, like the blind processes of nature in their unfolding, must find a way: it is not something given beforehand in a definite image any more than nature itself has a definite future. And although Dewey, for his part, thinks of artworks as unique transcripts of "the energy of the things of the world" ([1934a] 1989, 189), Alexander is not happy with the notion of a transcript, which gives the impression that the objects or things-meant by poem or painting exist already complete prior to their external or public expression. The difference with Dewey is purely verbal. The words in poem are not "purely a transcription," but there will always be alteration, selection, amplification, modification. Such progressive corrections are to be found, in fact, in all attempts at creative production, no matter what the genre. In Deweyan terms, a transcript is something active and in the case of an artwork, "unique," a creative transformation into another form.

In "Artistic Creation and Cosmic Creation," Alexander continued to foreground the centrality of the notion of the material quality of an artwork, its distinctive feel or tone. A subject matter coming from all dimensions of life, with its distinctive feel, is embodied, and without this embodiment it is devoid of aesthetic power or force. As to this material embodiment, Alexander writes, "thus and thus only can the subject matter receive the significance he [the artist] imparts to it" ([1927a] 1939, 266). Material conditions both enable and constrain the creation of the work, even if in on occasion its production appears to be effortless, without resistance. Nevertheless, Dewey has it fundamentally right: "Suddenness of emergence belongs to appearance of material above the threshold of consciousness, not to the process of its generation" ([1925] 1988, 82), with its long periods of latency.

The subject matter of a work of art "goes out into" the material and takes on form. The creative nisus of artistic creation involves both push and pull, just like nature itself. Alexander writes that while the eye of the artist is directed on the subject matter, the "thing-meant" is "partly present to his mind in all manner of conscious perceptions, images, and thoughts, and which partly affects him unconsciously" ([1927a] 1939, 266–267). These unconscious elements, Alexander contends, "belong to the subject matter and not to the art . . . artistic impulse lies in the choice of . . . materials, to which there corresponds in the work of art its design which gives it form" (267). But while there is a designer with an evolving design in art, there is for Alexander and for Dewey no such external designer in nature which inspires Muse-like. There is the ongoing nisus, the creative flux of *natura naturans*, a kind of divine fire that kindles and quickens our creative impulses.

As Dewey puts it in *Art as Experience*: "Materials undergoing combustion because of intimate contacts and mutually exercised resistances constitute inspiration" ([1934a] 1989, 71). The self, caught in the perpetual flux of existence, is confronted with the emergence of desires, impulsions, images from prior experience, proceeding, Dewey writes, from the subconscious:

Not cold or in shapes that are identified with particulars of the past, not in chunks and lumps, but fused in the fire of internal commotion. They do not seem to come from the self, because they issue from a self not consciously known. Hence, by a just myth, the inspiration is attributed to a god, or to the muse. The inspiration, however, is initial. In itself, at the outset, it is still inchoate. Inflamed inner material must find objective fuel upon which to feed. Through the interaction of the fuel with material already under fire the refined and formed product comes into existence. The act of expression is not something

that supervenes upon an inspiration already complete. It is the carrying forward to completion of an inspiration by means of the objective
material of perception and imagery. (71–72)


## Open Nature of Experiencing

This unexpected set of intersections between Dewey and Alexander clearly
raises questions of more than anecdotal historical interest. Looking for the
sources of Dewey's aesthetics, which is a continuation of his own pragmatist account of the structures of experiencing as a web of mutually informing
interactions between an inquirer and the problematic situations in which and
over against which such an inquirer is located, the "usual suspects" are clearly
Peirce and James, two of the original "big three" of the pragmatist tradition.
But the closeness of expression between Alexander and Dewey is startling.

Dewey's aesthetics is, on the one side, fundamentally Peircean in that
it is a parallel, and in many respects independent, development and transformation of the aesthetic implications of Peirce's theory of quality: everything experienced has a distinctive quality, a distinctive feel, which artworks
paradigmatically try to capture in expressive forms. So, to allude to Peirce's
enumeration, the odor of attar, the sound of a railroad whistle, the drama
of *King Lear*, the feeling of being in love, a symphony of Beethoven, and so
forth have their own qualitative *tones*. Dewey considered this Peirce's most
important philosophical discovery, not his theory of signs or the theory of
categories. Quality is linked with "feeling." But feeling is nothing merely
subjective, a form of self-affection. It is intentional and world-oriented, the
modality in which the world is first "presented" to us and ourselves to ourselves. Dewey described a world that is presented to us not primarily as a
distinct set of objects but rather as a field of feeling tones within felt contexts
which are then discriminated or precipitated out as segmented wholes or
configurations held together in various forms of unity. The original relation
to the world involves a "turning" toward felt qualities that define "problematic situations."[2]

------

2. See "Action, Meaning, Quality," chap. 4 of Innis 1992, and chap. 2 of Innis 2020a.
The key text is Dewey's essay, "Context and Thought" (1931b).

Situations, in Dewey's account ([1934a] 1989, 72), are themselves "depressing, threatening, intolerable, triumphant." We do not project these moods onto situations. They are objective in the same way that the feel of a hammer is objective. Their correlation to a perceiving and acting organism does not make them subjective. Their *affective tone* lies at the center of the structure that makes up human being-in-the-world. Situations have auras just as much as artworks do. Thus Dewey's fundamental claim that aesthetic experience grows out of and potentiates the general structures of experience is matched by Alexander, who remarks in "Art and the Material" that "artistic experience is unmysteriously in line with the simplest revelation of physical objects in nature to the mind" ([1925] 1939, 229).

Dewey follows the Jamesian claim that the field of experience grows by its edges and is always haunted by what James called the "evermore," a kind of experiential felt surplus of anticipated sense. The pragmatically bounded character of the *objects* of experience does not mean that either experience or the universe itself is bounded by definite limits, a position that is certainly consonant with that of Alexander. To recur once again to a passage central to Dewey's aesthetic framework that is informed by the theme-field-margin schema of James:

> Things, objects, are only focal points of a here and now in a whole that stretches out indefinitely. This is the qualitative "background" which is defined and made definitely conscious in particular objects and specified properties and qualities. . . .
>
> For although there is a bounding horizon, it moves as we move. We are never wholly free from the sense of something that lies beyond. . . . We might expand the field from the narrower to the wider. But however broad the field, it is still felt as not the whole; the margins shade into that indefinite expanse beyond which imagination calls the universe. This sense of the including whole implicit in ordinary experiences is rendered intense within the frame of a painting or poem. ([1934a] 1989, 197–198)

Rendering experience intense within a frame—this is what artworks do. And the frame encompassing what Meyer Schapiro (1994, 1–32) called "field and vehicle" is the indispensable material medium without which the artwork, as a distinctive focal point in the perceptual field, would not exist. This process of embodiment is the source and foundation of the artwork as an expressive object.

Dewey had an openness to a wide range of artworks, especially painting, which was developed under the tutelage of Alfred Barnes, whose echo resonates throughout *Art as Experience*. Dewey was very concerned not to fall into the trap of setting up false alternatives either in terms of definition or in terms of preferences and valuations. Alexander took many of his examples from poetry, with other examples from a rather limited set of visual pieces, especially sculpture. He relied for poetry, as Dewey did, greatly on Lascelles Abercrombie, and specifically on the self-focusing of language as the medium or material support of a poem, which Roman Jakobson and others have discussed under the rubric of the *palpability of signs*.

Writing about the putative contrast between Classic Art and Romantic Art, Dewey criticizes Romanticism for degrading the object in favor of a predetermined type of appreciation while criticizing Classicism for making the focal point to be objective achievement with appreciation being defined as conformation to the object, with, as he puts it, the object "employed to compose sentiment and give it distinction." To this contrast Dewey offers an alternative, which he calls Complete Art. Such art is "art free from subjection to any 'ism.'" Such art has "movement, creation, as well as order, finality" ([1925] 1988, 282), a kind of synthesis of the organizing principles of the prior alternatives.

Dewey recognized already in *Experience and Nature* the legitimacy of the seeming downgrading or even repudiation of representation, a topic initiated in stages in the nineteenth and early twentieth centuries, which plays a very minor role in Alexander. "Economy in use of objective subject-matter may with experienced and trained minds go so far that what is ordinarily called 'representation' is much reduced. But what happens is a highly funded and generalized representation of the formal sources of ordinary emotional experience" ([1925] 1988, 292). So, while in Dewey's words, "Emotion is an indication of intimate participation, in a more or less excited way in some scene of nature or life" ([1925] 1988, 292), the scene of life encompasses the very life of consciousness as the locus of the appearing of the very forms of appearing (Seel 2005; Innis 2009). In abstract art, "the use of objective materials is economized to the minimum, and the evocation of the emotional response carried to its relative maximum" ([1925] 1988, 292). The emotional response is elicited by some objects and situations that "afford marked perceptual satisfactions; they do so because of their structural properties and relations." It is deliberate exploration of these properties and relations that lead to works of art that are "more formal and abstract" and, "at their best . . . they assist in ushering in new modes of art and by education of the organs of perception in new modes of consummatory objects they enlarge and enrich the world of human vision." Such art is "peculiarly instrumental in quality . . . a device in experimentation . . . a new training of modes of perception" and the opening of "new objects to be observed and enjoyed" (293).

## Metaphysical Links

Finally, to return to the inner metaphysical links between Dewey and Alexander, Dewey points out that abstract painting, like all art, deals with nature and involves "discrimination . . . with reference to the particular aspect and phase of nature in which the rhythms that mark all relationships of life and its setting are displayed" ([1934a] 1989, 156). For Dewey, the distinction between abstract and concrete is a distinction between tendencies and, as he correctly points out, "each is justified when form and matter achieve equilibrium" (317). Extreme simplification on the one hand and multiplication of internal specifications to the utmost "consistent with organization" on the other are both ideals, and at times they can be successfully merged. There is nothing in such notions that Alexander would object to, but it must be admitted that he did not travel far down this path, paved as it was for Dewey with the help of Barnes and his incomparable collection of artworks.

Alexander, with his great vision of nature as driven by a universal nisus, as a dynamic, churning fount of forms, both natural and artefactual, asks, "What makes the difference between natural beauty and the beauty of art?" His answer is that there is no difference in kind, but only one of "circumstances" ([1925] 1939, 231). He remarks that beauty in nature comes from an "impulsion" from nature itself, an impulsion leading to the riotous upsurge of forms and interactions, while in art it comes from the artist. Nature "intends" nothing. The use of the term *impulsion* is echoed throughout Dewey's own work to foreground the continuous dynamism of the flux of experiencing, a permanent nisus or striving that marks nature itself as a generative matrix of profundity. Alexander had a deep affinity with Baruch Spinoza and Ralph Waldo Emerson, the latter of whom Alexander cites with reference to the dynamism that "drives on 'the chemic lump' . . . to 'ascend to man'" (1927a, 273). The quality of beauty embodied in nature, he thinks, "requires the supplement of our imputations and penetration by them. But in the proportion of discovery and creation the emphasis is on discovery" (273). As to the contrast with artistic beauty, here is the closing paragraph of "Art and the Material": "In the work of art creativeness is palpable. It needs reflection to recognize that the artistic creation is discovery. . . . Therewith vanishes any ultimate disparity between natural and artificial beauty. Only the seeing and intelligent eye discovers natural beauty. Only the work of art reveals, or in the old usage of the word, 'discovers' to the eye its intelligence" ([1925] 1939, 232). This intelligence itself is one of Dewey's "emergent growths" arising out of nature.

In "Art and Instinct," another essay from 1927, which Dewey probably did not know, Alexander defended the thesis that "the aesthetic impulse and the aesthetic emotion which goes with that impulse and is part and parcel of it are an outgrowth from the impulse of constructiveness" (1927b, 236). This instinct of constructiveness is also found on much lower levels in the subhuman realm (Richards 2019; Rothenberg 2011; Maran 2020). The beautiful for Alexander is defined in this context as "that which satisfies the constructive instinct when it has reached the stage of contemplation." In short, "constructiveness becomes contemplative" ([1927b] 1939, 237). This opposition is a clear equivalent of Dewey's contrast between instrumental and consummatory, at least in the domain of art. Dewey, of course, extended it to all experiential occasions to the degree that they incorporate means of all sorts into ends such that they introduce harmonies and integration into life.

In conclusion, at the end of the chapter "Experience, Nature and Art" in *Experience and Nature*, we find the following passage: "In creative production, the external and physical world is more than a mere means or external condition of perceptions, ideas and emotions; it is subject-matter and sustainer of conscious activity; and thereby exhibit, so that he who runs may read, the fact that consciousness is not a separate realm of being, but is the manifest quality of existence when nature is most free and most active" ([1925] 1988, 294). Therefore, if Dewey could write such a passage before he encountered the aesthetic works of Alexander, it is no wonder that when he did, he did not merely see in them a goad or stimulation for the continuation of his own work but rather met an intellectual companion whose thought entered in places, by creative appropriation, into a symbiotic relation with his own.

# CHAPTER 5

# Between Nature and Art

## *Analytical Exemplifications of Dewey's Aesthetics*

### Nature as Matrix and Medium

In *Art as Experience* Dewey characterized the focal point of his lifelong philosophical project to be "the immense variety of interactions between the live creature and his world" ([1934a] 1989, 317). The originating matrix of these interactions is nature as a network of forces, energies, and situations, what he called in *Experience and Nature* the "moving unbalanced balance of things" ([1925] 1988, 314) within which we live and which engages us on all levels: physical, vital, psychological, and semiotic (Maran 2020). Life, in Dewey's account, is a constant interplay of endogenic impulsions toward the immediate environment and nature as a whole and exogenic processes of being affected or impacted by it. For Dewey, the basic condition of our relation to nature is the "felt relationship between doing and undergoing as the organism and environment interact" ([1934a] 1989, 217), an interplay elicited by features of the environment pressing upon us and the immanent demands of ourselves as organisms. These environmental features are marked by distinctive, luring determining qualities and forms of resistance to us. They challenge us and at the same time enable us by giving rise to various modes of accommodation and adaptation, with the aim of establishing equilibrium between the organism and multileveled nature as a whole.

Such an equilibrium in a universe permeated by the creative processes of the emergence of novelties—emergent growths—is never fully stable on any level. Our lives are marked by constant efforts to keep our balance and to utilize and transform the very resources of the environment so as to deal with it instrumentally and practically and to perceive it in its harmonies and luring qualities that we dwell in for their own sakes. In the cumulating heightened vitality that arises in our encounters with nature, Dewey writes that "there abides the deep-seated memory of an underlying harmony, the sense of which haunts life like the sense of being founded on a rock" ([1934a] 1989, 23). The lack, however, of such a memory is a mark of a life trajectory without an onto-logical ground. Rather than being present in memory, such an underlying har-mony then becomes the object of longing. Its absence can be due to multiple factors, from what Dewey characterizes as the "bustle and ado of modern life" to the desolate existential landscapes of poverty, starvation, and disease in the great struggle of life on both the individual and social planes. Dewey approv-ingly cites Santayana (1905–6, 65) to the effect that "every living experience owes its richness to … 'hushed reverberations.'" ([1934a] 1989, 23). These reverberations are grounded in the universal structure of the ideal of a rhyth-mic swing and sway of the organism's engagement with its environments if it is able, without ultimate deviation, to follow courses of development in unison with them. But clearly, life can also be often haunted by the absence of such reverberations and rendered experientially impoverished. Our existence can be mired in deadening situations of disorder and negative energies.

Dewey writes, looking at the "normal" structures of experiencing, that "in a world made after the pattern of ours, moments of fulfillment punctu-ate experience with rhythmically enjoyed intervals." These intervals are what make up the inner harmony of the consummatory experiences in which experience is brought by various means to a "fulfillment that reaches to the depths of our being—one that is an adjustment of our whole being with the conditions of existence." Such adjustments, coming to terms with the envi-ronment, are not permanent states. The achievement of equilibrium is only one phase in a continuous process and "is at the same time the initiation of a new relation to the environment, one that brings with it potency of new adjustments to be made through struggle" ([1934a] 1989, 23). Art and the development of the inner and outer conditions of aesthetic experiences are essential forms of realizing and employing the very powers and qualities of nature to institute new adjustments.

Dewey's fundamental picture of the organism-environment/nature rela-tionship is one, not just of oscillation between activity and passivity toward "the given," but also of a constant circuit or spiral of engagements that is par-ticipatory and reconstructive. In his classic paper criticizing the reflex arc account of experiencing, Dewey (1896) had pointed out that the organism never responds merely *to* the environment but rather responds *into* it. The organism is not a passive mirror but rather an agent that constitutes, or recognizes and responds to, the webs of meaning of the environment by its actions and its perceptual acts. The organism is self-moving, wandering in the field of nature, appropriating its powers for both its practical and vital uses and for its expressive uses when, as in the case of art, experience "goes out into symbolization" (Dewey 1930a, 205). Going out into symbolization, however, involves both the grasp *of*, and being grasped *by*, the richness of experience itself as *emblematic* of domains of meaning beyond the merely physical or instrumental or the analytically conceptual, themes developed in rich detail by Susanne Langer ([1942] 1957, 1953, 1967–82; Innis 2009). This "going out into symbolization" in art generates *presentational forms*, configurations of significance that elude capture in discursive language.

It is precisely art's role and power to use the very materials of nature, including our own bodies, to create artefacts with which we resonate at all levels of our existence. But, for Dewey, the aesthetic is by no means to be confined to the vast collections of artefacts that make up what we now, in one way or the other, call works of art. It extends to experience as a whole inasmuch as we do not pass over or through it to something else, using it as mere instruments or pointers, but inasmuch as, to use a phrase from Michael Polanyi (1958, 1966), we come to "dwell in" it and experience it for its own sake as a domain of harmonious wholes. There is an aesthetic dimension to, and perception of, nature, just as there is a specifically artistic transformation and exploitation of its natural powers and materials that enable us to construct a second nature that differentiates out into the varied forms of art in which we express the infinitely variable aspects of the world and give flesh to meanings of our existence in all their breadth and depth.

Dewey exemplifies the aesthetic dimension of nature itself as an object of consummatory experiences, not so much by his own descriptions as by adducing some passages from W. H. Hudson, Emerson, and George Eliot, as well as snatches of poetry, including the nature-loving Romantics. Fusing the descriptive and the normative, Dewey writes that "nature is the mother and habitat of man, even if sometimes a stepmother and an unfriendly home" ([1934a] 1989, 34). The mothering or nourishing side of nature is clearly outlined in passages Dewey cited from Hudson (1918, 3, 331, 231, 232).

Hudson writes, "I feel when I am out of sight of living, growing grass, and out of the sound of birds' voices and all rural sounds, that I am not properly alive" (quoted in Dewey [1934a] 1989, 35). Being "properly alive" means attending to what Dewey called the "sensuous surface of the world," as exemplified in Hudson's account of his childhood as being "just a little wild animal running around on its hind legs, amazingly interested in the world in which it found itself" (Dewey [1934a] 1989, 130). As if doing an inventory of the senses, Hudson writes that he

> rejoiced in colours, scents, in taste and touch: the blue of the sky, the verdure of earth, the sparkle of light on water, the taste of milk, of fruit, of honey, the smell of dry or moist soil, of wind and rain, of herbs and flowers; the mere feel of a blade of grass made me happy; and there were certain sounds and perfumes, and above all certain colours in flowers, and in the plumage and eggs of birds, such as the purple polished shell of the tinamou's eggs, which intoxicated me with delight. (Dewey [1934a] 1989, 130)

Dewey insightfully notes that what Hudson enumerates in these passages are not isolated sense qualities. The experiences he catalogs are of *objects*. "The sight, smell, and touch immediately appealed to are means through which the boy's entire being reveled in acute perception of the qualities of the world in which he lived—qualities of things experienced not of sensation." It is the object that has significance, not the sense organ alone. "The connection of qualities with objects is intrinsic in all experience having significance" ([1934a] 1989, 131). This connection occurs through the body which is bound to the natural world and which is quickened by the qualities that lure us through it toward deeper and more nuanced perceptions of the environment with their resonances and reverberations. In this respect Dewey writes, in tune with Hudson:

> It is not just the visual apparatus but the whole organism that interacts with the environment in all but routine action. The eye, ear, or whatever, is only the channel *through* which the total response takes place. A color as seen is always qualified by implicit reactions of many organs, those of the sympathetic system as well as touch. It is a funnel for the total energy put forth, not its well-spring. Colors are sumptuous and rich just because a total organic response is deeply implicated in them. ([1934a] 1989, 127)

Art's purpose is to engender such a total organic response, even if it such a response has many gradations and tones.

Hudson's love of sensory detail and particularity, of experiential uniqueness, is, as he importantly admits, rooted in his childhood and the freedom he had to safely wander in nature. It was first and foremost nature's diversity and rich blooming that attracted him and filled him with joy and that was carried over to his later life. Dewey contrasts Hudson's account with a cognate and famous passage from Emerson to which Dewey thinks it is spiritually linked. Emerson writes in *Nature*: "Crossing a bare common, in snow puddles, at twilight, under a clouded sky, without having in my thought any occurrence of special good fortune, I have enjoyed a perfect exhilaration. I am glad to the brink of fear" (1968, 6; cited in Dewey [1934a] 1989, 35). This passage exemplifies a metaphysical mood, a global all encompassing *tone* elicited by a situation and a place and not individual objects. Emerson's exhilaration and gladness on the brink of fear arose with no thematic or operative effort on his part. Such experiences happen to us, come to us, and are not something that we do or are explicitly searching for, although after they occur we realize their life-enhancing character as revealing and satisfying a deep longing. They interrupt us, both setting us in motion and at the same halting us and holding us in their embrace. Rollo May, in *My Quest for Beauty* (1985, chap. 1), describes such an experience in his existentially deep essay on kneeling before the "Poppies in Greece," which in their carefree, colorful swaying in the wind saved his life when he was on the cusp of despair.

Dewey also cites a passage from George Eliot's *The Mill on the Floss* (1900, 44), reminiscent of Proust, that captures the aesthetic aspect of our deep memory-laden existential bond with ordinary nature, if we only attend to or have access to it:

These familiar flowers, these well-remembered bird-notes, this sky with its fitful brightness, these furrowed and grassy fields, each with a sort of personality given to it by the capricious hedge, such things as these are the mother-tongue of our imagination, the language that is laden with all the subtle inextricable associations the fleeting hours of our childhood left behind them. Our delight in the sunshine on the deep-bladed grass to-day might be no more than the faint perception of wearied souls, if it were not for the sunshine and grass of far-off years, which still live in us and transform our perception into love. ([1934a] 1989, 23–24)

The "still living in us" of past perceptions, their sedimentation into habits of attending and feeling, Dewey calls "fundedness." These habits literally "fund," or ground, our existence, serving as a kind of existential capital, both earned and unearned, on which we rely to realize our lives.

Like a drumbeat, in *Art as Experience* ([1934a] 1989), Dewey returns time and again to the omnipresence of nature as the ground of our lives. It is the ultimate surrounding frame and system of constraints in which human life takes place. It also, in its potential expressive powers, enters into all art forms as their medium or substance transformed into form. "Matter becoming medium" is a core thesis or organizing principle of Dewey's aesthetics, a principle that also links him with Samuel Alexander. The grinding of pigments; the shaping and carving of stone; the organization of sound, whether produced by the human body or reed, drum, or string; the harnessing of bodily movement; the marking and construction of surfaces, including the surfaces of the human body; the development of chisel, pen, and brush; the building of dwellings that shelter us and our gods; and so forth, all belong to nature *in* art. They are the tools for the bodying forth of nature. They make up the "substance" of art in general and in the particular modes in which it appears.

The theme of nature as matrix and medium runs through *Art as Experience* (1934) as a central thread or motif and, of course, through the chapters in *Experience and Nature* ([1925] 1988) that are devoted to art. It important to realize, as discussed in chapter 4, that Dewey's aesthetics is fundamentally naturalistic in the literal sense. It is concerned with meaning-infused and meaningfully structured matter. Such matter is the ultimate support of all art, and as the dynamic forms of nature they are the original objects encountered in perception. Artworks engage and reveal these very forms. They teach us how to contemplatively dwell on and in the inexhaustible faces of the world. The transformation of nature into a materially and semiotically sheltering foundation of our lives in technology and the built world likewise gives us a specifically human "place" in nature, provided we attend to their inseparable linkages with the bodily matrices and measures of our lives and their demands for aesthetic rationality (Innis 1987).

Some further exemplifications, both those linked to and those offered by Dewey, make concrete the foundations of Dewey's account of the ultimate experiential roots, contours, and implications of the transformative interactions between ourselves and nature that take place in artistic creation and aesthetic perception.

The Scroll and the Smile: Experience Has No Edges

In a remarkable passage, which has been cited in different contexts in other chapters, Dewey argues, continuing James's insight, that the open field of experience is an encompassing moving and ever receding horizon. This is a central insight of his pragmatist account of the organism-environment relationship.

> Things, objects, are only focal points of a here and now in a whole that stretches out indefinitely. This is the qualitative "background" which is defined and made definitely conscious in particular objects and specified properties and qualities. . . .
>
> For although there is a bounding horizon, it moves as we move. We are never wholly free from the sense of something that lies beyond. . . . We might expand the field from the narrower to the wider. But however broad the field, it is still felt as not the whole; the margins shade into that indefinite expanse beyond which imagination calls the universe. This sense of the including whole implicit in ordinary experiences is rendered intense within the frame of a painting or poem. ([1934a] 1989, 197–198)

This phenomenologically accurate observation can be illustrated in three examples, two taken from Dewey and a remarkable parallel passage from another work written with no connection to Dewey but linked to one of the examples.

First of all, there are numerous references to Chinese painting in *Art as Experience*, although with rare exceptions the bulk of Dewey's allusions, interpretations, and judgments are to the art of the Western world. The references and juxtapositions are of great theoretical and analytical import in showing the essential openness of Dewey's aesthetics. Dewey had pointed out that in his opinion, "craftsmanship alone is not art" and that the "thorough relativity of technique to form in art" has been often ignored. What example does he give? He claims that the special form of Gothic sculpture was not due to lack of dexterity any more than the special kind of perspective found in Chinese painting was ([1934a] 1989, 147). Dewey had remarked, in line with his general model of experience, that "works of art express space as opportunity for movement and action," including, I would say, spiritual action. And, in light of the primacy of the category of quality in Dewey's aesthetics, such a space is, as Dewey says, "a matter of proportions qualitatively felt" ([1934a]

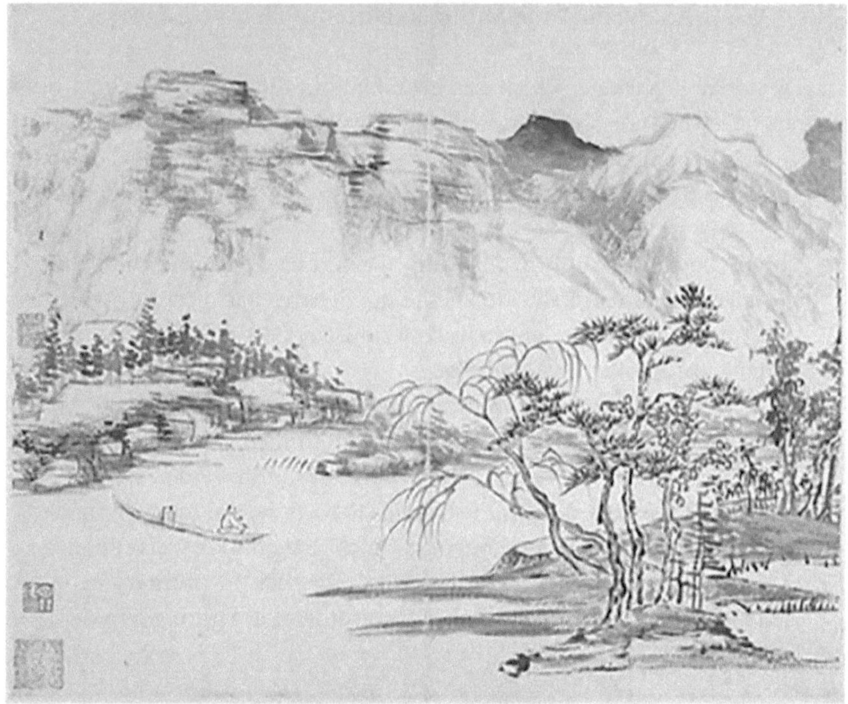

Fig. 5.1. Yi Bingshou, *Landscapes*, 1814. *Source*: Metropolitan Museum of Art, New York.

1989, 213), which is not dependent on the actual physical dimensions of a painting or a poem or even a social interaction (see figure 5.1).

Spaciousness, Dewey rightly remarks, is a characteristic feature of Chinese painting and especially the tradition of landscape painting, with its metaphysical import. Such paintings do not need frames because they are not centralized. Rather, "they move outwards, while panoramic scroll paintings present a world in which ordinary boundaries are transformed into invitations to proceed" ([1934a] 1989, 213). They have an auratic margin of an ever-receding "beyond." An invitation to proceed involves us, elicits participation. We do not just respond to such a painting, we respond into it and into the self-generating nature coming to appearance in it, within which we ourselves are. As Dewey puts it, "Nature in this meaning is not 'outside.' It is in us and we are in and of it" (336). Nature is the complex of generative processes into which and within which we enter into forms of relationships and participation that transcend our starting points, taking us out of ourselves and putting us into play. Works on Chinese painting emphasize this dynamic openness, which is bound to a profound stillness of contemplation and absence of agitation. Such painting holds in delicate balance both a displacement of the human and at the same time an image of the human ability and need to recognize displacement as their proper "place." What appears to be the strangeness of Chinese painting is really something that is proper to what all art demands of us: that "we install ourselves in modes of apprehending nature that at first are strange to us" (337), but that can lead to an "insensible melting" in which barriers and limiting prejudices are dissolved by our entering into a new "spirit," or qualitative matrix, embodied in and revealed by an artwork.

Being led in this way, both existentially in terms of being affected and attuned in different ways and in terms of seeing analytical connections, allows Dewey to note a remarkable parallel and intersection. Western painting, which was governed for a period of its existence by progressive attempts to picture the world through exact representation of its empirical properties, aimed to be a realization of the "objective eye." This involved the evolution, not just of monocular perspective, but also of very different uses of pigments and brushwork. Dewey nevertheless illuminatingly contended that by these different means Western painting, even in spite of its "highly centralized" form, was able to "create the sense of the extensive whole that encloses a scene that is carefully defined," that is, defined and organized objects with clearly defined edges and patterns of color and line. Dewey gives as an example Jan van Eyck's famous *Jean Arnolfini and Wife*, which Barnes had discussed in this way (see figure 5.2). This painting, Dewey observes, is able to "convey within a defined compass the explicit sense of the outdoors beyond the walls" ([1934a] 1989, 213). This is a remarkable insight, which is not mentioned in Barnes's analysis of this painting. It issues a challenge to us to scrape away the veneer of perceptual habits and to attend to the backgrounds of appearances and not just their foregrounds, even if we are also made aware of the gulf in metaphysical premises and worldviews out of which Chinese landscape painting and such a work as van Eyck's arose and were determined.

Going further, I want to adduce a third, quite unexpected, example of the importance of the background, which was not analyzed or even mentioned by Dewey but whose presence in our culture has been so domesticated that we have a very difficult time attending to or *being with* what is before us: the *Mona Lisa*, the exemplar par excellence of what François Cheng

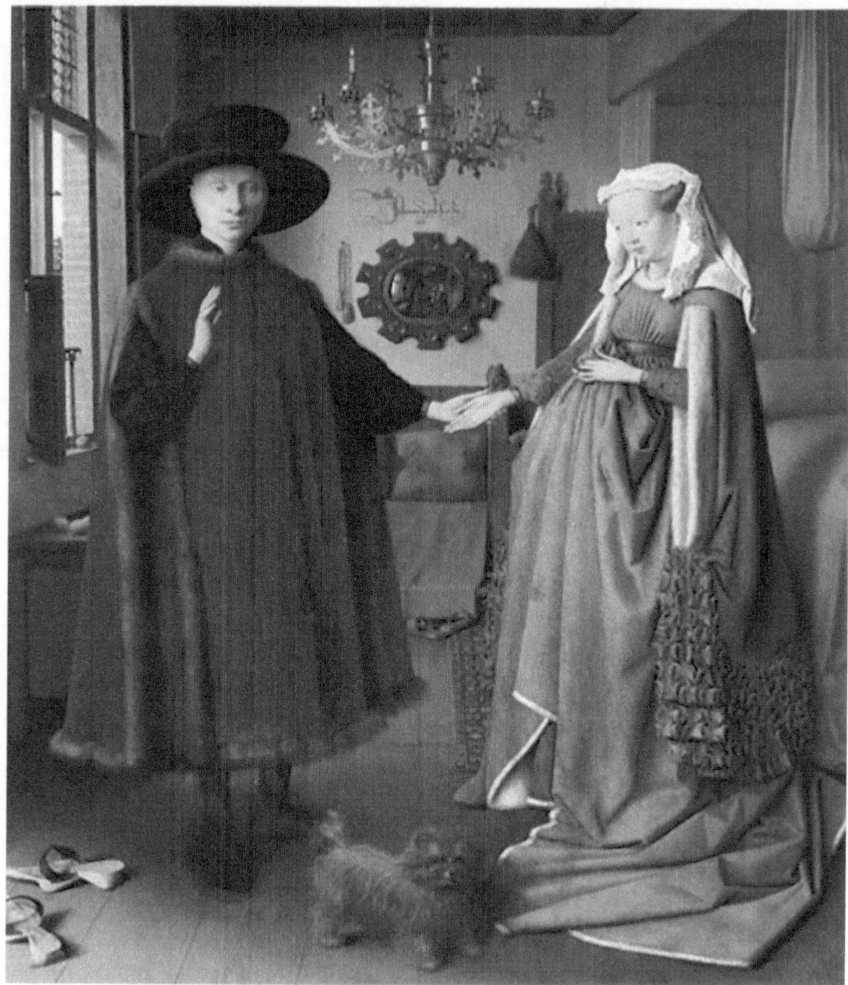

Fig. 5.2. Jan Van Eyck, *The Arnolfini Portrait*, 1434. *Source*: National Gallery, London.

called "an enigmatic smile that seems to want to say something" (2006, 44; see figure 5.3). This is true enough and universally recognized. Cheng, however, remarks on the "look" as a total quality, encompassing the eyes and the smile, a remark reminiscent of the centrality of the category of quality, the Peircean-Deweyan theme foregrounded and traced in these chapters. The look is indeed more than the eyes. Cheng claims, "The beauty of the look comes from a light that wells up from the depths of Being. It can also

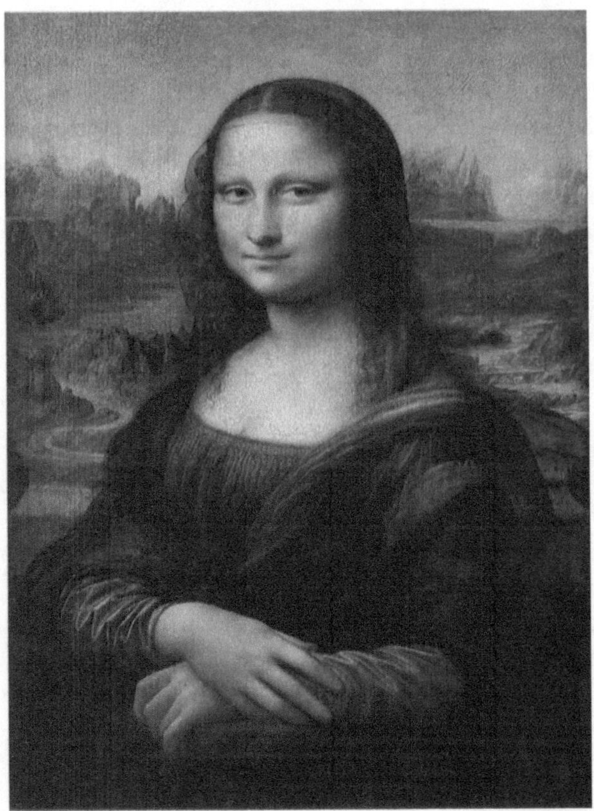

Fig. 5.3. Leonardo da Vinci, *The Mona Lisa*, 1503–1506. *Source*: Louvre, Paris.

come from an external light that illuminates it." Following St. Augustine's reflections in his "Sermon on Providence," Cheng writes about beauty that it "results from the encounter between the interior of a being and the splendor of the cosmos. . . . This encounter in some way annihilates the separation of the internal and external," which is precisely the core of Dewey's idea that the encounter between humans and the environing world involves participation and mutual penetration. Nature is as much in us as we are in nature, whose beauty forms a "landscape." Paul Verlaine, Cheng remarks, wrote that "your soul is a chosen landscape," which the Chinese aesthetic tradition called a "feeling-landscape" and is marked by forms of attunement. Cheng describes such a landscape in words very close to Dewey's characterization of *fundedness*. It is made up of "memories and dreams, fears and desires, experienced and anticipated scenarios" (47), which constitute the very quality of our lives, the ramified felt matrix of our existence.

Cheng goes further and indeed, by citing another analysis of the *Mona Lisa*, confirms the importance of Dewey's great insight into the edgelessness of our moving fields of experience and the decentering that Dewey ascribes to Chinese painting. The lesson of the analysis of *Mona Lisa* is nevertheless surprising and shows the analytical value of Dewey's core insight. The question Cheng poses is whether there is, as he puts it, a "key to unlock the mystery" of the Mona Lisa's look. The answer to this question is startling and unexpected, to say the least. He asks whether in fact the key is to be found in "that misty landscape behind her, both distant and near" (2006, 47). He cites a long passage from *Le Sel et le Vent* by France Quéré (1995, 150–152), which I reproduce here as a text consonant with Dewey's phenomenological orientation with its focusing on funded reverberations, resonances, organic responses, and memories.

> In forms of rocks and lakes burst the strange soundings of an interior world. . . . At the height of the [Mona Lisa's] shoulders, an ochre landscape of hilly terrain begins, which the efflorescence of the rock runs through. To the left, the path opens onto the gray waters of a lake, striated by the shadows of the overhanging rocks. These are thrust faults, manes, fierce necks, deformed muzzles that rise above the waters in a burst of petrified anger. A prehistoric violence blocks the view. . . . To the right, beside the young woman's turned-up mouth, the path follows the course of the muddy river, threading its way up from level to level, among the fallen rocks, finally reaching the shore of a second lake, higher than the first. . . . This is another world, immaterial, immensely contemplative, toward which the smile and the movement of the eyes subtly direct us. A dim glow makes the high altitude lake just barely iridescent. But the maledictions of the shadows and obstructions are vanquished. Other rocks rise, but they no longer shade or enclose anything. Their shadow traces a ring, suggests transparency, leaves the mirror of the waters intact. . . . Between the two purified shores opens a gap where the gold of the water and the light merge, and extend together toward infinity. Is this a god who welcomes the traveler? Is it the joy of an enlightened intelligence at the height of its meditation? . . . Is it childhood rediscovered, made more beautiful by the distances of memory? . . . A human dream begins there, at the height of the eyes and the pure forehead. Its dawns are even more beautiful than the hills of Florence in the sun's first rays. (2006, 47–48)

Cheng comments that looked at this way the Mona Lisa "no longer appears to us as the simple portrait of a socially prominent woman, but as the miraculous manifestation of that potential beauty the universe promises from the very first." The beauty of her face is not that of a single isolated face but rather the realization of a transfiguration arising from "the encounter of interior light and another light forever offered but so often obscured. *Transfiguration* is understood here as that which is transformed from within, and also as that which shows through in the space of life between the finite and the infinite, between the visible and the invisible" (49). The "space of life" that Cheng refers to has no firm or defined edges. Within life there are, as Dewey noted, pragmatic edges, but in the concrete world in which we live out our lives they are labile borders and not abstractions belonging to another ideal world. Life is lived both on and at the edge. We also see in the Quéré text the detailed engagement with the landscape, an oscillation between identifying and being grasped by the tone or determining quality of a landscape that becomes a mirror of the soul. We can see here in a different way the matrix of nature as determinate of an artwork, although it is clear that the global notion of a landscape is not able to fully encompass on its own the distinctiveness of Dewey's aesthetics and his approach to the analysis of artworks and of our relations to nature. Such relations, looked at in light of the role of action in Dewey's philosophical project, are not exclusively contemplative.

With respect to painting, Dewey had a special, but by no means exclusive, affection for the great impressionist and postimpressionist painters. Three artworks from the Barnes Foundation, Renoir's *The Bathers*, Cézanne's *Still Life with Peaches*, and Matisse's *Joie de Vivre*, are represented in the eight illustrations that were included in the original and critical edition of *Art as Experience* ([1934a] 1989). Renoir and Cézanne play central roles in exemplifying the point and fertility of Dewey's analytical framework. They are for him prime paradigms of painting and of major philosophical importance. It is worthwhile and very enlightening to see where they appear and what role they play in the development of Dewey's argument.


## Paradigms of Painting: On Representation, Expression, and Abstraction


First of all, as to Cézanne, references are strewn throughout *Art as Experience* ([1934a] 1989). They occur in different contexts of the general discussion of art and aesthetic experience and are linked with allusions, interpretations, and criticisms of various artists and artworks. Writing about the role of color and color qualities, Dewey writes that line generally, but not absolutely, has a stable constancy of *some* sort but that this is not the case with color. Changes of light and other conditions introduce variances. The motivation for this remark is what Dewey claims is the misplaced attempt to discover pure or simple qualities independent of relational contexts. Experiential qualities, even when studied scientifically, Dewey holds, "cannot shut out the resonances and transfers of value" due to their attachment to objects. Moreover, the attempt to separate design and color is misplaced. In this context Dewey has recourse to a passage from Cézanne: "Design and color are not distinct. In the degree in which color is really *painted*, design exists. The more colors harmonize with one another, the more defined is design. When color is at its richest, form is most complete. The secret of design, of everything marked by pattern, is contrast and relation of tones" ([1934a] 1989, 127; see also Hofmann 1967). For Dewey, the philosophical lesson is that opposing "quality as immediate and sensuous to relation as purely mediate and intellectual is false in general theory, psychological and philosophical" and, in the case of art, "absurd" ([1934a] 1989, 127). Relations go all the way down.

The interplay between doing and undergoing that makes up the spiral or circuit of experiencing that defines the ultimate contours of the organism-environment relation also undercuts any attempt to separate the "esthetic and artistic" as passive and active, respectively. Mere perfection in execution can end up as pure technique, Dewey claims, resulting in a product with a mechanical feeling. Indeed, for him "there are great artists who are not in the first ranks as technicians (witness Cézanne), just as there are great performers on the piano who are not great esthetically, and as Sargent is not a great painter" ([1934a] 1989, 54). Right after this critical observation, whose correctness cannot be discussed in this context, Dewey contends that technical perfection is not the same as true artistic craftsmanship.

What he says was surely influenced by the practice of Cézanne. For Dewey, for craftsmanship to be artistic entails that the craftsman must hold in view in the process of production those who will perceive and enjoy the product, including the artist, who must know when the work is finished and fulfills the felt schema, which Susanne Langer called the artist's "idea," out of which the artwork emerges and which it realizes. The artistic success of this process is determined by its being "loving." The craftsman "must care deeply for the subject matter upon which skill is exercised" so that it is "framed for enjoyed receptive perception" ([1934a] 1989, 54). When Dewey refers to the "constant observation" necessary for the artist as producer of the artwork, we cannot help but think of Cézanne's obsession with Mont Sainte-Victoire as a manifestation of telluric forces and an inexhaustible source of inspiration and lure for his painting, which exemplifies the synthesis of "outgoing and incoming energy" in perception and production.

Indeed, later on in the chapter on "The Expressive Object," when returning to the topic of whether "drawing" is essential to painting, Dewey establishes the pivotal nature of the distinction between recognizing and perceiving aesthetically. We do not go to painting to recognize objects because the artist has employed, with high skill, drawing as a "means of exact outline and definite shading," of reproducing reality as it is. Drawing for Dewey is

> drawing *out*; it is extraction of what the subject matter has to say in particular to the painter in his integrated experience. Because the painting is a unity of interrelated parts, every designation of a particular figure has, moreover, to be drawn *into* a relation of mutual enforcement with all other plastic means—color, light, the spatial planes and the placing of other parts. This integration may, and in fact does, involve what is, from the standpoint of the shape of the real thing, a physical distortion. ([1934a] 1989, 98)

But this very distortion does not contravene what Dewey thinks is the ultimate goal of art: to capture every shade of expressiveness of the world. The goal, that is, is not to copy the world but to make present or capture the *forms of the world*, the forms in which the world appears as configurations and fields of significance. Representing the significances of the world is not reproducing the world but rather producing expressive objects that draw out, shape, and inform the *how* of appearing.

It is at this point in Dewey's argument that the discussion about expressiveness and meaning turns to the central notion of *abstraction* and abstract art and their repudiation of representation as the highest goal of art. Cézanne, for Dewey, is a prime exemplar for showing the falseness of the opposition between representation and expressiveness and their connection with the putative goal of any so-called naturalism in painting in particular and art in general. Representation, Dewey thinks, is no more objective than expression. The absence of representation in a painting, as in the case of abstract art, does not make it "merely expressive" in the sense of a mirror of an individual subjectivity without any perceptual logic to it. Nor are the distortions present in Cézanne and El Greco or the blatant flatnesses of Matisse's painting, such as *The Red Studio* or *Joie du vivre*, merely expressive, with no links to the world (see Barnes 1937, 359–368). Dewey's conception of the nature of abstraction, especially in painting, has critical importance. Linear outlines that are restricted to merely accurately reproducing particular shapes have a limited expressiveness. They are either just realistic copies or they are the capturing of types, of generalized kinds of things, that allow us to recognize them. Aesthetically drawn lines, Dewey notes, have increasing expressiveness in that they can embody "the meaning of volume, of room and position; solidity and movement" such that "they enter into the force of all other parts of the picture, and they serve to relate all parts together so that the value of the whole is energetically expressed" ([1934a] 1989, 99). The force and scope of this remark extends, with obvious differences, to the realm of the what Dewey calls the automatic arts, where the "human organism, the mind-body of the artist" is the medium, such as in dancing and singing, bodily scarification, cultivation of bodily posture, and so forth, and the shaping arts, "which depend to a much greater extent upon materials external to the body" ([1934a] 1988, 231) that both enable and constrain what can be accomplished by their shaping activities. Such a distinction has nothing to do with ranking. "Each medium," Dewey rightly affirms, "has its own efficacy and value" (231)

Dewey claims, showing the deep but not always explicit influence of Barnes, that the history of painting has progressed "from giving a pleasing indication of a particular object to become a relationship of planes and harmonious merging of colors" ([1934a] 1989, 99), as in the work of his beloved Cézanne, Renoir, and many others who receive positive mention throughout *Art as Experience.*

As to abstract art proper in the strict sense, which was just emerging at that time, Dewey has recourse to citing a fertile passage from Barnes's *The Art in Painting* (1937, 36, 35). In this passage we can see how overcoming the tension or opposition between representation and expressiveness with regard to painting also illustrates a core feature of Dewey's whole aesthetic theory and can be extended to the art as a whole, *mutatis mutandis*:

> Reference to the real world does not disappear from art as forms cease to be those of actually existing things, any more than objectivity disappears from science when it ceases to talk in terms of earth, fire, air and water, and substitutes for these things the less easily recognizable

"hydrogen," "oxygen," "nitrogen," and "carbon." . . . When we cannot find in a picture representation of any particular object, what it represents may be the qualities which *all* particular objects share, such as color, extensity, solidity, movement, rhythm, etc. All particular things have these qualities; hence what serves, so to speak, as a paradigm of the visible essence of all things may hold in solution the emotions which individualized things provoke in a more highly specialized way. ([1934a] 1989, 100–101)

Dewey continues by drawing out the philosophical lesson of Barnes's exemplary formulation:

Art does not, in short, cease to be expressive because it renders in visible form relations of things, without any more indication of the particulars that have the relations than is necessary to compose a whole. Every work of art "abstracts" in some degree from the particular traits of objects expressed. . . . There is no *a priori* rule to decide how far abstraction may be carried. . . . Abstraction is usually associated with distinctively intellectual undertakings. Actually it is found in every work of art . . . for the sake of expressiveness of the object. ([1934a] 1989, 100–101)

The movement toward the impersonal and the abstract that marked the various forms of art when Dewey was composing his *Art as Experience* did not mean a movement away from a true naturalism, which aimed at capturing in forms what Schelling called the "potencies" in things, a notion functioning in the background of Peirce's thought that has been explored by Ivo Ibri (2009). Deweyan aesthetics sees no rigid opposition between the abstract and the concrete, between the drive toward simplification and the drive toward the proliferation of internal specifications, between direction and allusive indirection, between the overarching controlling *tone* of death and darkness in a presented subject matter and the light and air of another. The key is arriving at an equilibrium of form and matter, a unity that is the point of all art. It is the defining feature of art to be informed by and express "adequate sympathy" and not just instrumental dealings with "the immense variety of interactions between the live creature and his world" ([1934a] 1989, 317).

These interactions involve selection, whose directive source is interest, "an unconscious but organic bias toward certain aspects and values of the

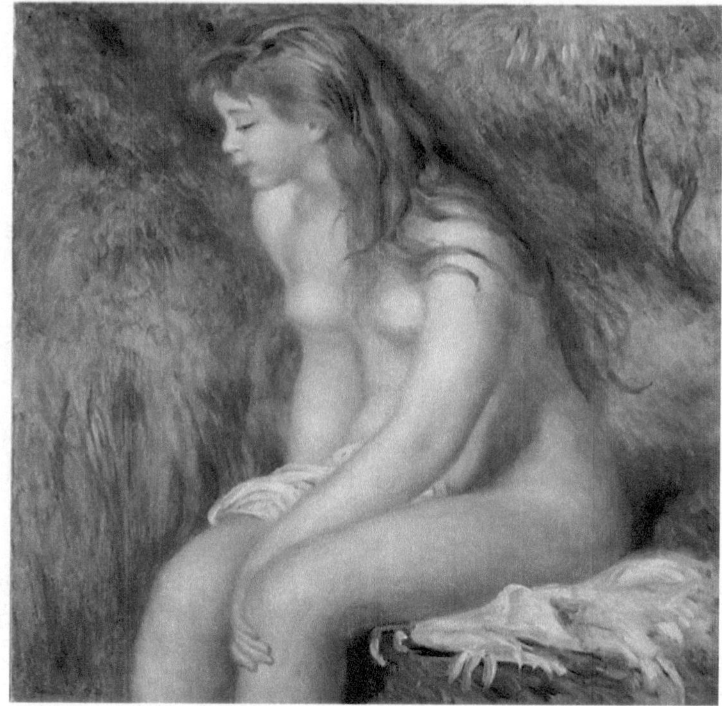

Fig. 5.4. Auguste Renoir, *Young Girl Bathing*, 1892. *Source*: Metropolitan Museum of Art, New York.

complex and variegated universe in which we live" ([1934a] 1989, 100). The artist works both with and within "the infinite concreteness of nature" and follows the logic of his selective interest while adding "to his selective bent an efflorescence or 'abounding' in the sense or direction in which he is drawn" (101). At the same time there has to be maintained some intrinsic reference, at some level of specificity, to the environment's qualities and structures, which make up some objective frame of reference that cannot be ignored, but which is transfigured in art in multiple ways.

A comment on the nudes of Renoir illustrates this theoretical or analytical point. They give delight, Dewey says, but are not in the least pornographic. This can be clearly seen from the reproduction in figure 5.4 of Renoir's *Young Girl Bathing*, which bears comparison with his *The Bathers*, reproduced in *Art as Experience*, a painting that has a more complex compositional logic but the same quality of efflorescence. While his nudes do not repudiate the "voluptuous qualities of flesh" but rather actually heighten our awareness of them, nevertheless Renoir abstracted *from* the conditions of their physical existence. There is a positive form of abstraction that is operating, which, through the medium of color, transfers naked (bare) bodies into a new dimension or realm. According to Dewey, the ordinary associations of naked bodies disappear: "The esthetic expels the physical, and heightening of qualities common to flesh with flowers ejects the erotic. The conception that objects have fixed and unalterable values is precisely the prejudice from which art emancipates us. The intrinsic qualities of things come out with startling vigor and freshness just because conventional associations are removed" ([1934a] 1989, 101). Dewey remarks that paradigmatically, in the case of Renoir, there is manifested a love of the substance of common life. Renoir exploited the power of "every plastic means—color, light, line, and planes, in themselves and in their interrelations—to convey a sense of abounding joy in intercourse with common things. . . . What is expressed is the experience Renoir himself had of the joy of perceiving the world" ([1934a] 1989, 134). This is precisely the goal that motivated Dewey both in his aesthetics and in his general philosophical project: to create an environment that satisfied our needs for stability and harmony in our everydayness which is not alien to the aesthetic dimension.

Dewey emphasizes Renoir's great ability to take hold of the phases of objects that especially interest him and, within the limits of the artwork under production, to grasp and embody "the total esthetic quality of an experience" ([1934a] 1989, 135), which has a property that Dewey called "livingness," a quality of moving from within and that can absorb us, as in Renoir's paintings of children reading or sewing. Renoir in Dewey's estimation shows us the richness of everydayness if it is properly attended to, provided, of course, that its frames, both natural and constructed, embody forms of what we could call aesthetic rationality. Nature is the omnipresent originating and shaping frame or matrix of our lives. Artworks, as Dewey has clearly shown, arise within this originating frame by the creative transformation and transfiguration of nature itself, on which they bear in multiple ways. They shape nature and our perception of nature, both human and nonhuman, by capturing in a unique way every aspect of an infinite play of forms as they manifest themselves in our experience, shaping us and locating us in places and times.

## Shaping Nature: Qualities of Space-Time in Art and Life

In line with his metaphysical vision, Dewey sees nature as a processive system of space-time. In the chapter in *Art as Experience* on "The Common Substance of the Arts," Dewey remarks that "space and time—or rather space-time—are found in the matter of every art product" ([1934a] 1989, 210). In painting, for example, space relates to, and is a factor in, the constitution of form. Dewey notes it is also felt directly or experienced as a quality. Dewey ascribes to James a key role in establishing that sounds had more than a temporal quality; they were also spatially voluminous, as musicians know. While science aims to reduce the qualities of space and time to relations captured in equations, it is the prime function of art to "make them abound in their own sense as significant values of the very substance of all things" (210–211). While the power drive of science is toward formal relations in a space-time field grasped mathematically, such relations in experience are "infinitely diversified and cannot be described, while in works of art they are *expressed*" (211). Art, in Dewey's account, involves significant selection—not universalization, but rather exemplification or exhibiting of a way of taking its thing-meant. The thing-meant, as well as the form in which it is embodied, is the uniquely significant result of intertwined processes of abstraction, compression, and intensification of experience, which push us across thresholds of habit and custom.

It is traditionally thought that the plastic arts—painting, drawing, sculpture, architecture—engage the spatial aspects of change while the literary arts and music focus on the temporal aspects of experience. However, the difference, Dewey says, is one of focus or emphasis. They share a common substance: the space-time matrix of our lives. Dewey adduces, or claims to adduce, a striking example of this: a close correspondence between the opening bars of Beethoven's fifth symphony and the "serial order of weights, of ponderous volumes, in Cézanne's 'Card Players'" ([1934a] 1989, 212). The "placed" figures have a "voluminous quality," conferring on them power, strength, and solidity—"like a massive, well-constructed bridge of stone," expressing the enduring and the structurally resistant (212). These are *felt* qualities that are embodied both spatially in a picture and temporally in a set of complex sounds (see figure 5.5).

Space and time, as experienced space-time, is "infinitely diversified in qualities" (212). Dewey is in full agreement with Peirce and James that existence itself is qualitatively defined, what Peirce called its "Firstness" and James foregrounded in his famous notion of the different feelings of "and,"

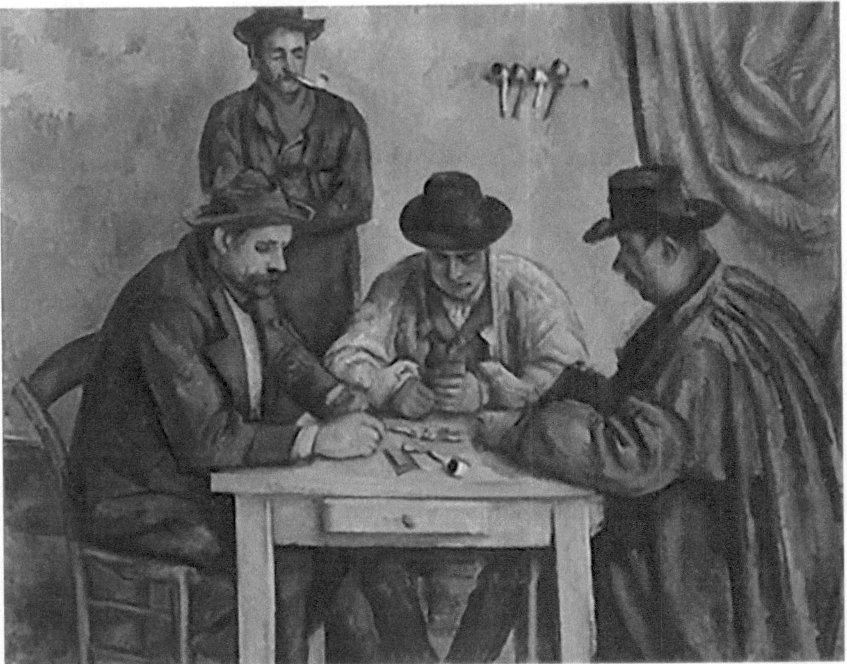

Fig. 5.5. Paul Cézanne, *The Card Players*, First Version, 1890–1992. *Source*: Metropolitan Museum of Art, New York.

"but," "then," "until," and so forth. This infinite diversification of space and time can be reduced, he claims, to three general themes: Room, Extent, Position—Spaciousness, Spatiality, Spacing—and the temporal correlates, Transition, Endurance, and Date. These dimensions, he claims, are distinguishable in thought but have no separate existence ([1934a] 1989, 212).

All three interlocked aspects of this space-time matrix manifest both aesthetic and everyday consequences. Space is first of all, as he puts it, *Raum*, roominess, not just in the physical sense but also in the existential sense of a "breathing space" that allows us to live with a sense of potentiality and to live and move in multiple dimensions. Likewise, there is a "space of time" which makes possible the accomplishment of anything significant. Inasmuch as *omnis determinatio est negatio*—that is, value arises out of limitation—infinite room, whether of time or space, leads to dispersion: "Limitations must bear a definite ratio to power; they involve cooperative choice; they cannot be imposed" ([1934a] 1989, 213). Dewey goes on to say that "works of art express space as opportunity for movement and action" whose proportions are "qualitatively felt" and notes that a lyric poem can have it while a "would-be" epic does not. Indeed, as many of us have experienced, a miniature painting can immensely surpass a canvas covered by acres of paint. This is clearly seen in the exceptional sense of spaciousness already noted in Chinese paintings and also, Dewey perspicuously notes, in an unnamed portrait of an individual by Titian in which "infinite space, not just the canvas, is behind the figure" (213).

Second, space and time in experience, Dewey writes, are also "occupancy, filling. . . . Spatiality is mass and volume, as temporality is endurance, not just abstract duration" ([1934a] 1989, 213). In our experience there is the shrinking and expanding of colors and sounds just as there is the rise and fall, the heightening and fading, of both colors and sounds. But neither colors nor sounds are free-floating and isolated. Colors especially belong to objects in a "world possessed of extent and volume" and sounds both return and proceed, displaying intervals and progressions that belong to them, and not just isolated tones. They have identity and continuation, but that does not mean, Dewey says, that they are associated with natural objects—although clearly they can be: brooks murmur, leaves whisper and rustle, waves ripple, surf and thunder roar, wind moans and whispers. Nevertheless, empty time, he states, does not exist, nor is there such an "entity" as time. "What exists are things acting and changing, and a constant quality of their behavior is temporal" (214). This is a matrix of artworks and not just of nature. Volume is an experiential quality independent of the physical characteristic of mere size and bulk, which can be objectively measured. Small landscapes, Dewey insightfully says, can open onto unlimited space or embody qualities of fragility and frailness without being aesthetically weak. Solidity and massiveness, or their reverse, can mark a wide range of artworks of different genres.

The third property, spacing, involves place or position, the "distribution of intervals through spacing," and contributes to realizing the individualization of parts. Rightness of placing is integral to the immediate qualitative value of a position, its just-right-ness, which is directly felt. This is also a mark of the fittingness or aura that is grasped in the encounter with a work that "works." What Dewey called the power of the concrete is manifested both in energy of position and also energy of motion. Intervals and spacings can be favorable, or unfavorable, to the manifestation of energy, while others frustrate and block. This is especially so, Dewey remarks, in the case of the "bustle and ado of modern life," which renders "nicety of placing the most difficult for artists to achieve" (216). But I think this remark bears more on life outside the projects of art and is a manifestation of Dewey's hesitation about the distortions of modern life, a topic I have explored elsewhere (Innis 1987, 2002).

Dewey summarizes his position in the following way, having recourse once again to the central and indispensable idea of quality.

> I have said that the three qualities of space and time reciprocally affect and qualify one another in experience. Space is inane save as occupied with active volumes. Pauses are holes when they do not accentuate masses and define figures as individuals. Extension sprawls and finally benumbs if it does not interact with place so as to assume intelligible distribution. Mass is nothing fixed. It contracts and expands, asserts itself and yields, according to its relations to other spatial and enduring things. While we may view these traits from the standpoint of form, of rhythm, balance and organization, the relations which thought grasps as ideas are present as *qualities* in perception and they inhere in the very substance of art. ([1934a] 1989 217)

## The Exemplary Place of Architecture

Dewey's schematization of the experienced qualities of space and time offers indispensable analytical tools for our understanding and evaluation of the exemplary place of architecture and its generative processes in human life. It complements and exemplifies the scope of his aesthetics in ways bearing on the very matrices of the lifeworld for all of us. The built world, the architectural world with its varying scales, is, as Dewey puts it, "supremely expressive of human interests and values" ([1934a] 1989, 225). In its spatial and temporal dimensions it influences the future, it records and conveys memories of the past, and it informs the present and our forms of attunement (Pérez-Gomez 2016). For Dewey, architecture "records and celebrates more than any other art the generic features of our common human life." ([1934a] 1989, 234). It is the fusion of *building* and *dwelling*, as Heidegger wrote, a theme taken up in different ways by Richard Sennett (2018), John McDermott (1976, 1987, 2007), and Tim Ingold (2000, 2013). Such a fusion marks humanity's universal activity to make a place for ourselves and *ground* ourselves *on* and sometimes *in* the earth. Dewey writes that buildings, in intent if not in reality, come the nearest to expressing "the stability and endurance of existence. They are to mountains what music is to the sea" ([1934a] 1989, 234).

Dewey does not claim that architecture is the highest art form. He leans for various reasons toward the priority of literature and painting. But the designed and built world exists all around us. It engages us on all levels in our everyday life and exemplifies and confirms in the highest degree Dewey's assertion that aesthetic experience is, first and foremost, a matter of *perception* in the fullest sense, including imaginative perception. It involves, at the ideal limit, a "total organic response." The products of architecture and its subsidiary and connected arts of design (doorknobs and handles, light fixtures, furniture of all sorts, teakettles and beer glasses) are universally accessible. We can test the aesthetic status and import of architecture and the built world by measuring their perceptual and symbolic richness without having to go to museums or concert halls.

*Art as Experience* is deeply critical of many, but certainly not all, architectural practices, especially in the United States, in that period of industrial capitalism in which it appeared, although its scope is by no means restricted to that time.

> As long as art is the beauty parlor of civilization, neither art nor civilization is secure. Why is the architecture of our large cities so unworthy of a fine civilization? It is not from lack of materials nor from lack of technical capacity. And yet it is not merely slums but the apartments of the well-to-do that are esthetically repellent, because they are so destitute of imagination. Their character is determined by an economic system in which land is used—and kept out of use—for the sake of gain, because of profit derived from rental and sale. Until land is freed from this economic burden, beautiful buildings may occasionally be erected, but there is little hope for the rise of general architectural construction worthy of a noble civilization. ([1934a] 1989, 346)

In this passage, which was written in the time of the Great Depression, Dewey offers, not just a descriptive, but also a multileveled, normative framework for an analysis of architecture. It is, however, not principally a social and political normative framework concerning the tension between use values and exchange values or between the well-to-do and those dwelling in slums. For Dewey, the social and political critiques are themselves based, or should be based, on a kind of ideal of aesthetic rationality, which is rooted in the body as the matrix of our encounter, or rather, intertwining with the world (Innis 1987). About this intertwining, Dewey writes that it is "an act of perception [that] proceeds by waves that extend serially throughout the entire organism" ([1934a] 1989, 59). Steen Eiler Rasmussen remarked, in his classic *Experiencing Architecture*, on how difficult it is to find the right words for "how we perceive things that surround us" (1959, 8). Living in the built world affects us "all the way" down—and, of course, all "the way up"—to the symbolic level. Architectural practices of design and building, according to Deweyan principles, must be carried out not just with full recognition of the perceptual *effects* of its products. Dewey and, as I will argue, the Finnish architect Juhani Pallasmaa have also foregrounded the perceptual *roots* of the formative factors of the processes of *design and production* that enter into and inform these effects.

Yi-Fu Tuan, a cultural geographer, has a passage in *Space and Place* (1977, 106–107) that bears on the perceptual matrices of this problem:

> Building is a complex activity. It makes people aware and take heed at different levels: at the level of having to make pragmatic decisions; of envisioning architectural spaces in the mind and on paper; and of committing one's whole being, mind and body, to the creation of a material form that captures an ideal. Once achieved, architectural form is an environment for man. How does it then influence human feeling and consciousness? The analogy of language throws light on the question. Words contain and intensify feeling. Without words feeling reaches a momentary peak and quickly disappears. Perhaps one reason why animal emotions do not reach the intensity and duration of human ones is that animals have no language to hold emotions so that they can either grow or fester. The built environment, like language, has the power to define and refine sensibility. It can sharpen and enlarge consciousness. Without architecture feelings about space must remain diffuse and fleeting.

The contours of the experiential side of this phenomenon are also engaged by E. V. Walter in his *Placeways: A Theory of the Human Environment* (1988), which is devoted to the development of *topistics* (from Greek topos, "place"). Walter writes: "Human experience makes a place, but a place lives in its own way. Its form of experience occupies persons—the place locates experience in people. A place is a matrix of energies, generating representations and causing changes in awareness" (131). The idea of a place "locating" experience in people is a provocative one, as is the contention that "the energies of place flow through its meanings" (12). Joseph Grange, in his book *The City: An Urban Ecology* (1999), writes, against the background of his roots in the South Bronx, that there is a "certain tone of feeling that pervades a particular urban region, structure, or event" (97). These meanings of place, in distinctive configurations of form, rhythm, balance, and organization, are not just in or addressed to the "head" but are materially embodied and become "located" in our bodies within assemblages of diverse placeways and meshed lifelines (Innis 2017a; Ingold 2015, 2017). The relations of form, rhythm, balance, and organization, Dewey points out (following Peirce), are present as *qualities* in perception, giving it, too, a distinctive tone or quale.

Dewey's philosophical naturalism strongly affirms our essential rootedness in the material world in all its dimensions. Dewey sees the surroundings arising from large-scale industrialization that humans have made or are forced to live in as offering meager fulfillments and eliciting repulsions of an unprecedented order. He sees in the midst of the Great Depression the continuing effects of the "Satanic mills" of modern industry and of an unregulated economic system of production for private gain at public expense. John Ruskin, independently of the analyses of Marx, subjected the lived logic of this system to devastating aesthetic criticism. Still, Dewey writes:

> There are, however, certain considerations that should deter one from concluding that industrial conditions render impossible an integration of art in civilization. . . . Every well-constructed object and machine has form, but there is esthetic form only when the object having this external form fits into a larger experience. Interaction of the material of this experience with the utensil or machine cannot be left out of account. . . . There is something clean in the esthetic sense about a piece of machinery that has a logical structure that fits it for its work, and the polish of steel and copper that is essential to good performance is intrinsically pleasing in perception. . . . The external architecture of city apartments remains box-like but internally there is hardly less than an esthetic revolution brought about by better adaptation to need. ([1934a] 1989, 344)

This need is an aesthetic need in the broadest sense. Dewey writes that the "organism hungers naturally for satisfaction in the material of experience. . . . The hunger of the organism for satisfaction through the eye is hardly less than its urgent impulsion for food" ([1934a] 1989, 345). It is not just the eye, but rather the living body in its full reality that hungers, caught up as it is in the tension filled fields of life and embedded in nature and the constructed second nature of the built world.

There is ample support in our own experiences and life contexts for Dewey's valuable observations and demands. Dewey's guidelines, as well as those of Tuan and Walter, point us toward the "pressure points" where a pragmatist aesthetics, especially in Dewey's mode, as inspired by Peirce's theory of quality and James's theme-field-margin schema of experience, comes into contact with the omnipresent pressing reality of the built world in all its variety.

These pressure points are foregrounded in the work of the philosophically sophisticated practicing Finnish architect, Juhani Pallasmaa. Pallasmaa offers novel links to, and extensions of, Dewey's pragmatist experiential aesthetics and its bearing on architecture. In *The Eyes of the Skin: Architecture and the Senses*, Pallasmaa (2005) "fleshes out" in the case of architecture a central Deweyan descriptive and normative claim: the built world should be held to the measure of how well its construction activates us on all levels of our bodily being. In *The Thinking Hand: Existential and Embodied Wisdom in Architecture* (2009), Pallasmaa confirms and illustrates the "handed" or "hand-guided" generative matrix of processes of organizing energies that are involved in the creative design of the built world. Pallasmaa sees the hand as the key to the processes of architectural design that respect the contribution of embodied imagination to the realization of the *haptic* dimension. This dimension, he claims, is central to taking the measure of architecture's reaching of its goal. Works of architecture are designed and produced and dwelt in as repositories of existential meaning that "touch us" and evoke the "total organic response," which Dewey sees as integral to "having an experience" and not just passing through it.

I will focus on three important links between Dewey and Pallasmaa: (a) the foregrounding of the "handedness" of design, (b) the relation between feeling and materiality in architecture, and (c) architecture as the articulation of an existential space of meaning.

## On Design and the Hand

A passage in *Art as Experience* anticipates Pallasmaa's philosophically and experientially rooted account of the design primacy of the thinking hand.

Writer, composer of music, sculptor, or painter can retrace, during the process of production, what they have previously done. When it is not satisfactory in the undergoing or perceptual phase of experience, they can to some degree start afresh. This retracing is not readily accomplished in the case of architecture—which is perhaps one reason why there are so many ugly buildings. Architects are obliged to complete their idea before its translation into a complete object of perception takes place. Inability to build up simultaneously the idea and its objective embodiment imposes a handicap. Nevertheless, they too are obliged to think out their ideas in terms of the medium of embodiment and the object of ultimate perception unless they work mechanically and by rote. Probably the esthetic quality of medieval cathedrals is due in some measure to the fact that their constructions were not so much controlled by plans and specifications made in advance as is now the case. Plans grew as the building grew. But even a Minerva-like product, if it is artistic, presupposes a prior period of gestation in which doings and perceptions projected in imagination interact and mutually modify one another. Every work of art follows the plan of, and pattern of, a complete experience, rendering it more intensely and concentratedly felt. ([1934a] 1989, 58)

Pallasmaa goes further and deeper than Dewey in specifying the lessons of architectural practice and not just its results, issues that were engaged from a rather different, though related, background by Spuybroek (2016, 2020). Pallasmaa sees, in the dependence on the computer of modern architectural design, a gross undervaluing of the "tacit understanding of the body in the making of architecture" due to the "quasi-rationality and arrogant self-consciousness" of today's culture (2009, 15; see also Robinson and Pallasmaa 2015). For him—and also for the Finnish tradition in which he has lived and worked—architecture is a "product of the knowing hand. The hand grasps the physicality and materiality of thought and turns it into a concrete image. In the arduous processes of designing, the hand often takes the lead in probing for a vision, a vague inkling that it eventually turns into a sketch, a materialisation of an idea" (Pallasmaa 2009, 16–17).

Pallasmaa has serious reservations about the ascendance of the computer at the initial stages of designing or imagining an architectural work as a complex whole, topics taken up in great detail by Spuybroek and Ingold. Computer imaging in Pallasmaa's conception involves a flattening of the active multisensory and synchronic imagining of the emerging architectural idea of the design process, thus turning the process into a "passive visual manipulation, a retinal journey" (2005, 12), the result of which is discussed with critical nuance by Bardt (2019) in his chapter on "design tools and their roles" in his *Material and Mind*, the relevance of which extends far beyond architecture to a social and material aesthetics. But it is not, in Pallasmaa's opinion, only flattening. His claim is that the computer creates "distance" between the maker of a design and its object. The process of drawing by hand and working with physical models, analog procedures *par excellence*, has a haptic dimension that is absent from the abstract mathematized and digital space of the computer model that is taking form in front of the architect, who chooses from a continuum of pregiven points, which are then subject to easy manipulation. They leave no "trace" in the literal sense of being grounded in the prior groping with charcoal, pen, or pencil to find the feel of appropriate form on paper. In the processes of manual drawing, the object to be created that is taking shape in the imagination is, Pallasmaa argues, "held in the hand and inside the head" (2005, 12–13). This is, he holds, the source of the necessary empathy and compassion that allow us to project ourselves into the space that is to be filled by and to determine a structure in which life and movement are to be situated and take place.

## Feeling and Materiality

As to the relations between feeling in the broadest sense and materiality, Pallasmaa makes the contentious claim, which we should all reflect on depending on the built-environmental situations in which we each live, that "modernist design at large has housed the intellect and the eye, but it has left the body and the other senses, as well as our memories, imagination and dreams, homeless" (2005, 19). The impact of modernist design on the experience of architecture, Pallasmaa claims, has been profound. For Pallasmaa, authentic architectural experiences do not consist in apprehending a façade, or a constellation of façades, in a formal manner, as if that were a building's essence and the ground of its relations to other buildings (something that many of us do or are inclined to do). Pallasmaa recognizes rather that we move *into*, *in*, and *among* buildings. The building or building complex is approached and entered, but generally not as if we were entering contemplatively into the world of a painting or a stage set—although there are certainly many successful instances of this, such as the lovely Piazza Sant'Ignazio in Rome or the quite different spatial feel of Piazza del

Popolo. Indeed, Gernot Böhme (Böhme 2017a, 2017b) has shown how the "art of staging" is a heuristic clue to an aesthetics of atmospheres, including those autodefining atmospheres that are embodied in buildings as distinct felt spaces.

In the paradigmatic case of a single domestic building, Pallasmaa argues (although the point is quite general), we have to think in *verbal* forms. It is the act of *entering* and not simply the visual design of the door or gate, the act of *looking* in or out through a window or along a perspective rather than the window itself as a material object to be merely seen in relation to other windows (and that are primarily looked at from the outside as part of the building's surface), or the feeling of *occupying* a sphere of warmth, whether physical or atmospheric. *Entering, looking, occupying*: do these not also correspond to our engagement with the Baroque *sceneggiatura* of Piazza Sant'Ignazio or the Neoclassical reconfiguration of the space encountered entering through the Porta del Popolo, the Porta Flaminia of ancient Rome? As Pallasmaa puts it in a passage with deep connections to Dewey's differentiation of space: "Architectural space is lived space rather than physical space, and lived space always transcends geometry and measurability" (2005, 64), even if it respects it and relies on it. The lived geometry of Piazza Sant'Ignazio differs radically *in feel* from that of the Piazza del Popolo, just as the cities of Boston, São Paulo, New York, Chicago, Rome, Buenos Aires, and so forth differ radically. We do not need such "famous" exemplars, however, to illustrate the point, which has an eminently local relevance.

Pallasmaa argues, paralleling Dewey, that in the design process, the architect must first of all imaginatively *feel* him- or herself into the space, thus internalizing

> the landscape, the entire context, and the functional requirements as well as his/her conceived building: movement, balance and scale are felt unconsciously through the body as tensions in the muscular system and in the positions of the skeleton and inner organs. As the work interacts with the body of the observer, the experience mirrors the bodily sensations of the maker. Consequently, architecture is communication from the body of the architect directly to the body of the person who encounters the work, perhaps centuries later. (2005, 66–67)

Looked at this way, the meaning or significance of a building—or a built and occupied space framed by buildings—is not merely conceptual or a function of being constructed according to some set of coded elements or "orders," although such orders have played key roles in the evolution of architectural practices.

A passage in *Art as Experience* (Dewey [1934a] 1989, 233–234) goes further in foregrounding the bodily materiality of a building—or configuration of buildings that make up a village, town, city, or even region.

> The trait that characterizes architecture in an emphatic sense is that its media are the (relatively) raw materials of nature and of the fundamental modes of natural energy. Its effects are dependent upon features that belong in dominant measure to just these materials. All of the "shaping" arts bend natural materials and forms of energy to serve some human desire. . . . Compare buildings with other artistic products and you are at once struck by the indefinitely wide range of materials it adopts to its ends—wood, stone, steel, cement, burnt clay, glass, rushes, . . . as compared with the relatively restricted number of materials available in painting, sculpture, poetry.

Can we not think of architecture and the built or designed world as a kind of Wagnerian *Gesamtkunstwerk*, part of the staging of the human opera of life? Architecture takes up the natural energies of gravity, stress, thrust as well as the perceived qualities of these materials to express what Dewey calls the "enduring values of collective human life." Or—in the case of much "monumental architecture"—the enduring disvalues and contradictions, too, as the contentious debate on the status of Confederate monuments in the United States has shown. This debate was already framed by Dewey's remark about the "esthetic vulgarity" of "our terrible civil-war monuments" ([1934a] 1989, 173).

## Architecture and the Articulation of the Existential Space of Meaning

As to the relation between architecture and the articulation of the existential space of meaning, Dewey thinks of the "representational"—or semiotic—dimension of architecture as encompassing the "memories, hopes, fears, purposes, and sacred values" ([1934a] 1989, 230) of those who dwell in and act in the different types of structures—palaces, fortresses, temples, domestic dwellings, public fora, law courts, museums, prisons, and so forth. This dimension is what Langer (1953, 95) called the "ethnic domain." It is the *pattern of relations* between these types of structures that a critical pragmatism (and a pragmatist semiotics) must attend to. There is no reason to assume that there cannot be severe contrasts and tensions between those who interact and engage one another within the contexts of the social, political, and cultural forces located in and symbolized by these structures, whose material quality or degree of aesthetic value are indicative of social relations. A building such as a prison does not have an inevitable connection only with engineering, but also with power, especially the power to control and constrain human affects and the occupation of preferential spaces. Dewey sees aesthetic values in architecture—or the lack thereof and the presence of other "values"—as "peculiarly dependent upon meanings drawn from collective human life" ([1934a] 1989, 242). We must hesitate, however, to always think of "aesthetic" here in a laudatory sense. There is an aesthetics of control and power that *encloses* just as there is an aesthetics that engages us in or furthers the *open* play of embodied meaning.

Clearly, however, if we tried to respond with full attention to every perceptual detail of the environing built world we would be paralyzed, although we can also be both enriched as well as paralyzed against our will by the overpowering prevalence of tacit apprehensions of our surroundings. Nevertheless, we can still agree with Pallasmaa's contention, which mirrors Dewey's own position as well as those of Tuan and Walter: "In memorable experiences of architecture, space, matter and time fuse into one singular dimension, into the basic substance of being, that penetrates our consciousness. We identify ourselves with this space, this place, this moment, and these dimensions become ingredients of our very existence. Architecture is the art of reconciliation between ourselves and the world, and this mediation takes place through the senses" (2005, 72). This penetration occurs in many ways behind our backs or at least without any thematic action on our part by means of the tacit assimilation of the affordances furnished in the environmental array that we do not focally attend to but embody ourselves in and are steered by. Architecture and the built world are not concerned with mere visual aestheticization functioning as a kind of veneer on something that would putatively perform its function without it. Architecture's power is rooted in the deep structures and processes of *aesthesis* quite generally, as Böhme has convincingly argued with conceptual tools consonant with Dewey's analytical thrust.

Pallasmaa ascribes a higher calling to architecture, even if it is permanently situated in an "aisthetic" or polysensory matrix. Architecture in his view is most fundamentally a "mode of existential and metaphysical philosophising through the means of space, structure, matter, gravity and light.

Profound architecture does not merely beautify the settings of dwelling: great buildings articulate the experiences of our very existence" (2009, 19). They "articulate" in the sense of "make manifest" or "exemplify" or "materially" embody these experiences and their constitutive conditions. We can authentically dwell in them to the degree that they, as Polanyi puts it, "effect the integration of the diffuse aspects of our existence in time into a felt unity" (Polanyi and Prosch 1975, 75) and, in this way, function as material symbols to which we surrender ourselves and for which we feel deep affection.

While Pallasmaa clearly is thinking of articulation as something positive, clearly any building or conglomeration of buildings also can articulate experiences that lack the quickening power of "profound" architecture or built surroundings by being either functionally transparent or deadening. Like Dewey, Pallasmaa recognizes this negative side of architecture: "Architectural ugliness or existential falseness can make us experience alienation and weakening of the sense of self, and finally make us fall mentally and somatically ill" (2009, 133). Is this not, as in the case of the United States and clearly in other nations around the world, a by-product of slums or racially segregated communities, egregiously decrepit public housing projects, prisons, public offices, and so forth, one of the architectural sources of the increasingly widespread politics of resentment and anger and the widespread ruling of our lives by negative comparisons? Pallasmaa argues that we need an architecture "that makes us experience the world rather than itself" (2009, 133). A work of architecture, he says, "places itself directly in our existential experience. . . . Architecture does not invent meaning; it can move us only if it is capable of touching something already buried deep in our embodied memories" (2009, 135–136)—or fail to move or touch us in some positive fashion because something else is buried deep and is reenforced by the material circumstances of our lives.

Societies, and different groups within them, have structured—or been forced to structure—and live in different existential spaces that ground their collective identities and senses of togetherness or apartness. Pallasmaa is right, as is Dewey, to affirm that it is the essential purpose of architecture, whether monumental or not, to structure and articulate the existential flesh of the world that makes up our exosomatic bodies and gives it specific meanings. "Architecture turns the soulless physical world into a home of man. We know and remember who we are and where we belong fundamentally through our cities and buildings, our constructed world, the human—architecturally humanised—microcosm"; or, as the case may be, the architecturally dehumanized microcosm (2009, 128).

Pallasmaa cites a passage from Wittgenstein (1984, 74), who famously and paradoxically designed a dwelling for his sister that was incompatible with the living logic of domestic space: "Architecture immortalises and glorifies something. Hence, there can be no architecture, where there is nothing to glorify." In such circumstances, loss of the ideal dimension of life implies architecture's disappearance—even at the most pedestrian level. What Pallasmaa calls "meaningful buildings" "arise from tradition and they constitute and continue a tradition" (2009, 146). They "articulate" a tradition both positively and negatively and in this way perhaps stand as a permanent measure of what we have to live up to or try to escape from.

Pallasmaa's approach to architecture may seem to focus inordinately on aesthetically remarkable architecture and forms. But his concern for hapticity and the permeating omnipresence of our perception and indwelling in the environment is central to the critical bite of his analyses and proposals. They bear on the wide theme of the politics of architecture and its philosophical import. Pallasmaa cites another rather startling statement from Wittgenstein's *Culture and Value*: "Work on philosophy—like work in architecture in many respects—is really more work on oneself. On one's own conception. On how one sees things. (And what one expects of them.)" (1984, 24).

What does one expect of the self-work of an architect? For Pallasmaa, an architect is, first and foremost, a craftsman attuned to the demands of the materials that support his or her work and, most important, one attuned to the demands of those for *whom* one is working and *where* one is working, issues concerning the technical and social matrices of craftsmanship taken up in different ways by Sennett (2009) and Bardt (2019). Pallasmaa contends that the architect must have the kind of knowledge of the lived contexts of building that, for example, a skilled athlete has in operating in a "field inhabited by a 'knowing body'" (Pallasmaa 2009, 124). Just as a musician pours him- or herself into the music, so the architect has also, at least ideally, poured his or her life and existential knowledge into what he or she has built and the materials—or has failed to do so for various reasons, whether political, economic, or technical.

The authentic or ideal architect, Pallasmaa argues, "needs to internalise the client, the other, and develop the design for his altered self" (2009, 125), that is, to design so that a truly habitable "existential space" is constructed for whomever it is intended. The ultimate client is we ourselves, in our different orientations and life contexts. Indeed, "the architect needs to create his/her ideal client in the process of design" (2009, 125), not by imposing a rigid philosophical schema on the evolving structure but rather by following the culturally diversified lived logics of our being in space and place and of coming to dwell in a locus where our energies are organized and we come to rest in place, at home in the world—whatever that world may be. Not every work of architecture or habitat need be, or can be, profound. One needs a background matrix, with its own distinctive quality, that informs and frames one's everydayness, but one also needs forms of buildings and lived spaces that not only embody and activate one's individual and collective memory but also to point toward ideals that should bind us together and not tear us apart. For Pallasmaa as for Dewey, "Architecture provides our most important existential icons by which we can understand both our culture and ourselves" (2009, 147). The architect must "defend the enigma of life and the eroticism of the life world" (2009, 148)—in the face of existential emptiness and erotic or sensuous impoverishment.

Pallasmaa thinks of architecture as opposing the speeding up of things that marks modernity—and of those who seek in vain to catch up to it. But it is hard, in light of a world in turmoil marked by the spreading clamor of megalopolises, to find a way for architecture "to slow down experience, halt time, and defend the natural slowness and diversity of experience . . . to maintain and defend silence" (2009, 150). This is clearly a Nordic or Baltic preference, but it is perhaps best thought of more as a dimension than as a predominant frame for lived existential space and time. A city or urban conglomeration is not a monastery. If the duty of architecture in the broadest sense, as Pallasmaa conceives it, is to "to survey ideals and new modes of perception and experience, and thus open up and widen the boundaries of our lived world" (150), it must become an art form—and the generative core of a life form—of "[the] eye, the hand, the head and the heart" (147), both in its construction and in our existential indwelling in it.

## Conclusion

Pallasmaa's phenomenology of the eyes of the skin and the thinking hand is deeply pragmatist and adds confirmation, nuance, and detail grounded in architectural practice to Dewey's comprehensive experiential aesthetics. Dewey writes that art—and by extension architecture—as a "unique transcript of the energy of things of the world" operates by "selecting those potencies in things by which an experience—any experience—has significance and value," that is, by which experiences "act upon us and interest us" ([1934a] 1989, 189). Dewey's aesthetic approach is far from focusing on the monumental. It encompasses all the forms of everydayness in which we live out our lives and which we both assimilate and are assimilated to in the formation of habits.

Around all the objects, situations, and events that determine and inform the affective, actional, and conceptual fields making up the existential space of our lives is found a Jamesian margin or aura of resonances that mark the infinite iridescences of consciousness that are bound together by a defining quality. The art of life is played out in all the forms of experiencing. Dewey writes that "in every experience, there is the pervading underlying qualitative whole that corresponds to and manifests the whole organization of activities which constitute the mysterious human frame" ([1934a] 1989, 200). We are located in dynamic fields of experiencing that grow by their edges. Dewey and Pallasmaa recognize that the seemingly arrhythmic "bustle and ado of modern life" presents special problems for architects and for all of us who must live in a primarily built and designed world marked by a profusion of materials and activities that seem to run on their own with no concern for us and that pull us in against our will. But it is incumbent on us, following Dewey and Pallasmaa, to attempt to construct an environment composed and rhythmically marked by orders exemplifying a "rationality among qualities" (1934, 174), an aesthetic norm (Innis 1987, 2002, chapters 4, 5, and 6) that transcends art in the strict sense.

A pragmatist approach to architecture, following Dewey and Pallasmaa, sees every structure, whether important or not, as, in Dewey's words, a "treasury of storied memories" or a "registering of cherished expectancies for the future" ([1934a] 1989, 230), and also as a present existing repository of affective, perceptual, and symbolic valences. We need to see and measure them through the eyes of the skin, recognizing that no perceptual occasion ultimately leaves us indifferent or unchanged. They operate behind our backs and often against our will. We should see the multiform structures of architecture, like literature, working with what Dewey called "loaded dice," their materials "charged with meanings they have absorbed through immemorial time" and presenting the values of collective life ([1934a] 1989, 249). It is up to us to determine whether the meanings and values embodied in these structures enliven or deaden us and whether they exemplify and further the ideals of a life worthy of living in all its dimensions—and, if not, why not.

# CHAPTER 6

# Pragmatism and the Challenge of a Cosmopolitan Aesthetics

## *On Theory beyond Borders*

### The Problem—Scharfstein's Challenge

In his *Art without Borders: A Philosophical Exploration of Art and Humanity*, Ben-Ami Scharfstein, writing against the background of his deeply pragmatic *The Dilemma of Context* (1989), contends that "art is not a single problem, nor does it have a single solution, rational or mystical" (2009, 179). Art's multiple contexts, and its types of contexts, are, he argues, the sources of this radical plurality, which characterizes thought itself. In this, art mirrors life. Nevertheless, in spite of the admitted plurality, he issues a call for an "open aesthetics" and an "aesthetic pluralism" and asks, "Is there really an aesthetics that cuts across all human cultures?" (404). It may be that there is, but it is not immediately clear how openness and pluralism can be accommodated to the putative demand of cosmopolitanism to be universal and not provincial. This is the core issue of the project of developing a cosmopolitan aesthetics, an aesthetics that is not limited to, or based on, any one place, either *temperamental, geographical, conceptual*, or *political*. These types of places are deeply intertwined, and each marks a space of difference with potentially, but not necessarily, deleterious consequences in many dimensions of life. Such places other than our own, whatever they may be, may strike us as strange, and often we may treat them and those who inhabit them as dangerous or threatening to our entrenched forms of self-understanding, which get valorized in forms of power and dominance embodied in state institutions with the aim to control the Other.

A cosmopolitan aesthetics would recognize in a spirit of affirmation the validity or value of temperamental differences; accept the rootedness of aesthetic values in different ecological or geographical frames; acknowledge that the conceptual tools used in aesthetic theories have links to other conceptual commitments, especially metaphysical world visions, and need not have the same weight or focus in every tradition and their paradigmatic art forms; and be wary of the political enforcement of official art.

Scharfstein points out the ineluctable and irreducible "difference between generalizations and their examples" (2009, 434), a difference known to everyone who has read a book on aesthetic theory or reflected on their own aesthetic experience. A recognition of this difference runs throughout these chapters. Theories need exemplifications, to be sure, but aesthetic theories are notoriously connected with the tastes and preferences of the theorist, a point foregrounded in Hume's classic essay on the standard of taste. But exemplifications likewise need theories, in some sense of that term, in order to be placed in an intelligible context and validated. A cursory look at John Dewey's examples, including the original illustrations in *Art as Experience* ([1934a] 1989) or in Santayana's own cosmopolitan *The Sense of Beauty* ([1896] 1988), bears out this reciprocity between theory and exemplification, but one could choose practically any book at random, from any tradition from Aristotle to the present day, to illustrate the point. It is to Scharfstein's great merit—and a challenge to us—that he tries to avoid both the perils of an ungrounded or unreflecting provincialism and an aesthetic version of Hegel's complaint about Schelling's Absolute, that it was "the night in which, as the saying goes, all cows are black" (Hegel 1807, 9).

Still, the nonflattening universal implications of a cosmopolitan aesthetics is gestured toward in Scharfstein's not unambiguous remark that "it is its universalization that distinguishes aesthetic from ordinary experience" (2009, 420). Here the reference point of universalization is not *art* in an essentialist sense, but a principled contrast drawn between dimensions, phases, or types of *exemplified experiences* of certain types of objects or situations, whether they are art in any predefined sense or not. Aesthetic experience, as well as its objects, would seem to have more than a merely local or idiosyncratic appeal if the notion of some kind of universality or intelligibility is to have any validity at all. Art and aesthetic experiences, while necessarily embedded in, as well as creating, particular contexts, must in some sense be able to transcend these contexts and their boundaries, or at least in principle not be limited to them. They must be in some way open to everyone but not necessarily on their own terms, and there has to be a context, or at least an interpretive process, that contextualizes these contexts, perhaps a kind of metacontext that allows mutual and nonreductive engagement. This metacontext does not have to be universal theory but simply a set of hermeneutical practices that Gadamer ([1960] 1991) characterized as the fusion of horizons. Such practices will accept the permanent tension between cosmopolitan, open, and universal. *Cosmopolitan* foregrounds the self-conscious or self-reflective non-provinciality of an aesthetic theory or aesthetic practice; *open* foregrounds the consequent unbounded willingness to accept new instances of aesthetic values; and *universal* foregrounds the aspect of general import of aesthetic products or their demand on us for recognition. While clearly not identical, these labels have substantial overlap and relations of mutual implication.

Scharfstein's challenge is clear. A cosmopolitan aesthetics must find a way of surmounting multiple boundaries, between (a) historical artistic traditions, with radically different forms of art and their cultural, including philosophical, matrices, (b) forms and genera of art and their rankings, (c) the experience of art and other forms of (aesthetic and nonaesthetic) experience, (d) art and nonart, and so forth. Obviously, it is not possible to deal with all these issues in the course of a single chapter; nor could Scharfstein do so even in the course of 500 dense and nuanced pages.

It is primarily, though not exclusively, the first type of boundary that I will be concerned with, although each boundary type bears on the problem at hand. It is a commonplace in the history of art and of the forms of experiencing associated with it that different cultures have deep preferences as to paradigmatic art forms as well as different levels and standards of excellence and achievement. Whether music, literature, painting, sculpture, architecture, or whatever is the highest form of art and the source of the greatest pleasure and insight is not central to the specific theme at hand. But, once again, such rankings, or temptations to engage in rankings, illustrate the substantive problems facing the intertwined themes of a cosmopolitan, open, and universal aesthetics. Moreover, the concept of aesthetic *experience* does not initially have to be connected to art at all. As Dewey clearly showed in *Art as Experience*, it is more general than art. As to being able to draw a line between art and nonart, unless one has an antecedently accepted or postulated universal concept of art as such, the task would seem not just impossible, but also unnecessary.

## Some Analytical Complexities

It is clear, and Scharfstein's book confronts this boundary problem unflinch-ingly, that there are many artistic traditions and many different institutional-ized and entrenched aesthetic habits of attending in and to the world. These traditions make up a kind of aesthetic pluralistic universe, a vast stream of eddies and currents of products and contexts that intersect, fuse, repel, and challenge one another. There are many different aesthetically relevant con-ceptions of art and the aesthetic, with multiple focal points that compete and strive to subordinate or reduce the others to themselves. For example, the classical Western aesthetic tradition's focus on beauty is entangled with other putatively general analytical and critical categories such as form, meaning, expression, and so forth, which struggle for conceptual primacy and strive to put beauty in its place—and perhaps even "*dis*place" it. Clearly, some approaches and categories are richer than others. Form, meaning, and expression are semiotic in essence, but they also have to have experiential cash value, as I have argued elsewhere (Innis 1994, 2009). Such categories have more than merely local validity and appeal. They challenge us to "*dis*-locate" ourselves from our self-evident, individually, and socially egocentric premises.

Stendhal famously wrote in his *On Love* (1822), in the existential, not the analytical, mode, that beauty was only the promise of happiness, but he also qualified this assertion by linking the many styles of beauty with cor-relative visions of happiness. However, focusing on beauty as essentially or necessarily connected with happiness restricts the content of a promised, or hoped for, cosmopolitan aesthetics. While beauty and happiness are clearly not merely local categories, they do not have, if we follow Stendhal, a uni-vocal meaning. It could be objected that Stendhal is trying to explicate an already contentious, obscure, and problematic notion, namely, *beauty*, by recourse to the even more contentious, obscure, and problematic one, that is, *happiness*.

Stendhal, a cosmopolite himself, is, however, clearly onto something in the attempt to hold on to both poles. One might think it self-evident that one would never pursue beauty if doing so did not offer some intrinsic, internal, noninstrumental reward, such as happiness. Beauty is clearly not a mere tool for obtaining something else external to it. Still, as the sinol-ogist François Jullien has convincingly argued in his *Vital Nourishment:*

*Departing from Happiness* (2007b), there is a way of thinking of the vital nourishment we get from art and the aesthetic as precisely involving *departing* from happiness rather than seeking it. Perhaps, following Jullien, one is seeking—or being lured by—something else entirely, for example, ontological attunement or a way of manifesting and participating in the invisible originative matrix of the visible, as in the Taoist tradition and, to a certain extent, in the Confucian tradition's concern with being in balance with "the way of Heaven." There is a seeming radical theological divide between Plotinus's framing of art and beauty (and its Christianizing continuation in Augustine and the high Scholastic tradition) in terms of eternal forms and our participation in them and the Taoist framing of parallel issues in terms of processivity. However, there are, at the same time, remarkable intersections in terms of contemplating the cosmos as a play of forms emerging from and manifesting a primal unity, as John Scotus Eriugena proposed in his *De Divisione Naturae.*

Crispin Sartwell (2004) has shown, in his *Six Names of Beauty*, how different cultural matrices, with their different terminological accents and focal points, can supply other, albeit not completely foreign and novel, conceptual tools that foreground or conceptually place other aspects of our encounters with beauty, or at least one of its placeholders, and in this way effectively explode a unitary meaning to such a term. Sartwell rotates the notion of beauty through six frames and matrices that locate various experiential occasions and their objects and place them in the spectrum of our lives, both individual and social. Beauty is explored: (a) as satisfaction of an existential lack, hence the link between happiness and beauty (Plato's *Symposium* and Stendhal's differently focused "this worldly quest"), (b) as openness to sensory glowing and blooming, to forms of appearing as appearing, (c) as the experienced decentering, transcending, even loss, of the self's movement toward the holy, (d) as participation in ideality and rational order, (e) as engagement in forms of modest, even poor, everydayness, and (f) as pursuit of wholeness, health, and environmental harmony.

Just as in the Islamic tradition Allah has many names, not even the sum of which can encompass his unlimited reality, so even the most cursory look at the history of aesthetic reflection reveals a open spiral of corresponding partial mappings of beauty or its correlates or substitutes. The aesthetic dimension spreads itself over the whole field of experience and the multiple contexts in which it occurs.

## Engaging Boundaries and Affinities:
## The Great Image Has No Form

A truly cosmopolitan aesthetics or any aesthetics claiming some sort of universal relevance, then, needs to acknowledge and accept differences but learn not to pass beyond or over them but rather to pass *between* them or even over *to* them, as Sartwell did in his "album of instances" (2004). One has to proceed by following a kind of hermeneutical principle of charity. Such a principle is meant to root out all temptations to theoretical self-assertion without falling into an easy relativism and avoiding the hard work of an honest engagement with *the other*. Indeed, it is only when we have passed over to another frame that we recognize the outlines and limits, as well as the powers, of our own.

To that effect I propose to explore, as a test case, how relying on some critical elements, primarily from John Dewey's pragmatist and experiential approach to the aesthetic, can enable us to establish deep and hidden affinities of general import and mutual confirmation between Dewey's aesthetic analytical scheme and the philosophical approach embodied in one major strand of Chinese art and aesthetics as propounded by François Jullien (2009) in his *The Great Image Has No Form, or On the Nonobject through Painting.* Using such a comparison and contrast shines a bright light on how a Deweyan pragmatist aesthetics can supply, in this case, analytical tools for understanding deep linkages between an aesthetic tradition and metaphysical vision that emerged in radically different circumstances from the pragmatist philosophical tradition. They have much in common and are mutually enriching.

As a first point of contrast and contact, Dewey writes in *Art as Experience* of "the penetrating quality that runs through all the parts of a work of art and binds them in an individualized whole. . . . The different elements and specific qualities of a work of art blend and fuse in a way which physical things cannot emulate. This fusion is the felt presence of the same qualitative unity in all of them" ([1934a] 1989, 196). Dewey's phenomenological point, in spite of his qualification, is quite general. It is not restricted to the aesthetic dimension and indeed can be applied to our perception of physical things and problematic situations of all sorts (Innis 1994, 44–68). For Dewey, the center of any occasion of experience is an "intuited enveloping quality" ([1934a] 1989, 196), which runs through all its differentiations. In the case of a work of art "the resulting sense of totality is commemorative, expectant, insinuating, premonitory." However, as Dewey says, "there is no name to be given it" (197).

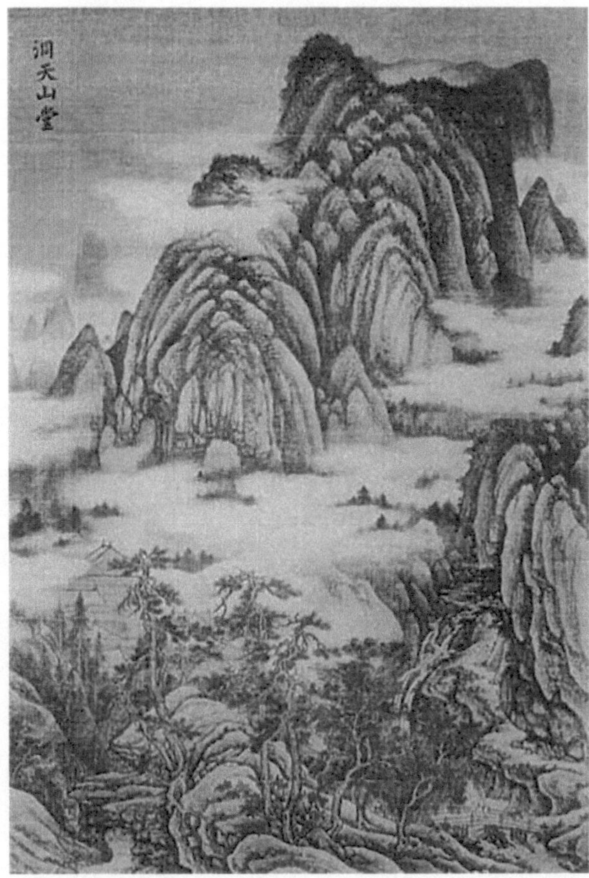

Fig. 6.1. Shitao, *Landscape for Yongweng*, 1642–1707. *Source*: St. Louis Art Museum.

It is what it is, with its own idiom, which stamps it with individuality and singularity.

This sense of totality, Dewey writes, is the background that "enters into and qualifies everything in its focus, everything distinguished as a part and member" ([1934a] 1989, 197). Dewey puts at the heart of his aesthetic project, appropriating and extending James's rich phenomenological descriptions, the essential openness of experience as a process that "grows by its edges" with an aura or margin of felt tendencies and transitive relations. The following text will help us see a first fertile point of intersection, or overlap, between Dewey's valorizing approach to aesthetics from the experiential side and François Jullien's presentation of Chinese literati painting from the metaphysical side (see figure 6.1). The problem of a cosmopolitan aesthetics will be seen, even starting low on the experiential level, to bear on the problem of a metaphysical or cosmic vision embodied in and informing aesthetic and artistic contexts. In two long passages (also cited in various places and contexts in other chapters), Dewey frames key dimensions of the following discussion:

> We are accustomed to think of physical objects as having bounded edges; things like rocks, chairs, books, houses, trade, and science, with its efforts at precise measurement, have confirmed the belief. Then we unconsciously carry over this belief in the bounded character of all *objects* of experience (a belief founded ultimately in the practical exigencies of our dealings with things) into our conception of experience itself. We suppose the experience has the same definite limits as the things with which it is concerned. But any experience, the most ordinary, has an indefinite total setting. Things, objects, are only focal points of a here and now in a whole that stretches out indefinitely. This is the qualitative "background" which is defined and made definitely conscious in particular objects and specified properties and qualities. . . . For although there is a bounding horizon, it moves as we move. We are never wholly free from the sense of something that lies beyond. We might expand the field from the narrower to the wider. But however broad the field, it is still felt as not the whole; the margins shade into that indefinite expanse beyond which imagination calls the universe. This sense of the including whole implicit in ordinary experiences is rendered intense within the frame of a painting or poem. ([1934a] 1989, 197)

Dewey's phenomenology is concerned from the experiential side with the feeling of "the unlimited envelope" that becomes, or is made, intense in our experience of an object of art but is also present in other occasions of experience, especially of landscapes, the paradigmatic Chinese art form.

Jullien argues that Chinese landscape painting will try to paint—*as a non-object*—this unlimited envelope, such that it makes manifest the fact that, in Dewey's words, "We are never wholly free from the sense of something that lies beyond" ([1934a] 1989, 197). Everything that is experienced as a focal object, Dewey writes, is "part of a larger whole and inclusive whole." Dewey then avails himself of the fundamental Jamesian triad of theme-field-margin. The focal object is a Jamesian *theme*, the part of the stream of consciousness that "focuses our experience." The theme is located within a field, which may be narrower or wider. As Dewey writes, "However broad the field, it is still felt as not the whole; the margins shade into that indefinite expanse beyond which imagination calls the universe." Hence, still speaking from the experiential perspective, Dewey remarks that "about every explicit and focal object there is a recession into the implicit which is not intellectually grasped. . . . The sense of extensive and underlying whole is the context of every experience and it is the essence of sanity" (198). The sanity referred to here is a feature of experience, but, if we can trust Jullien, it has ontological and existential relevance, without being reduced to the realm of subjectivity.

Chinese literati painting, according to Jullien, "unfocuses" our experience from "the object" and the semiotically charged task of *representation*, one of the great themes of Western art and its philosophical companion and tutor. In his *The Great Image Has No Form, or On the Nonobject through Painting* (2009, 33), Jullien characterizes classic literati painting as an attempt to silence and soften "representation's power to figure"—that is, to present objects—and to bring us, paradoxically, by means of an image of the great image that has no form to the "brink of the undifferentiated," the Chinese equivalent of Peircean Firstness as metaphysical category. To be sure, according to Jullien, while "the concrete is refined but not left behind" (95), "once we get to China . . . we leave behind the autonomous consistency of forms, and the status of the perceived object dissolves," although in light of the development of abstract painting such a dissolution of the object is not unique to Chinese painting. In Jullien's conception, Chinese painting has as its goal to make manifest *breath-resonance/ energy-consonance*, and this is "ineffable" and "nonsubstantial" in the strong sense. It is, as the *Tao te Ching* says, beyond names and, as Jullien contends, beyond images, too. What is made manifest in the painting is, according to Jullien, the "undifferentiating-harmonizing fount" (98) which is no "objective that" to which we can point (see figure 6.2). "If there is a 'that' which Chinese painting paints, it is truly the primordial 'that' of breath-energy, from which the world endlessly comes forth and which animates the world" (99).

This is another way of speaking in a different rhetorical (creative metaphorical) register about *natura naturans* or *nature naturing* that is the core concept or principle of philosophical naturalism (Crosby 2002, 2008; for a different approach, see Corrington, 1997, 2013, 2016). It likewise takes, in the Chinese context, a nontheistic form. Breath-energy is not a substance, not a thing, not a cosmic person, not "the wholeness of the divine All" of the Stoics, Jullien remarks (2009, 102). It escapes, maybe even sidesteps, the grip of ontotheology altogether. It is beyond being and nonbeing. While Dewey

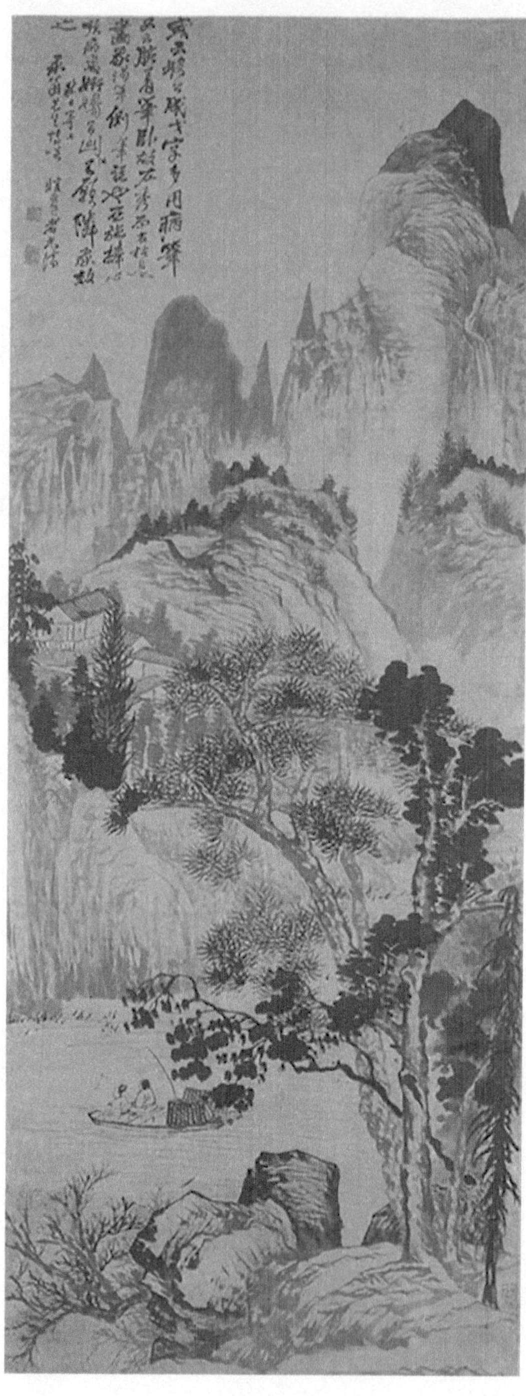

Fig. 6.2. Dong Yuan, *Taoist Temple in the Mountains*, 934–962. *Source*: National Palace Museum, Taipei.

clearly admits the deep affinity between the mystical sense of participation in an encompassing whole and the deep structures of aesthetic perception, he is also close to the Chinese position as laid out by Jullien: "China is not haunted by that hidden God" of traditional philosophy. "It has no interest in deciphering the Promise nor has it been anxious about Lack" (2009, 102). That is, it is not symbolic or compensatory or waiting for a revelation from or of another world—and neither is a Deweyan or Dewey-inspired naturalist aesthetics or metaphysics. Jullien argues that for Chinese painting, the painted world—the world itself—is the "phenomenal site of a transformation" and its object—or rather its nonobject—is what he calls "the fount of invisibility." That fount, following Jullien, in spite of being manifested, does not enter into the realm of form, even if it is impossible for us to leave this realm. "That is the realism inherent in painting" (104), even if form itself is *not* the nonobjective-object, which appears *in* and *through* it, but not *as* it.

There is a deep, even if seemingly paradoxical, affinity between Dewey's experiential approach and the Taoist recession from experience, an affinity that reveals something fundamental about the project of a cosmopolitan, open, and non-content-determined universal aesthetics. Dewey, as noted in chapter 5, remarks in *Art as Experience* that "emphasis on spaciousness is a characteristic of Chinese paintings," that "move outwards" and, for example, in the case of panoramic scroll paintings, "present a world in which ordinary boundaries are transformed into invitations to proceed" ([1934a] 1989, 217). Participation in an unfolding process has a remarkable similarity to Dewey's profound and pivotal notion of the *organization of energies*, which marks both the artwork and the participant observer, who is turned into a live creature by the work (the theme explored in chapter 2).

Dewey's aesthetics, which extend James's crucial insights into the dynamic structures of experiencing, is on one level oriented toward perceptual completion or at least completion in perception—or, paradoxically, an experience of incompletion or dynamic openness. It sees art's fundamental role as capturing objects in their intensity and in their surrounding fields in terms of their shades of expression, that is, their forms of appearing against an ultimately indeterminate background. The literati paintings that Jullien brings forth for discussion in their philosophical import do not intend to uncover fixed objects or fixed meanings. Dewey thought it was precisely art's role to disabuse us of the notion that objects had permanent, fixed properties. Indeed, Peircean semiotics proposes that the complex sign structure of artworks induces an unending play of interpretants, or proper significate effects, in, through, and by means of which its object/nonobject is grasped. The following passage from Jullien about China is, in many though not in all ways, deeply compatible with the essential thrust of a pragmatist aesthetics: "China never conceived of the contemplation of images as an operation of recognition or as the pleasure of recognition. The aim of figuration is not to fix essences but to record the play of energies in continuous interaction, whose coherence figuration unveils and indicates how to use" (2009, 108). The Western tradition with its organizing principle of representation certainly has implemented, in some ways unwittingly, a metaphysical project clearly different from the Chinese, until it ran its course. With the rise of abstraction, it found its pleasure not in the contemplation of objects but rather in the energies of objects and the principles by which objects obtain their energies and their nonobjective reverberations. While representation certainly is a legitimate goal of painting as an art (and a goal of other art forms, of course), it does not entail the production of an exact copy. It is a *re*presentation, not a duplication. The relation of representation to figuration, to be sure, is defined by their relative placement within different conceptual systems and different material practices. However, according to a cosmopolitan aesthetics, acceptance of the aesthetic validity of one conceptual system or system of practices does not contravene acceptance of the other.

A historically sensitive and pragmatist cosmopolitan aesthetics would not try to fix essences in an ontologically constituted and critically oriented meta-context or metaframe, a project that Jullien, in *Detour and Access: Strategies of Meaning in China and Greece* (2000), ascribes essentially to the West in general and Greece in particular. Such an ascription is clearly true to one of the central features of the classical strand in Western aesthetic theory, the normative status of which was gradually weakened by artistic practices, in multiple genera, within that tradition itself, as has been charted by art historians in great detail. Aristotelian mimesis and the Chinese project of *figuration*, Jullien argues, have important and quite different conceptual contexts and ontological points of origin. Still, the differences are not absolute if we attend to the processual side of Aristotle's own dynamic vision of nature and his criticism of any aesthetic norms beyond nature itself. We have to accept Jullien's claim that he is not proposing any intrinsic superiority of one over the other, although one can question whether the contrasts, while being principled, are as absolute as he claims. It is true that the Chinese tradition, as characterized by Jullien, places the origin of painting in the "great Process of the world, which exceeds human beings to the point of being 'unfathomable' and encompasses all human activity" (2009, 108), but this is not a position foreign to, for example, major strands in the Romantic tradition of nature painting or to such theorist-artists as Goethe. Again, Jullien claims that China "conceived and justified the power of images in a completely different way" from the Greeks, for in their case "lying at the heart of the image is not some capacity both representative and cognitive but rather an efficacy" (109).

But one could ask, is this clearly and emphatically nonmagical efficacy not the phenomenon of the organization of energies, the play of felt tendencies, that lies that at the core of Dewey's also James-based aesthetics? Are not the artwork and the participants, both creative and receptive, the locus of this play (a central theme treated in chapters 1and 2)?

Jullien speaks of the Chinese image phenomenon "as an energetic condensation and as a convocation of powers" that early on "took its distance from the requirement for resemblance, or at least from resemblance of form," without, however, repudiating them altogether. The philosophical premise of this distance taking is that the painted image bears upon the "Great Emptiness," which is the "nonobject par excellence" (2009, 110) and a focal point of the Taoist philosophical position. The consequence for the philosophical aesthetics immanent in and governing the pictorial traditions that Jullien is proposing in contrast to the dominant Western tradition is that "rather than the imitation of an external object set up as a model and considered only from a perceptual point of view, what is at issue is the power of figuration that anticipates the entreaty emanating from beings and things and joins with them in the internal aspiration that makes them exist, leading them to deploy" (111). This entreaty is a *spiritual resonance*, a term Dewey also uses, that strives to achieve a kind of closure but not completeness, a closure that is always finite and transitory. Such a resonance gives the processive figuration—*not the figure*—a live presence, which also, Jullien argues elsewhere (2007a), accounts for the absence of the nude in Chinese painting. "If spiritual resonance does not emanate from all sides, you will deploy the resemblance of form to no avail" (2009, 112).

Spiritual resonance is a phenomenologically apt notion, a kind of Chinese analog to Dewey's point about the felt difference between living and dead forms of appearing. Forms do appear, to be sure, but the *form* of appearing can lack energy or power to quicken us by being too easy or slack, with no auratic margins or fields of implications, such as James describes in the famous chapter of his *Principles of Psychology* ([1890] 1983). In such cases, there is nothing in the presentation—not the *re*presentation—that elicits from us a response that leads us on and *into* a field of felt implications. The contrast that Jullien makes between resonance and resemblance is a fruitful one, but the relation between them, as Jullien shows in spite of himself, is not absolute. Jullien writes that resonance is the "prolonged reverberation of an internal timbre, while resemblance is the specific reproduction of external traits. Resonance opens onto infinite vibration, while reproduction dries up on the surface" (2009, 114). Paradoxically, infinite vibration and resonance belong first and foremost to the object and only as a consequence to the perceiver. The object that is appearing is a dynamic, even at times evanescent, locus or congelation of activity and power, which emerges from and makes its ground appear—which, in the Chinese view, is *no-thing-at-all*, the cosmic marginal field.

As to the second pole of the resonance-resemblance contrast, Jullien writes of a "resemblance that does not resemble"; that is, it is not compelled by (formal) resemblance but "deploys indefinitely *through* form" (2009, 117). Indeed, in the case of painting, true resemblance, according to Jullien, "lies in that allusivity to the invisible dimension that permeates the concrete particularity of all the strokes" (113). Looked at from the point of view of pragmatist semiotics, this concrete particularity is the signifying power resident in the material quality of the image-sign, what Meyer Schapiro (1994) ascribed to the two principal nonrepresentational components in an image-sign, namely, the vehicle that by its very perceptual materiality makes forms appear and the field in which they appear that becomes progressively more and more framed. The persistent emphasis of the Chinese literati paintings that Jullien has taken as his theme is paradoxically to paint within, or construct, a frame that makes appear on the margins the presence of another frame that can never be encompassed, as Dewey affirmed in his discussion of van Eyck's *Arnofini Wedding*. It is out of this frame that an infinite vibration emerges and is embodied in concrete, though transient, forms. Thus, paradoxically, resemblance, as correspondence to its object, can be seen to be at work even when there is no object at all, and in this way it is precisely in the material visible's allusive power that it is able to make manifest the invisible.

Readers of the two chapters in *Art as Experience* on the common and varied substance of the arts will recall that Dewey makes much of the fact that "every product of art is matter and matter only" ([1934a] 1989, 198) and that "sensitivity to a medium as a medium is the very heart of all artistic creation and esthetic perception." Indeed, as Dewey writes, "media and esthetic effect are completely fused" (207). This is precisely the point Jullien is making. As discussed in chapter 3, Dewey saw Peirce's great contribution to an experiential philosophy to lie in his theory of quality, including the material quality of any sign-configuration: that everything, every situation, every object, every moment of consciousness, every life, has its own distinctive quale, and a fortiori, so does every work of art. The concrete particularity of the *stroke* in Chinese painting is based on the embodied—that is, indexically configured—semiotics of the wrist and the utilization of the method of one stroke by which a medium becomes the locus of an appearing of something, but not some *thing* that cannot itself appear but is still made manifest. This profound notion of the stroke has been explored in the rich text of Shih Taʾo on the philosophy of painting (Coleman 1978).

For one familiar with Peirce's idea of Firstness as a plenum of possibility, such a notion is reminiscent of his striking image of the mark on the cosmic slate board that introduces difference in the plenum, setting possibility into play, that is, into actuality. Whether the mark comes from an original sporting without agency or from an immanent agency at work in the world is, of course, not unambiguously settled by Peirce. According to the Western tradition, the agent is the artist, however much the artist may be inspired by an outside power (the Muses or divine inspiration) or dependent on the available material means of introducing differences on the marked surface, whatever it should be, and thus creating a material field of appearances.

In connection with the foregoing idea of the mark or the stroke, when Jullien offers up the contentious yet defensible assertion that the essence of Chinese painting is *de*-picting, that is *un*-picturing, he argues that it rests on an (achieved) effortless fusion of wrist, brush, and ink, culminating in, or exemplified in, the ink wash, which has its own qualitative feel or distinctive quality, which every material configuration has. Jullien writes, with respect to the aesthetic revolution of the Tang dynasty in the eighth and ninth centuries:

> It was exclusively to the ink wash that the Chinese literati assigned the play of variation between pale and dark, wet and dry, between there is—there is not, to render the evanescent character of things in the process or emergence or resorption. These things, born of the gradual saturation of the silk or paper by the ink, deploy in a haze, and this halo keeps them evasive. . . . Depending on the state of dilution of the ink, these gradations foster the continuous transition of beings and things from physical concretion to spirit dimension. (2009, 194)

Of course, looked at semiotically, this is the *indexical* dimension that supports, in its qualitative materiality, the paradoxical *iconic symbolization* of the nonobject. Jullien remarks, however, that it is the brush, *not the form*, that is paired with ink, with the implication that the Western approach pairs color with the form, the brush being a mere instrument. This is an enlightening difference and a clue to how to read the produced image. But its import is as much hermeneutical as it is metaphysical. Both dimensions, as Jullien shows, are intertwined in the respective ultimate premise systems of the various aesthetic traditions of practice and concomitant theory. The fusion of the metaphysical and the aesthetic in the joining of brush and ink in Chinese painting in the following passage has distinctively Peircean overtones: "Chinese painting was being conceived ever more consciously, not as a practice of representation that transfers given forms from the model to the support, but as an operation of actualization and engenderment in which what takes precedence is its character as a differentiating process from an undifferentiated foundation-fount, in this case silk or paper" (2009, 194). Such a materially embodied semiotic-constructive process is, Jullien asserts, isomorphic with the Chinese conception of world process or cosmic processivity. Production and process run together.

According to Jullien, "Every engenderment of the line in the art of painting and writing stems in the first place from the integration of a vital rhythm and not from a capacity to represent" (2009, 203). Writing in *Art as Experience* that rhythm is "ordered variation of energy," Dewey goes on to further say that "variation is not only as important as order, but it is an indispensable coefficient of esthetic order" ([1934a] 1989, 170). Variation in the material foundation-fount engenders Jullien's integration of a vital rhythm, which Dewey also characterizes as "rationality among qualities" (175), *not* the representation or construction of an ideal preexisting order of objects and forms. The integration that Jullien refers to involves, or stems from, "the figuration of a continuous transformation of forms in accordance with the rhythm animating them and not from the reproduction of forms to be contemplated, whether ideal or perceived, given or invented (but always definitive, perfect). In short, they confirm that in China, painting stems more from a kinetic-energetic apprehension than from an aesthetic perception" (2009, 203). Such a notion of kinetic-energetic apprehension is in full accord with Dewey's reflections on resistances, tendencies, intensities, and the essential materiality of the art product. This product becomes the artwork in being experienced and worked out in the hermeneutical process of interpretation communities whose worldviews are embodied in these works. This aesthetic effect has metaphysical implications for Dewey just as much as it does for the Chinese traditions presented by Jullien. Dewey characterizes this effect as "due to art's unique transcript of the energy of the things of the world." It is not a transcript of things alone, or even primarily of things, but rather of their energies, and it "operates by selecting those potencies in things by which an experience—any experience—has significance and value" ([1934a] 1989, 192). It is to these potencies that we are to respond with "commensurate perception" and surrender ourselves "in devotion" (193).

## On Blandness and the Circle of the Perceived

Jullien wrote a provocative book on blandness as a central category of Chinese aesthetics (2004), which seems both to refute the notion of a distinctive quality as marking any work of art and any experiential occasion and to exemplify it at the same time. As Jullien remarks in a striking metaphor, blandness as an aesthetic category in Chinese thought strives toward the limpidity of water and utter transparency, where everything is in balance and nothing stands forth. It is, however, for most aesthetic theories (including the pragmatist aesthetics developed by Dewey), precisely the standing forth that gives each work of art its unique affective tone and idiom. But are we really faced with a contradiction or irreducible contrast here? The paradox of blandness is that it is both noticed and not noticed at the same time. Blandness is the quality of being just right, but one cannot put it into words. As Jullien puts it, the "sole characterization [of blandness] is to elude characterization" (2004, 23). This is, as I see, actually a positive, not a negative, quality (27). Jullien writes, in a passage that captures the upshot of the types of intersections adduced in the preceding pages, that "the motif of the bland distances us from theory but does not, at the other end, commit us to mysticism." The bland, however, does not eschew discourse or render experience vacuous. "With the bland, we remain in the realm of perceived experience, even if it situates us at the very limit of perception, where it becomes most tenuous" (33). The circle of the perceived is our experiential home and the locus of the aesthetic, but *its* circle is the ever-receding horizon or margin where tenuousness opens onto plenitude, a phenomenon that galvanized Emerson in his ecstatic moments.

A cosmopolitan aesthetics must be prepared to accept and attend to occasions of experiencing in all their manifold forms of appearing. Such an open aesthetics, in Scharfstein's sense, is not a theory comprised of universal concepts that apply in all contexts. Rather, it is a practice of self-reflective engagement that prepares us for an inexhaustible set of encounters with, and production of, forms that carry and express what James called the "infinite iridescences of consciousness" ([1890] 1983, 229). It is marked by a radical perspectival and experiential pluralism. Cosmopolitan aesthetics is not itself an aesthetic theory. Scharfstein is right, and the conflicts of aesthetic theory bear witness that there is no one-size-fits-all framework that can unify aesthetic and artistic traditions. Each aesthetic tradition has its matrix of premises and ways of working that make these premises appear. The conceptual, as opposed to the aesthetic and hermeneutical, task of a cosmopolitan aesthetics is to engage these premises and make them explicit. While the primary hermeneutical task is to engage the artworks themselves in their own terms, the job of philosophy is to reflect on the premises embodied in the works themselves and their background conditions. But, as Jullien puts it, in the Chinese mode, "tasting substitutes for knowing; it is the only true aspiration" (123).

Philosophy, in the pragmatist mode, encompasses both tasting and knowing and does not set them in opposition. A truly cosmopolitan aesthetics in the pragmatist mode is a variegated set of hermeneutical exercises in learning to attend to the world and to our modes of attending, including becoming aware of their limits, their heuristic powers, their material supports, and their affinities. A pragmatist aesthetics, in both its receptive and constructive phases, would focus specifically on the heightening of these iridescences and thus lead to transformations in our consciousnesses from the local to the nonlocal. It would also, and most important, allow us to accept irreducible differences as enriching rather than as leading to existential and interpretive frustration or to psychic or sociocultural violence. But it would not lead to a slack relativism nor to an easy irenic reconciliation of truly opposing metaphysical visions. The real oppositions must be properly identified and submitted to critical examination.

In light of competing metaphysical lattices or frames, each with its own distinctive heuristic powers, the very idea of a cosmopolitan aesthetics is an *injunction* to engage in hermeneutical and existential self-reflective *practices*. There is no privileged *conceptual* place for a cosmopolitan aesthetics. In principle a cosmopolitan aesthetics is at home nowhere and everywhere, even where, paradoxically, it does not feel at home. Cosmopolitan aesthetics in the pragmatist mode is the aesthetics of the rooted wanderer who has given up, but without despair, anxiety, or frustration, his search to find a permanent place to lay his head. The flux of experience and the emergence of novel forms with their distinctive qualities pull us on. As Jullien says, "When, rather than favoring one flavor over another, we remain equally open to all of them, we evolve freely through the different flavors and so do away with their incompatibility" (2004, 121).

Putting such an injunction into practice is the essence of a cosmopolitan aesthetics. In the following section I illustrate another way of doing so by charting the intersections between Peirce's metaphysical vision and another presentation of the Taoist way of beauty.

## Peirce's Aesthetics and the Way of Beauty

### *The Poem of the Universe and the Primacy of Quality*

The extreme technicality of Peirce's philosophical project does not preclude it having profound existential and existential consequences for how we live our lives. Ivo Ibri, in his *Kósmos Noetós: The Metaphysical Architecture of Charles S. Peirce* (2017) and in other essays (2009. 2010, 2020), and John Sheriff in his *Charles Peirce's Guess at the Riddle: Grounds for Human Significance* (1994) have foregrounded how Peirce's systematic reflections, from cosmological and metaphysical speculation to the theory of signs, can guide us to conduct ourselves in accord with the deepest laws of the universe. There is, we must note, a vague anthropomorphism lying at the base of Peirce's picture of a universe in process, such that we are not to think of ourselves as strangers wandering in a lawless cosmic desert. Nor are we to think, however, that we are immune from the ravages of time and tragic endings of our own particular life projects. The universe is not directionless, nor is it clear that Peirce, in any naïve way, thought of it as directed by an external force that "has the whole world in its hand" and so is in a position to rescue us, no matter what we do, from existential shipwreck. Peirce, however, does see the universe as progressively taking on rational habits, being informed by a concrete rationality whose triumph in the long run is worth cooperating with and betting our lives on it.

Peirce's metaphysical picture of the universe appears in both an extremely technical form, relying on his theory of categories of Firstness, Secondness, and Thirdness and their semiotic correlates, and in a more poetic form. For example, "The Universe is a vast representamen, a great symbol of God's purpose, working out its conclusions in living realities" (1998, 193). The universe as a great symbol is also assimilated to an argument and further to a great work of art.

Now, as to their function in the economy of the Universe, . . . the Universe as an argument is necessarily a great work of art, a great poem, . . . for every fine argument is a poem and symphony, . . . just as every true poem is a sound argument. But let us compare it rather with a painting, . . . with an impressionist seashore piece, . . . then every Quality in a premiss is one of the elementary colored particles of the painting; they are all meant to go together to make up the intended Quality that belongs to the whole as a whole. That total effect is beyond our ken; but we can appreciate in some measure the resultant Quality of parts of the whole, . . . which Qualities result from the combinations of elementary Qualities that belong to the premises. (1998, 194)

This is a radical aestheticization of the universe, with its pivotal distinction of elementary Qualities and resultant Quality. Of special importance with relevance to the universe as a whole is Peirce's comment that the total effect is beyond our ken.

On Peirce's position, our engagement with the universe as a work of art involves three aspects, consonant with Peirce's most basic schema of the categories of consciousness: (a) an apprehension of qualities or tones in experience, (b) a sense of being interrupted by something over which we have no control that imposes itself on us and constrains and steers our attention, and (c) a grasp of a complex unity or whole in an act of synthesis, which can elude full articulation or explication in discursive terms. These are essential dimensions of an aesthetic encounter, which Peirce himself only fragmentarily treated. While he claimed, "I am still a perfect ignoramus in esthetics" (1931–58, 5:111), he was nevertheless convinced that the phenomenological and semiotic core of it lay in the domain of quality and its apprehension by feeling, a theme running throughout this book.

Consider again the following text from Peirce's "The Seven Systems of Metaphysics":

It is esthetic enjoyment which concerns us; and ignorant as I am of Art, I have a fair share of capacity for esthetic enjoyment, and it seems to me that while in esthetic enjoyment we attend to the totality of Feeling, . . . and especially to the total resultant Quality of Feeling presented in the work of art we are contemplating, . . . yet it is a sort of intellectual sympathy, a sense that here is a feeling that one can comprehend, a reasonable feeling. I do not succeed in saying exactly what it is, but it is a consciousness belonging to the category of Representation through representing something in the Category of Quality of Feeling. (1998, 190)

Perceiving the universe aesthetically and perceiving a work of art are thus joined at a deep level. Both involve a sort of intellectual sympathy and a sense that there is a reasonable feeling to be grasped that nevertheless eludes capture in words but seizes us by what the painter Eugène Delacroix, who is cited prominently by Dewey, called its "magical accord" as an "harmonious ensemble" (Dewey [1934a] 1989, 151). It is this total massive quality, without a name, that controls attention, a pervading qualitative unity, appearing, as Peirce wrote, in "the emotion of the *tout ensemble*." which defines "every operation of the mind, however complex" ((1931–58, 1:311). This is the *total felt significance* of our interpretative and existential responses to nature and to artworks, which we contemplate, Peirce says, "as they are" (1998, 6) in their "direct positive presentness." Indeed, for Peirce, "qualities of feeling show myriad-fold variety . . . as they are in their presentness, each is sole and unique" (150).

Presentness and uniqueness are inextricably joined, grasped by and in practices of attending embedded in processes unfolding in time, arising on a manifold of previous impressions, which insensibly pass into one another but whose Peircean, emergent, total resultant quality can be experienced as a rupture or as the felt passing of a perceptual threshold. Thus, Peirce holds, aesthetics (esthetics) considers "those things whose ends are to embody qualities of feeling," although, it is clear, the Peircean conception of the self involves three levels or interwoven dimensions. We are also engaged with "those things whose ends lie in action" and must achieve a coherent and true picture of the world by constructing symbolic forms or systems of signs, "those things whose end is to represent something" (1998, 200). Feeling, action, and thought make up the defining intertwined contours of the Peircean model of the semiotic self (Innis 1994; Colapietro 1989; Wiley 1994). It is the whole self, embodied in webs of feeling, action, and thought, that is put into play when truly contemplating the universe and works of art.

Dewey followed up Peircean hints to develop a phenomenologically rich, open, and nonprovincial experiential aesthetic that opens onto a cosmopolitan aesthetics. Peirce's heuristic indications about the nature and scope of aesthetics and art, however, can also be explicitly linked with, informed by, and enriched by attending to the way of beauty articulated in and practiced in the Taoist tradition, as illustrated in François Cheng's *The Way of Beauty: Five*

*Meditations for Spiritual Transformation* (Cheng 2006). They share mutually defining and reinforcing metaphysical and aesthetic visions, although they are expressed in different philosophical and rhetorical registers. Cheng's book combines disarming intellectual sophistication with existential depth. It likewise engages, in agreement with Ibri and Sheriff, with the grounds of human significance from the twin angles of metaphysics and aesthetics that inform Peirce's intellectual project and illustrates another way of reflecting on the nature and import of a cosmopolitan aesthetics.

### Peircean Parallels in the Taoist Way of Beauty

Cheng proceeds, as Peirce claimed to do, as a "slightly naïve phenomenologist." But he is not just describing the appearing of the world in Taoist terms but reflecting in a self-activating manner on the groundlines of how to live in the world, how to conduct a life over against and within the cosmos. Following the Way of the Tao, he writes, involves, indeed is constituted by, "moving toward open life," seeing the emergence of things as both "gift and promise." It means eschewing vain seekings after control, "hollowing out in myself the capacity for receptivity," to become the "ravine of the world," into which world process pours and through which it runs (12). Each thing in the order of life is a unity that cannot be explained by universal theorems. In the order of life, "all unity is unique," but not alone or isolated. Uniqueness "solicits other uniquenesses." Moments are also unique, situations that prompt in us "feelings accompanied by infinite longing," a longing that lures us beyond the finite and the definite to an encompassing matrix of the way of the world. Uniqueness "transforms each being into presence," and while it is tempting to think of the universe as made up of "a set of figures," that is, abstractions or types and forms of things, Cheng thinks that the Taoist framework reveals it as a "set of presences" (15). A "presence not reducible to anything else is a transcendence," that is, an emergent novelty, yet not something isolated and separated but embedded in a "complex network of circulation and interconnections" (16), which is precisely a central claim of Peirce's metaphysical vision.

Taoism, in Cheng's presentation, is governed by a picture or image of a "self-generating universe" with a drive toward complexity that produces imagination and mind (21). The universe obeys "some intentionality of a more ontological nature" (20), an immanent trend toward beauty in as much as matter contained from the beginning "a promise of beauty" (21), some seeds, an image used by Ibri (2010). Cheng asserts that the Taoist frame-work, like Greek thought, recognizes that the sense of the sacred or the divine comes from "witnessing beauty ... something that is striking for its enig-matic splendor, that dazzles and enthralls," and not just because of its formal beauty or external traits. Cheng goes further when he asserts that "our sense of sense, our sense of a universe possessing sense, also comes from beauty" (22). Reflecting on the multiple meanings of the French word *sens*, Cheng sees it as composed of three semantic trajectories: sensation, direction, and signification. Strangely enough, this triad is reminiscent of the Peircean triad of feeling, reaction, and thought as the ultimate dimensions of the processes of the universe, although it is perhaps the universal categories of Firstness, Secondness, and Thirdness as the matrix of the play of the universe that evokes the deeper point. Indeed, true beauty is assimilated to a *becoming* in Cheng's reckoning, which resonates with Peircean themes, to the realization of a desire on the part of the universe, following the "course of the Way," to proceed on its "irresistible progress toward open life ... a principle of life that keeps its whole promise open" (23).

Such a position, however, does not entail an externally willed or imposed finality or teleology, although the language at times seems to border on it. The Tao is not a person or a creator but rather a dynamic principle that informs the universe, analogous to the Whiteheadian principle of creativity in pro-cess philosophy's view of the world. Cheng thinks of it as, in some way, an "inexhaustible fountain" or "line of force" (25) that propagates and embodies itself in "rhythmic waves," exemplified, for Cheng, in the case of the rose, on which he meditates at length, alluding along the way to Angelus Silesius's remark that the rose has no why; it blooms because it blooms. As an instance of beauty, it "bursts forth from within being, or Being, like an inexhaustible fountain" (24). The core notion, for Cheng, is that of "a universe that makes itself, creates itself" (27), a "sense of origin and engendering ... the living universe as a created work" (28), although there is no creator outside it. Cheng adduces the Taoist notion of *yi*, an invisible essence that drives world process, producing in rhythmic waves of scent and resonance an impulse of Being toward life that in its salient moments "leaps toward the Open" as a place of manifestation. There is clearly an echo of Heidegger here but also a parallel to Peirce's conception of a universe open to ever new forms of novelty. This leaping toward the Open is also the key notion of the ecstatic natural-ism of Robert Corrington (1997, 2013, 2016), which has its roots in Peirce's work. Such a series of leaps, which make up the melody of our lives in time, is marked on the one hand by nostalgic retention of what is no longer and on the other hand by hope in the promise of new advents of beauty linked in "a qualitative continuity in which those things experienced and dreamed of form an organic present" (34), binding our lives in time.

In addition to *yi*, Cheng also adduces the central notion of *qi*, "the Breath that animates the movements of the earth" (40)—but not just the earth. *Qi* is the cosmic breath of the Tao, generating Peirce's great poem or vast representamen. Of course, the Western tradition has, in pregnant images, conjoined breath with word in a cosmic anthropomorphic way, which is not to be taken literally. But we can see a Peircean echo of the rise of Thirdness in the notion that we, as cosmic emergent manifestations of thirdness, are the "awakened consciousness and beating heart of the material world . . . we can be the gaze and the speech of the living universe, or at least its interlocutors" (41). Looked at from the point of view of aesthetic perception, as illuminating our role as interlocutors, the Taoist way of art and a Peircean aesthetics both aim to foster the ability and the task to "resonate with the 'continuo' of another"—the "continuo" that defines each being—its determinative quality, in Peircean and Deweyan terms—"located on a deeper, more intimate level than consciousness" (49). The continuo can be thought of as the ineffable focal point, beyond mere particular properties, that attracts and draws us toward each locus of unique presence that points us toward the "direction of open life" (53).

Cheng quotes Zhuangzi to the effect that "between heaven and earth there is great beauty" and that "nature has the power to transmute the withered and rotten into marvels" ( 62). These marvels, to the degree that it is also through us that they arise in art, and the abilities to perceive the cosmos as a work of art, involve the cultivation of a "uniquely human beauty, that fire of the spirit that burns, if it burns, beyond the tragic" and is manifested in "the inner dignity of those who confront the terrible, in the name of life" (55). In other words, it is manifested in those who pursue, as Peirce demanded, the true, the good, and the beautiful, the three dimensions of the truly admirable. Such cultivation Zhuangzi considered to be the task of the true man who pursues "spiritual wandering" in the universe, which is a perfect characterization of Peirce's own practice of universal inquiry. It involves a "total opening to universal resonance," and, as Cheng puts it, "The me of the subject participates in the universal becoming" (65), which is precisely what Peircean aesthetics, and its Deweyan extension, invite us to do. We are to meet the world as "gift, reception, bypassing appearance by dwelling in the full presence of the other, opening to the universal resonance" (66). The practice of life and the experience of beauty are inseparable.

Returning to the Breath, the Taoist analog of Peircean creativity without a creator, Cheng writes that it is "a unitary, organic conception of the universe in which everything is linked and held together. The Primordial Breath that ensures the original unity continues to animate all beings, linking them into a gigantic, interwoven, engendering network called the Tao, the Way." From the human side, we can distinguish, following Cheng, a threefold breath that is correlative to the rhythmic nature of the universe, which is a procedure Peirce himself followed with his correlation of ontological categories and the categories of consciousness. The Taoist threefold breath of Cheng's aesthetic meditations does not correlate exactly in a one to one fashion with the Peircean metaphysical categories, yet they have deep phenomenological relevance and are clearly in tune with Dewey's Peircean experiential aesthetics. Yin Breath corresponds to Dewey's notion of undergoing, a receptive process, receptive gentleness. Yang Breath corresponds to Dewey's notion of active engagement or power. The Breath of the Median void "draws its power from the original Void" and "has the gift of pulling them into positive interaction" (67), embodying the "necessary intermediary space of encounter and circulation needed to enter into effective, and insofar as possible, harmonious interaction (104), constituting "the between" (105).

Thus, receptivity, active attending, and mediation or unification/synthesis are the very swing and sway of the processes of consciousness delineated by Peirce and exemplified in Dewey. The movement of the life of beauty takes place "within a network of constant exchanges and interconnections—generalized interaction" (68), the core of a pragmatist aesthetics. The result is a "miraculous state of symbiosis" (72), exemplified in the affinity between Cézanne's fascination with Mont Sainte-Victoire and the "mist and cloud of Mount Lu" of the Taoist tradition, both embodying the cosmic/human logic of the "hidden-revealed" structure of our chiasmic perception of the world. In these cases, as Cheng writes, "at the same time the human becomes the landscape's interior, so the landscape becomes the interior of man" (73).

For Cheng, authentic art, not propaganda or the instrumental use of art, "tends toward open life by breaking down the barriers of habit and prompting a new way of perceiving and living" (87). It is "always the crystallization of an apparently provisional here and now. The elevation of a presence in time as advent. These achieved forms that reactivate the great rhythms are the highest means by which humans can defy destiny and death" (88) and, once again, they constitute the grounds of human significance. Peirce, it is well known (Ibri 2009), was deeply influenced by Friedrich Schelling. Cheng, for his part, asserts that Schelling's vision was closest to the one underlying Chinese arts and letters, although, in his contestable opinion, it is "too fixed, too static" (95). But he sees, nevertheless, in perhaps an unknown distancing from Peirce's abstract speculative bent, that Schelling "gives true artistic creation the highest place, even above pure philosophical speculation . . . a quest for the identity of the self and of the world. . . . This higher identity . . . only realized through art" (94).

Peirce's philosophy, in spite of its objective idealism dimension, is not a philosophy of identity, but it certainly allows us to see "the face of the infinite in the finite" (95) stretched out in time in the play of objectification and subjectification and of infinite intentions and possibilities that are displayed in art. This dialogue with nature, giving rise to beauty, has three levels: (1) the level of represented Nature, including human nature and humans *in* nature, where there is the encounter between the hidden and the revealed, (2) the level of the artistic act, the encounter between brushstrokes and between the colors applied, and (3) the salient and decisive moment of the encounter of the human spirit and the landscape, bringing it to life and serving as the locus of its energies. Art gives *life* more than pleasure. It gives us a place or space for indefinite *sojourn* and not just the passing glance, which nevertheless can be caught and brought to a halt.

Cheng proposes that the Way of art that is looked at within the Taoist framework culminates in three fundamental ideas. They specify the necessary qualities that any work of art must have and can "serve as criteria for judging the value of a work art" (107), to be found not by recourse to form or taste that has ruled Western aesthetics. They are located "further upstream, closer to the very source of Creation," for "the course of the Way is itself continuous Creation," in which humans participate. Any proper aesthetics, on this account, has a cosmological dimension "according to which human gestures are bound to the 'universal gestation'" (108). The three fundamental ideas put forward by Cheng, which have clear Peircean relevance, are (a) unifying interaction (*yin-yun*), (b) rhythmic breath (*qi-yun*), and (c) divine resonance (*shen-yun*).

The category of *unifying interaction*, which also is a key Deweyan notion, pinpoints in, for example, a pictorial artwork "a perpetual dynamic movement of contrast and union that underlies the living matter of a pictorial work and is indispensable to it." The source of such movement is prefigured in Shitao's "one stroke," the originating brushstroke that "implicates all possible imaginable brushstrokes" (109). This is the "decisive moment when the artist's brush encounters ink to give birth to a figure or scene . . . the ink embodies all that is virtual in nature," the vast realm of Peircean possibility and sporting. Is this not the idea close to, if not identical with, Peirce's image of the introduction of difference into the cosmic and semiotic blank slate board by a stroke that opens and at the same time defines?

The category of *rhythmic breath* points to what "structures a work at its depth and makes it radiate" (110). This is the Taoist equivalent of what Dewey called the "livingness" of a work of art, which is rooted in the "organization of energies" (discussed in chapter 2). The work appears as animated from within and is a locus of intersections, entanglements, and clashes whose ultimate finality is a dynamic harmony and a continuing upsurge of "unforeseen forms and unexpected echoes," all of them entering into the total resultant "Quality" foregrounded by Peirce. The rhythmic breath unifies and produces metamorphosis and transformation by continuous structuring and merging of a work's elements in a spiral movement that generates the open work that Umberto Eco discussed in detail with regard to literature. The rhythmic breath both operates in and informs the median voids that enable a work to breathe, introducing novelty and multiple patterns instead of mere repetition. Cheng's discussion here is perhaps closer to Dewey's development of Peircean insights than to Peirce, but is clearly in deep accord with Peirce's innermost intentions.

The category of *divine resonance*, the third pivotal notion, Cheng calls the highest degree of value; it is the "supreme quality" needed for a work to be great in the first degree. Defining such a quality is extremely difficult since, in one way, it has no name. *Shen*, Ching holds, is the superior state of $qi$, the divine spirit, the animating Breath of all forms of life, but now extended to the whole universe, considered as living thing, with no distinction between matter and spirit. *Life* is the dynamic core of a nature in constant process with its many orders in synechistic continuity. While such a notion may seem to border on panpsychism or pantheism, Cheng interprets it as signifying "all that life always contains as promise" as an "inalienable, open principle" with which we, in privileged moments, find ourselves in resonance. Such a musical notion transcends musicality, and with respect to poetry and painting it extends to vision and the idea of presence. In a landscape painting, for example, there are manifold qualities embodied in it: loftiness or tempestuousness, density or ethereality, suffused with light or perfused by mystery. But the essential thing is that going beyond representation alone offers us the "advent of a presence . . . that can be felt or sensed," an "image beyond images" (115), which has no *form*. Such a presence is self-generating, but, as Cheng puts it, while beyond the screen of phenomena, it is experienced as, echoing Plotinus, "a generous gift that makes all that exists *there*, miraculously *there*" (116).

Our understanding of this gift will never be complete. It pulls us unceasingly toward the Open and "harbors a waiting, a listening that is ready to welcome a new advent." Both the artist and the perceiver must let themselves be "inhaled by the space of the work," and also of the cosmos. It is up to us, in the movement of letting-go, what Martin Heidegger called *Gelassenheit*, to respond to this supreme gift. Cheng's meditations on the way of beauty not only extend and deepen our understanding of the dimensions of aesthetic experience but also inform our pursuit of beauty, which, along with truth, as Cheng concludes, is "for man, more than an acquisition[;] it will always be a challenge, a wager" (116).

CHAPTER 7

# Filling the Hole in Sense

## *Between Art and Philosophy*

### The Wound in Consciousness

In his *Summers of Discontent*, Raymond Tallis claims that human beings suffer from a permanent "wound in consciousness." In a kind of echo of Saint Augustine, he writes: "There is an incurable wound in the present tense—the only tense that human consciousness really has" (2014, 46)—into which the past and the future tenses are enfolded. Such a wound, Tallis argues, keeps us absent from *experiencing our experience*. It is a factor in our permanent tendency as the "explicit animal" caught in its diaphanous discursive web to substitute a conceptual scheme for [the] experience itself, which will always outrun, surpass, or fail to live up to our concepts and the expectations based on them, which are "surrounded by a nimbus of the unsaid" (66). The "summers of discontent" that the title of Tallis's book alludes to are exemplified in the common experience of looking forward to something, such as going on vacation, yet when the time arrives, of being haunted by its not measuring up to expectations or being anxious or distressed about its imminent coming to an end while undergoing constant interruptions that impede our ever *being* fully "on vacation" or *being with* the present.

Such a situation, according to Tallis (2014), is due to a tendency latent, but not always active, in the overweening double-faced effects of the semiotically creative logic of discursivity. This logic defines not just the analytical master tool of philosophy but ourselves as the language animal (Innis 2008, 2018b) and allows us, or induces us, to make the absent present in such a way that paradoxically the present becomes absent.

Such a permanent tendency, according to Tallis's way of putting it, is rooted in the contrast between ideality, which is abstract, and actuality, which is concrete, one of Dewey's oppositions and contrasts. It is art's role to fuse the two. Tallis explores this contrast in his *Michelangelo's Finger* (2010), focusing on the shaded differences between the paradigmatic gesture of the pointing finger and systems of linguistic symbols that both name and relate. The dual processes of indication, as rooted in the pointing finger, and of a consequent symbolization, as effected by language, divide up the significant joints in reality. They discern the differential markers in the sensory field and produce a web of abstract terms and relations by means of which they are stabilized and captured. This is completely consonant with the pragmatist approach to the relation of language to experience: language, and the body's intentional gesturing, serve as an instrument of control in the broadest sense. The uses of indication and symbolization, in both Tallis's and Dewey's account, are first and foremost oriented toward the control or formulation of experience, both practically and intellectually. It must be said that from a semiotic perspective indication and symbolization also, in their own ways as forms of mediation, bring us close to experience, but paradoxically they also distance us from it. The movement from mere pointing and relying on perceptual indices to symbolization based on general classifications and relations clearly is the work of a specific kind of abstraction and of higher-order intellectual processes. But Langer has shown and made the core of her aesthetics that there is another kind of abstraction that, rather than distancing us from experience for the sake of mediating generalizations, makes the forms of experiencing themselves present in novel and inexhaustible ways, as was exemplified in chapter 2 in Iris Murdoch's paradigmatic presentation in language itself of an aesthetic encounter.

In *Art as Experience* ([1934a] 1989), Dewey speaks generally and loosely of the nonaesthetic, two-factored indicative and symbolic uses of language in which we pass through a sign-configuration functioning as a conceptual lens to what it brings into focus as being "instrumental." He does not deny the utter uniqueness and defining feature of human language as effecting or enabling the emergence of new forms of meanings far beyond the instrumental in any restricted way. In *Experience and Nature*, Dewey famously called language "the tool of tools, the nourishing mother of all significance" ([1925] 1988, 134). However, a nourishing mother is not identical with her offspring, of which art in its many forms is clearly one of the most striking. Her offspring's unique signifying powers may not mirror her in some essential ways, and indeed the mother of all significance may, in the last analysis, not be language itself but rather something even more fundamental, something anterior to language, a felt sense of the significance of forms with symbolic pregnance: objects, gestures, images, events.

Language's discursive uniqueness and usefulness lead us to what Langer called the open ambient that makes up the distinctively human world, a world of self-potentiating articulated meanings and meaning systems. This is a creative achievement that marks us as the explicit animal. Language in the discursive mode aims, not just to map the territory of experience, but also to create new territories of meaning or even the sense of new territories that can be, or are, accessed in multiple other ways, both linguistically and in ways beyond language. There are many different linguistic maps of the territory of experience, with different formal, notational, and rhetorical structures. Language's semiotic instrumentality, or use value, does not lose itself in making the world present through abstract naming and relating. It is accomplished by nonisomorphic linguistic systems, where the material medium of language becomes irretrievably and inseparably part of the territory itself, as in poetry and fiction and in song (Innis 2007b). Language here has a different use, to enhance and create forms of perception in the presentational mode, where the linguistic frame and what it frames are constitutively correlative. These linguistically embodied forms of perception *realize* an experience, rather than just pointing us toward one. Stanley Burnshaw in *The Seamless Web* (1979) has shown with provocative nuance how the poetic form of language heals the wound or closes the rift that the language animal inflicts necessarily upon itself.

## Art and the "Far Side of Use": Being in the Presence of Something

Tallis ascribes to art and aesthetic experience a distinctive power, "on the far side of use" (2014, 47). Such a power is not able to permanently heal the wound in consciousness introduced by the rift between ideality and its future expectations, weighted down by the past, of fulfillment in the actualities of experience. It is rather to minister to it and help us live with it. This is precisely the role of Dewey's consummatory experiences. An artwork, Tallis argues, gives us a sense of arrival, a sense of *being in the presence of something*, and not just *being on the way* to, or being given directions to, something we have not yet attained or something that is merely an instance of a class or a natural kind or some form of classification in a natural language surrounded by the nimbus-like tacit dimension of the unsaid. Indeed, being in the presence of something as an artwork is being in the presence of *this thing* with its fullness of felt significance or with its failure to achieve such a fullness.

On Tallis's thoroughly naturalist position, which parallels Dewey's, art's essence is "to enhance human awareness: to italicize that useless thing called human consciousness" (2014, 119). This enhancement is the concentration and enlargement of immediate experience that Dewey ascribed to aesthetic experience, an experience that is beyond use in a merely instrumental sense. Such highlighting is performed by occasions of experience, spontaneous or contrived, of any sort that constitute or reveal unique, and not just generalized, oases of sense in the disparate and unintegrated dimensions of our everyday lives, which are carried out in existential situations and contexts with many factors. Art performs its italicizing function, Tallis argues, by embodying consciousness in forms—by realizing an idea concretely and not abstractly in the discursive sense, in the way language works with concepts. "A work of art," Tallis writes, "is a concretely realized idea. . . . The fundamental tendency of art is to extend the 'mindful' through form" (51). This idea is extended to experience as a whole by Dewey: "Form is a character of every experience that is *an* experience. . . . *Form may then be defined as the operation of forces that carry the experience of an agent, object, scene, and situation to its own integral fulfillment*" ([1934a] 1989, 142). Integral fulfillment can take many forms and is not restricted to art but rather is the defining feature of the "aesthetic" quite generally, a way of attending to experience that dwells in it for its own sake and that does not lead us *to* experience but, rather, constitutes one. This way of attending is not merely passive but rather is interpretive and constructive. It is part of the flowering out of experience into works of art through exploitation of the symbolic pregnancy of potencies and energies of experience itself, as was discussed in chapter 2 with reliance on Dewey and Langer.

Writing in her *Philosophy in a New Key*, and expanding on insights from Gestalt psychology, Langer outlined the many ways in which "meaning accrues essentially to forms" ([1942] 1957, 91) or enters into organized wholes in the sensory field. These forms emerge out of, and are seen in, the continuum of experience and enter into symbolic transformations of experience in both discursive and nondiscursive modes, processes that Dewey in his essay "Qualitative Thought" (1930a) called "going out into symbolization" (205n4). For Tallis the artistic forms in which ideas are realized are exemplars and mediators of presence. They satisfy the "hunger to *be* entirely where one *is*" and show, but do not explain to us, the lived logic of such presencing. The goal of both art and philosophy is to fill "the hole in sense" (2014, 46), but "sense" is meant differently in the two cases. If we follow Tallis, arriving through the artwork at the "filled time" of the present and having the sense of being there with what fills it is an experience, not an argument or a theory. In art, according to Tallis, we are not thinking *about* or describing a form, we are thinking *with* or constructing *in* a form. By actively attending to its production and through it to what it makes present, we encounter a significance surrounded by the aforementioned concretely realized idea, surrounded by the ever-present nimbus of what is unsaid but nevertheless meant, Dufrenne's "dim evidences" (referred to in chapter 1).

Such an experience with an artwork is what Vladimir Jankélévitch, speaking of music in *Music and the Ineffable* (2003), called the "drastic" encounter with art, an encounter that interrupts us and brings us to a halt without "saying" anything to us. For Tallis, an artwork is "at once experienceable in minutiae . . . and known as a whole: the idea and the experience, the moment in time and the arrested form, are brought together and we, who could not arrive, arrive. The world is captured in a moment and the moment flowers out into a world—the world we could not, when we lived it moment by moment, grasp as a whole—so that we reciprocate its grip on us with a grip as strong" (2014, 67). Such a passage evokes Murdoch's fictional and Hustvedt's personal accounts of encountering their Giorgiones (discussed in chapters 1 and 2). Speaking of music but clearly extendable to all art, Jankélévitch ascribes this "grip" to the work's "charme" (analogous to Dewey's aura), which grasps us prior to all analysis, its "magical accord" that effects vibrating resonances in what Peirce called "the bottomless lake of consciousness" (Peirce 1931–58, 7:547). In such encounters, one's life is, as Tallis puts it in a vivid image, a veritable "river of succession—the moments that passed through us as a procession of inchoate and warring forms—broadens and deepens to a lagoon" (2014, 67). But the lagoon, it must be admitted, has hidden currents and is not stable or placid, since, as Jankélévitch writes, in the wake of a work of art we often find not existential complacency but an "incomprehensible disquiet churned up" (2003, 75), a vortex of resonances, which can be reevoked by future encounters, as in recapitulation and repetition in music, with the tensive feel of both backward reference and augmentation and deepening of "the same." Philosophical discourse, in the form it takes in this book, also exhibits this tensive feel inasmuch as, to continue Colapietro's idea, it appropriates and reconfigures a past reservoir of attempts to "think things over." This is Dewey's funded nature of thought and experience.

The river of succession that makes up our lives pulls or carries us on toward other experiences, other pragmatic concerns, and other seekings after explanations that attempt to make our ideas clear. But art does not explain; it opens onto realms where explanations play no role. The forms of attending induced by art are embedded in experience as a whole, even if they cannot be permanently practiced in the multiple universes of meanings in which life takes place, with its constant oscillation between undergoing and doing that is the hinge of Dewey's model of the self-environment relation as a spiral or widening gyre of interactions, both instrumental and consummatory. Art works and our consummatory experiences of them, to use one of Dewey's memorable images, are like mountains arising on or out of a plain.

Moreover, while the paradigmatic aesthetic experience is the experience generated by artworks, nature itself offers inexhaustible occasions for an aesthetic experience, as was shown in different ways in chapters 5 and 6. Such experience, Dewey pointed out, is marked by (a) *completeness*, in that the material that is experienced "runs its course to fulfillment" ([1934a] 1989, 36); (b) *uniqueness*, due to the experienced whole or form carrying with it "its own individualizing quality and self-sufficiency" (37); and (c) a unifying and nonreified *emotion* functioning as a kind of "moving and cementing force" that "provides unity in and through the varied parts of an experience" (44). In the classic chapter "Having an Experience," Dewey enumerates more explicitly these further aesthetic characteristics of the aesthetic interaction: *continuity* of experiencing, as opposed to breaking the experiential occasion; *cumulation* of items, entailing the increasing fullness of elements; *conservation* of elements, so that nothing is lost in a self-enfolding and funded stretch of experience; *tension*, due to differential weightings of elements in the process of being integrated due to the organization of energies resident in and informing the experience; and *anticipation*, rooted in the dynamic vectorial nature of the various components of the stream of consciousness, with what James (1971, 274) called its "ever not quite" quality drawing it toward completion. At the same time Dewey wanted to draw special attention to the factor of resistance or difficulty, which is manifested in the interruptive nature of the artwork.

## Form between Symbolization and Abstraction

An artwork is first and foremost an articulate form embodied in a medium, just as language itself is. But anterior to language and art is the comprehension of form itself. This is an indispensable contribution of Langer to outlining the semiotic dimensions of art and aesthetic encounters, which was discussed in chapter 2. Now let us reconsider, in the context of the challenges raised by Dewey, Tallis, and Jankélévitch, the following pivotal text from *Feeling and Form*:

> The comprehension of form itself, through its exemplification in formed perceptions or "intuitions," is spontaneous and natural *abstraction*, but the recognition of a metaphorical value of some intuitions, which springs from the perception of their forms, is spontaneous and natural *interpretation*. Both abstraction and interpretation are intuitive, and may deal with non-discursive forms. They lie at the base of all human mentality, and are the roots from which both language and art take rise. (1953, 378)

The pivotal human process of going out into symbolization from experience follows two different paths or trajectories carried out in two forms of abstraction: *generalizing abstraction* in the case of discursive symbolization and *presentational abstraction* in the case of presentational symbolization. This semiotic rift, which is rather different from the experiential rift (which both Dewey and Tallis are also concerned with in different ways), cannot be stitched up in any permanent way, although core terms in the passage—form, exemplification, abstraction, metaphorical value, interpretation—transcend a rigid separation. The distinction between forms of abstraction, based on two different "logics," is fundamental, even if it is only beings endowed with self-reflexive discursive powers that have developed both spontaneously and systematically another autonomous path of presentational symbolization in which art, along with myth and ritual, are grounded. Their logics have a common root: the perception of forms or symbolic pregnancies rooted in the physiognomic and affect-laden qualities of undergone experience and embodied in the diversely shaped materials of artworks.

Generalizing abstraction divides experience into classes and abstract patterns of relations (which are rooted in perception, to be sure), relying on the diacritical power of recognizing differences in its sortings and relatings of the significant joints and relations in experience. The primal drive of language is that it tries to extend its power over all of experience and leads to what we could call the logocentric temptation: to put everything in its ordered place. Langer, however, shows that presentational abstraction divides or shapes the field of experience into forms that articulate or make explicit a significance resident in an object or natural occurrence that enables it, as embodied in a shaped image, to function as a symbol: a natural symbol or a ritual or a work of art that semiotically exploits the natural object or event. The very materials of experience, circumscribed wholes, are transformed into symbolic structures—visual forms, sounds, gestures, and so forth—whose untranslatable *import*, which is a distinct physiognomy, is inseparable from their material embodiment. These forms, when transformed into artworks, become what Polanyi called in *Meaning* "so many closed packages of clues, portable and lasting" (Polanyi and Prosch 1975, 87). It is these remarkably open "closed packages" that hold us in their grip for those integral moments of aesthetic encounters, examples of which have been reviewed in the preceding chapters.

Presentational abstraction, which is situated in a different way in Peirce's semiotics (Innis 2013), is one of the semiotic keys to understanding how artworks as material artifacts can engender the experiencing of experience, which Tallis held to be the task and achievement of art. As Langer writes in *Philosophy in a New Key*, the rise and development of presentational symbolism quite generally effected

> a new departure in semantic. . . . The recognition of vague, vital meanings in physical forms—perhaps the first dawn of symbolism—gave us our idols, emblems, and totems; the primitive function of dream permits our first envisagement of events. The momentous discovery of nature-symbolism, of the pattern of life reflected in natural phenomena, produced the first universal insights. Every mode of thought is bestowed on us, like a gift, with some new principle of symbolic expression. It has a logical development, which is simply the exploitation of all the uses to which that symbolism lends itself. ([1942] 1957, 200–201)

This "exploitation" is realized in shaped materials, including the human body itself, that make explicit, articulate, and embody what Langer calls the forms of feeling, and they do so by potentiating the symbolic pregnancies of experience itself. Emerson showed in *Nature* ([1836] 1992, 3–39) that we can apprehend and exploit natural symbols—fire, water, air, breath, and so forth—independently of formal art. Indeed, for him they are art's ground as well as the ground of language. Such symbols open onto an unsurveyable network of connections. Their import bears on the unlimited that manifests itself in the finite. Such forms are not by any necessity linked by a discursive logic to other forms in a system or to life with its conflicting demands and multiple dimensions of concern. But their affective bonds do, nevertheless, have deep affinities and art works exploit and reveal them in multitudinous ways.

Each art form, which is a significant whole but incapable of being the whole *of* significance, is a unique unit composed out of materially unique elements. It does not have, to use Polanyi's distinction, a representative meaning but, rather, it has an existential meaning constituted by multileveled patterns of internal relations of ordered wholes or contexts. Both types of meaning are forms of semiotic articulation. Writing in his *Personal Knowledge*, Polanyi remarks: "A patch of colour, a musical note are so substantial in themselves, that they can speak their part in articulating a relationship with other patches of colour, or other musical notes, without pointing beyond themselves. Instead of denoting something—whether an external object or their own use—they emphatically present their own striking sensuous presence" (1958, 193–194). Objects and relations can and do appear in this play of sensuous presences, but Langer is surely right to hold that it is the *form of appearing* that determines the unspeakable *felt import* that is made explicit and presented for our contemplation and interpretation in the formed material before us, which manifests the *morphology of feeling*. This is especially the case with music, whose paradigmatic importance for and challenge to philosophy as a set of discursive practices has been discussed by Vladimir Jankélévitch in his *Music and the Ineffable* (2003).

## Philosophy as Epiphanic and Episodic

Jankélévitch ascribes to the experience of musical works an essentially *episodic* or *epiphanic* character. This is a character not restricted to music. It belongs to other art forms as well, especially painting, in which one is caught by a kind of sudden magical aura immanent in and emanating from the work (a phenomenon noted in other chapters). This is the distinctive quality that grips us without an explicit effort on our part. *Being gripped* is something undergone, not something we do. Dewey, as has been shown in the preceding chapters, makes this notion one of the central pillars of aesthetic experience, not just in *Art as Experience*, but also in his seminal essays on qualitative thought, affective thought, and the analytical ultimacy of Peirce's theory of quality (1930a, 1931a, 1935). Such a sense of being gripped by a defining quality is the heart of Peirce's contribution to aesthetics. There is a certain spontaneity to the event, which clearly also is dependent on a kind of openness on the part of the perceiver. Such an openness is a kind of antecedent willingness embedded in habits of receptive attending. These habits have to be cultivated against the inertial force of language's dynamic drive toward general classifications or social manipulation.

Jankélévitch, like Langer but perhaps for different reasons, is insistent that music is not a kind of language, although it has a variety of complex formal structures, themselves evolving, that govern its products. It does not have ideas "to line up logically with one another" (2003, 18). It is not that music has no "ideas" lined up and (to be) developed, since it clearly does, and there are constraints—which can be overcome or transformed into other systems of constraints. For Jankélévitch there is certainly a compositional logic governing the types of musical forms he is most devoted to or has an affinity with—predominantly the works of French modernism—but it is not essential to his argument. The ideas are musical ideas, products of a form of reverie governed by improvisation that "means nothing and yet means everything," while at the same time expressing no communicable sense, outside of the very forms of experience it confronts us with. Rather, Jankélévitch thinks that a musical form is "an image of life, spontaneous outpouring and progress that cannot be foreseen" (21). We are caught up in the dynamics of its shaped time, just as we are caught up in the shaped spaces of a painting emerging out of what Kandinsky called its "elements"—point, line, plane, color, form.

Another challenge to philosophy here is to foreground the epiphanic or episodic nature or possibilities of philosophical reflection rather than its predominantly argumentative character. It is questionable whether in fact these philosophical modes are ineluctably opposed to one another, as the complex variety of philosophical writing attests (Lysaker 2017, 2018a, 2018b). The paradoxical achievement of artistic forms as finite fragments, as what Iris Murdoch in *Metaphysics as a Guide to Morals* called "authoritative limited wholes" (1992, 3), is to intimate and express, and to both force and train us, as she shows in *The Sovereignty of Good* (1970), to attend to a surplus of sense. They do so by being significant wholes that, while being unable to capture in their symbolically pregnant forms the whole *of* significance, nevertheless can make it or its exhibited dimensions appear *in nuce* in and through themselves, as in Bach's *Mass in B Minor*, Mozart's *Requiem*, and Mahler's *Symphony No. 7*. Jankélévitch argues that music, in its essential "objectlessness," cures us or at least relieves us temporarily of the search for discursively explicit meanings, while admitting that there is no absolutely "tacit" music that does not articulate an experienced felt content, which itself can be seen as "illuminating" something inconceivable, yet paradoxically thought *about* and understood, not in concepts but rather in ordered sounds that present the dynamic play of the morphology of feelings and affective tones.

The mysterious, inconceivable origin of the universe in the big bang, the physicist Victor Weisskopf used to say in his lectures, is perhaps better made intelligible in the opening chords of Haydn's *The Creation* than in the elegant equations of physics (Corry 1984). This oratorio is what Tallis (2014) called a *concretely realized idea*. Music is audible, something in the world, and is yet paradoxically caught in a peculiar dialectical tension between noise and silence: through sound, it silences for a finite time the noise of existence, which in itself leans toward chaos and elicits from us a blessed rage for order—or at least a sense of its possible presence or origin, as Weisskopf claimed. Philosophy tries not just to make sense of the noise of existence, but also to make sense of the variety of ways in which we attempt to do so. Its putatively diaphanous medium is concepts, while music, and all art as well, overcomes the noise of existence with embodied "Ideas" that carry us away by the intrinsic powers of their material embodiments, in whose very materials the felt significances of our lives in time are inextricably incarnated.

## Being Affected: The Ineffable and the Invisible

While Jankélévitch explores the implications of the epiphanic nature of music, or musical forms, for philosophical reflection, in *Seeing the Invisible* ([1988] 2009), Michel Henry, relying on a conceptual framework based on Husserlian phenomenology and far from a pragmatist or semiotic approach to experience, uses a similar reflection on the foundations of abstract art as formulated in Kandinsky's theoretical writings to situate painting as paradigm art within a nonrepresentational framework, linking it in a specific way with music. Henry's claim is that, like music, painting in its essence is not "about" the world—not about representing a world that is already complete and in no need of duplication, which is a position close to Jankélévitch's repudiation of "resaying." Thinking that there is such a need is to exacerbate the wound of consciousness introduced by the achievements of conceptual abstraction and the unrest and sense of incompletion and dispersion of everydayness. Henry's book engages a profound paradox: the content of a painting and, a fortiori of all art, is not its theme or object, which can be named or seen. It is life or subjectivity. Life, as he characterizes it, is invisible. It is not an object, but is nevertheless accessible through the visible and felt in our bodies with what Dewey called a "total organic resonance." The inner and the outer, according to Henry, are inextricably joined but not identical. While the visible belongs to the domain of objectivity, the invisible belongs to the domain of the flux of life, of embodied subjectivity, with its accompanying somatic tonus. It is precisely the epiphanic experiences of integrated subjectivity mediated by art, experiences in which we dwell for their own sakes even for the briefest of moments, that minister to the wound, which, paradoxically, belongs to or defines the essentially tragic being-toward-death that marks our existence. Painting is a way of "listening to the inner resonance dwelling in each particular object" (Henry [1988] 2009, 134).

Life, as Henry puts it in a way that will not be unfamiliar to readers of Peirce, James, Langer, and Dewey, is at the fundamental level a flux of what he calls "tones and tonalities," arising from processes of *being affected* by the inner resonances of objects. According to Henry's interpretation of Kandinsky, we are not primarily affected by *what* appears in a painting. The essence of a painting is not primarily to "tell" us *about* the world or represent the world again as a collection of objects in relation to each other. Its logic is, by means of its sensible "elements"—point, line, plane, color, form—to embody, exploit, and reveal the expressive possibilities of the variable engendering energies of the felt tones and tonalities of *appearing itself*, and not just of *an* appearance. It is these linked toned forms of appearing, what Peirce (1998) called "the total resultant Quality of Feeling presented in the work of art we are contemplating" (190), that augment and inform the subjective flux of our lives and give it what Peirce called its material quality, or *quale*, which we are made aware of by means of our encounter with artworks as their embodiments. In making us aware of these toned forms of life, painting—and indeed all art forms—makes us aware of, or present to, ourselves and leads us to experience our experience and not just the world as an indifferent configuration of objects.

Reflection on Henry leads us once again to the centrality of the theory of quality that informs the analyses of Peirce and Dewey. Dewey ([1934a] 1989, 99) quotes approvingly the following passage from Albert Barnes's *The*

*Art in Painting* (1937, 52): "When we cannot find in a picture representation of any particular object, what it represents may be the qualities which *all* particular objects share, such as color, extensity, solidity, movement, rhythm, etc. All particular things have these qualities; hence what serves, so to speak, as a paradigm of the visible essence of things may hold in solution the emotions which individualized things provoke in a more specialized way." It is the exploitation of these elements as the generative matrix of painting, and not the representation of the objects alone, that mediates the experiencing our experience that Henry (1988) describes under the rubric of "life," the ultimate "content" of painting. The experiential interaction with a painting is a paradigm of being led by the felt magical accord of an appearing form, which is a materially embodied creative gathering gaze. Our being gathered in the moments of appearing is another way of describing healing the wound in consciousness or filling the hole in sense by letting go of argumentation and giving oneself over to the present in its fullness.

## Art, Philosophy, and the Noise of Meaninglessness: Letting Go of Argumentation

Jankélévitch explores this topic of letting go with regard to the nondenotative character of music, with its "countless associations" (1983, 74) occurring in a kind of Peircean play of musement. There is, in Jankélévitch's account, a certain passivity to "following the music," of "being with" or "being in" the sound, or being with the internal movements and directions of a painting, which is not dissimilar to Paul Klee's notions of letting a line wander or go for a walk (see Sallis 2015, especially chapters 6 and 12), with us alongside it. Is there not something similar happening in Emerson (and in others, to be sure): letting a thought wander, with thoughts pulling other thoughts out? Are not, perhaps, the essay form and the aphorism close to the epiphanic and episodic nature of art? Is there not an essential place for this kind of writing in the future tasks of philosophy, which must perform the past as well as engage the present, as John Lysaker (2017, 2018a, 2018b) has demonstrated? Lysaker exemplifies thought as a process of self-interruption, as reflexive sequences of breaking off and returning through reformulations to the matter at hand, which Colapietro saw as the world's omnipresent challenge to philosophy. Jankélévitch (2003) writes of philosophical dialogue being a kind of "interrupted serenade."

Perhaps we could also think of philosophical discussion and reflection as analogous to playing chamber music, with different voices performing different lines with the joint aim of "realizing the topic" or coming to an understanding of vitally important aspects of the complex, multivoiced, and often discordant melody of existence or, in this case, dimensions of aesthetic experience. John Stuhr, in his *Pragmatic Fashions* (2015) and his "Lost, Looking Around, Looking Ahead," has provocatively argued that such discussion and reflection do not just involve a philosophical approach to, or use of, a wide variety of arts such as poetry, drama, music, graphic novels, music, and addresses. For him, as he proposes, rightly understood, "these arts *are* philosophy" (2018, 46), not just as what Dewey calls "creative criticism" but also as uncovering and fostering the social process of oriented striving toward ideals that recede from full realization, which both Dewey and Tallis foregrounded with different aesthetic emphases.

Jankélévitch points out that forms of music do not have to be "expressive" in the normal sense of imposing themselves massively on us by trying to make a point via a kind of gigantism and striving toward grandiosity. Such a remark is partly to be explained by his aesthetic preferences for musical modernism and its self-imposed minimalism. There are clearly miniatures in music as well as in painting and other art forms—and also in the varied forms of philosophy. Monumental painting exists alongside the miniature in museums and concerts are planned with complex mixtures of large-scale and small-scale works. In art as well as philosophy, one size does not fit all. This is an important philosophical lesson. Beethoven's string quartets are no less embodiments of musical significance than his symphonies, and philosophical insight is not wedded to the treatise or "the big book." Dewey wrote in his *Essays in Experimental Logic* that "thinking is a reconstructive movement of actual contents of experience to each other" (1916, 176). Such thinking occurs in different scales and modes.

The notion of a reconstructive movement of thought is essential to philosophy and to understanding artistic creation. Artworks emerge against a large background of previous works but without attempting to displace them. Each is a way of exhibiting or organizing experience, just as the philosophical essay can be seen as exhibiting or organizing a thought against the complex background of philosophical traditions, performing or furthering those traditions in multiple ways and modes. And indeed, as an example connected with the present topic, Dewey's great 1896 paper on the inadequacy of the reflex arc concept presented *in nuce* the approach to an intricate web of topics regarding the intertwining of perceiving and acting that would occupy him reconstructively in later years. The great fragments of Peirce are rich mines or reservoirs of insights whose systematization, including aesthetic systematization, has been left to others. Thus, just as Peirce held that we are in thought rather than thought being in us, so in the case of our experience of art it is perhaps better to say that we are in or taken up into the experiences presented in them, just as we are in a play or game or are put into play by them.

There is another possible lesson here for philosophical reflection and writing. The originary agon of philosophy is an agon of wresting meaning from the noise of meaninglessness, not just of winning an argument. Even the inexpressiveness or abnegation of striving for effect of the type of music to which Jankélévitch is devoted consists in its implying "innumerable possibilities of interpretation, because it allows us to choose between them" (1983, 74), recognizing that they are not mutually exclusive. This is something attempted in these chapters, which are devoted to some conceptually and historically linked complementary analytical frameworks for making sense of the dimensions of aesthetic encounters without repudiating the ideal of objectivity or the need for awareness of the limits of one's own proposals or the completeness of one's conceptual tools. These possibilities of interpretation are manifested in what Jankélévitch called the "incomprehensible disquiet churned up" in the wake of a work of art (1983, 75) or, more broadly, in the wake of our encounters with "limit situations" in life that confront us and are articulated in multiple modes, including the aesthetic mode of the sublime and transcendent, in what Karl Jaspers called "ciphers" (see Corrington 2007, 2013, 2016). Such situations heighten subjectivity and bring us to ourselves, putting our awareness "into italics," as Tallis (2014, 119) so felicitously put it. By reason of their disquieting power they give us a heightened sense of being present to something that pulls us out of ourselves and discloses to us the space of our own existence by shattering its taken-for-grantedness.

Polanyi describes such an ecstatic engagement, which pulls us away from the discursive lattices of our lives, under the rubric of "dwelling in and breaking out" (1958, 195–202). Observers and manipulators are "guided *by* experience and pass *through* experience without experiencing it *in itself*" by reason of the interpolation of a conceptual framework that functions as a screen. The contemplative encounter with art works, or the cosmic panorama of nature, "dissolves the screen, stops our movement through experience and pours us straight into experience; we cease to handle things and become immersed in them. . . . As we lose ourselves in contemplation, we take on an impersonal life in the objects of our contemplation" (197). This is the form of dwelling in and breaking out that marks aesthetic encounters. A child fascinated by a slug moving across a stone and oblivious to everything else, which Tallis (2014) mentions, is in its own way as remarkable or exemplary such an immersion as the enraptured activity of the creative mathematician or artist or mystic. They manifest, as Polanyi puts it, the "impersonality of intense contemplation [as] a complete participation of the person in that which he contemplates and not in his complete detachment from it" (1958, 197). Such complete participation has wide scope: "a valid articulate framework may be a theory, or a mathematical discovery, or symphony. Whichever it is, it will be used by dwelling in it, and this indwelling can be consciously experienced" (195).

Artworks are articulate frameworks, so constructed out of materials transformed into expressive mediums that they give rise to a felt modification and steering of consciousness by reason of their material qualities and patterns, in which we dwell and lose ourselves. The experience of crossing of a threshold in encountering a work of art or a wondrous spectacle of nature lights up the present moment and gives it a new distinctive tone. Such moments are of many different scales and are not by any means always monumental, but they bring about our presence in the moment, with its felt import and its luring perceptual qualities.

## Art's Challenge to Philosophy

On the last page of the chapter "The Challenge to Philosophy," in Dewey's *Art as Experience*, we find the following passage:

> My intention throughout this chapter has not been to criticize various philosophies of art as such, but to elicit the significance that art has for philosophy in its broadest scope. For philosophy like art moves in the medium of imaginative mind, and, since art is the most direct and complete manifestation there is of experience *as* experience, it provides a unique control for the imaginative ventures of philosophy. . . . The significance of art as experience is, therefore, incomparable for the adventure of philosophical thought. ([1934a] 1989, 309)

Art, in this conception, is not to be conceived of primarily or exclusively as a problem *of* or *for* philosophy to resolve. Rather, art in its various forms could be considered as exemplifying ways of arriving at solutions *to* focal problems that philosophy itself as a reflective conceptual practice has given rise to: its claim to totality and comprehensiveness and the need for system, the primacy of discursive rationality as ultimate measure for delimiting the thresholds of sense, and the existential need to integrate experience in light of the gap between actuality and possibility that marks the dispersal of our lives in time and in the structures of everydayness.

There is also another type of gap, different from that between actuality and possibility, pointed out by William James, whose work informs Dewey's aesthetics at the deepest background level. This gap is found in the radical pluralism of multiple realities or universes of meaning in which we live. These universes of meaning make up the web of intentional bonds linking us to various dimensions of experience, each with its own distinctive feel and organizing principle. In James's *Some Problems of Philosophy* we find the following passage: "Different universes of thought thus arise, with specific sorts of relation among their ingredients. The world of common-sense 'things'; the world of material tasks to be done; the mathematical world of pure forms; the world of ethical propositions; the worlds of logic, of music, etc.—all abstracted and generalized from long-forgotten perceptual instances from which they have as it were flowered out—return and merge themselves again in the particulars of our present and future perception" (1911, 52). A central descriptive and critical task of philosophy is to reflect on and mediate between these universes of thought, which clearly involve different patterns of experience with different subjective feels and intentional structures. Philosophy is not to duplicate, or substitute for, the knowledge embodied in these universes. Rather, its task is to uncover and to analyze the types of knowledge and forms of experience, spontaneous and constructed, that they exemplify, based on what James called the "specific sorts of relation among their ingredients" (52).

It is these specific sorts of relations in aesthetic experiences and also in artistic production that are exemplified and linked in different ways in the preceding chapters by means of a sort of method of rotation and following a trail of linkages and intersections of complementary approaches to the dimensions of aesthetic encounters. These approaches, both philosophical and nonphilosophical, are not surveyed but rather put to work and measured by their respective heuristic powers to illuminate just how and why art, and aesthetic experience in general, "moves in the medium of imaginative mind" and manifests the contours of "experience *as* experience."

A special merit of the pragmatist tradition in its various configurations is not to devalue or rank any form of knowledge or experience against some a priori standard. Instead it aims to do justice to all modes of experiencing and to discern and develop ways of outlining and relating the complementary factors entering into the root model that underlies the "flowering out" of the various worlds of meanings that make up the matrices of our lives. The pragmatist tradition foregrounds the experiential and participatory matrices of our forms of world engagement, criticizing especially the spectator, or what Dewey called the "kodak fixation," models. Peirce's semiotic characterization of the bottomless lake of consciousness and the play of signs (Innis 1994), James's fine-meshed descriptions of the theme-field-margin structure of the flux of consciousness culminating in his radical empiricism, and Dewey's expansion of his core idea of a spiraling, open-ended, and dynamic circuit of behavior offer sets of analytical matrices focusing on how we respond constructively, in multiple modes, *into* experiential situations and not just *to* them.

In Dewey's conception, pragmatism's principal goal, in the attaining of which art plays a distinctive and informing role, both in its practices and in its products, is to show us how to maintain and restore, however intermittently, experiential and existential balance in our various forms of participation in what he called in *Experience and Nature* the "moving unbalanced balance of things" ([1925] 1988, 314). Such is nature in process, a nature out of which we have emerged, in which we follow our life paths, and into which we shall return. Maintaining and restoring our balance through art and aesthetic experience in general is to *bring us close to experience* so that, interrupted or enriched, we do not just pass through experience but, rather, come to affectively dwell in its configurations of qualities, harmonies, and vital messages as ends in themselves that hold us in their grip and organize us in new ways by the engendering of their proper significate effects or interpretants.

This is the existential point of Dewey's pivotal and well-known distinction between instrumental and consummatory experiences. It is exemplified in Dewey's distinction between a kind of generalized indexical use of tools and signs, things that point beyond themselves in various ways, and the construction of objective forms *of* and *for* experience, where the Jamesian "ingredients" are indwelt for their own sake and produce or express by their distinctive configuration a distinctive kind of significance. This is the originating matrix of the intertwined domains of art and the aesthetic. Art and the aesthetic dimension quite generally for Dewey are, as he writes in *Art as Experience*, a transfiguration of significance grounded in various forms of *integrations*: of "actuality and possibility or ideality, the new and the old, objective material and personal response, the individual and the universal, surface and depth, sense and meaning" ([1934a] 1989, 301). When Dewey claimed that it is "to esthetic experience ... the philosopher must go to understand what experience is" (278), the aim was not just to understand it but to be challenged by it and to live up to its demands. What a work of art does, Dewey argues, is to "concentrate and enlarge an immediate experience. . . . [T]he meanings imaginatively summoned, assembled, and integrated are embodied in material existence that here and now interacts with the self. The work of art is thus a challenge to the performance of a like act of evocation and organization, through imagination, on the part of the one who experiences it" (278). These processes of concentration and enlargement in aesthetic experience, both receptive and productive, are what the diverse complementary analytical resources from different frameworks employed in these chapters throw powerful, indeed, indispensable light on.

Art challenges philosophy to come to grips with our models of experience and of meaning-making by engaging the radical diversity and novelty of experience and by exploring the nature and origin of the material forms of presentation in which works of art appear and their relevance for philosophical reflection. This book has followed a trail of conceptual and historical linkages between a range of aesthetic theories, models, and examples of aesthetic encounters not just with art works but also with the universe, which Peirce called the poem of God, or which Lao-tzu named the Tao, while recognizing that it itself is beyond naming. Bringing different aesthetic frameworks into complementary, not competitive, relations to one another enables one to avoid the fallacy of false alternatives or a striving toward totality and comprehensiveness by the imposition of an iron grid of concepts. Such a grid, with its nearly irresistible temptation to systematic completion and universality, is confronted with the phenomenon of the immense variety and scope of aesthetic experiences and their contexts. Dimensions of aesthetic experience inform our experience all the way up to the highest levels of symbolic articulation and all the way down to the fundamental somatic tonus of our being. While it may not be possible to develop a full account of these dimensions with only the analytical tools I have employed, one can make a strong claim, as I have tried to show, that it would not be possible to do so without them.

REFERENCES

===

Alexander, Samuel. 1920. *Space, Time, and Deity*, 2 vols. London: Macmillan.

Alexander, Samuel. 1933. *Beauty and Other Forms of Value*. London: Macmillan.

Alexander, Samuel. (1925) 1939. "Art and the Material." The Adamson Lecture, 1925. Manchester University Lectures, no. 23. Manchester: At the University Press. Reprinted in Samuel Alexander, *Philosophical and Literary Pieces*. Edited, and with a memoir, by John Laird, 211–232. Westport, CT: Greenwood Press.

Alexander, Samuel. (1927a) 1939. "Artistic Creation and Cosmic Creation." Reprinted in Samuel Alexander, *Philosophical and Literary Pieces*. Edited, and with a memoir, by John Laird, 256–278. Westport, CT: Greenwood Press.

Alexander, Samuel. (1927b) 1939. "Art and Instinct." The Herbert Spencer Lecture, May 23, 1927. Reprinted in Samuel Alexander, *Philosophical and Literary Pieces*. Edited, and with a memoir, by John Laird, 233–255. Westport, CT: Greenwood Press.

Alexander, Samuel. 1939. *Philosophical and Literary Pieces*. Edited, and with a memoir, by John Laird. Westport, CT: Greenwood Press.

Alexander, Thomas. 1987. *John Dewey's Theory of Art, Experience and Nature: The Horizons of Feeling*. Albany: State University of New York Press.

Alexander, Thomas. 2013. *The Human Eros*. New York: Fordham University Press.

Armstrong, John. 2000. *Move Closer: An Intimate Philosophy of Art*. New York: Farrar, Straus, and Giroux.

Bardt, Christopher. 2019. *Material and Mind*. Cambridge, MA: MIT Press.

Barnes, Albert C. 1937. *The Art in Painting*. 3rd ed., revised and enlarged. Boston: Harcourt.

Benjamin, Walter. 1969. "Some Reflections on Kafka." In *Illuminations*. Translated by Harry Zohn, 141–146. Edited, with an Introduction, by Hannah Arendt. New York: Schocken Books.

Böhme, Gernot. 2017a. *The Aesthetics of Atmospheres*. Edited by Jean Paul Thibaud. London: Routledge.

Böhme, Gernot. 2017b. *Atmospheric Architectures*. Edited and translated by Tina Engels-Schwarzpaul. London: Routledge.

Broch, Hermann. 1945. *The Death of Virgil*. Translated by Jean Starr Untermeyer. New York: Pantheon.

Browning, R. 1917. "The 'Moses' of Michael Angelo." In Joseph Friedlander, comp., *The Standard Book of Jewish Verse*. New York: Dodd, Mead and Company. https://www.bartleby.com/98/76.html.

Buchler, Justus. 1966. *Nature and Judgment*. New York: Grosset and Dunlap.

Buchler, Justus. 1974. *The Main of Light*. New York: Oxford University Press.

Buchler, Justus. 1979. *Toward a General Theory of Judgment.* 2nd ed. New York: Dover Publications.

Bunn, James. 2002. *Wave Forms: A Natural Syntax for Rhythmic Languages.* Stanford, CA: Stanford University Press.

Burnshaw, Stanley. 1979. *The Seamless Web.* New York: George Braziller.

Cassirer, Ernst. 1957. *The Phenomenology of Knowledge.* Vol. 3 of *The Philosophy of Symbolic Forms.* Translated by R. Manheim. Introduction by C. W. Hendel. New Haven: Yale University Press. Original German publication 1929.

Cassirer. Ernst. (1942) 2000. *The Logic of the Cultural Sciences.* Translated and with an Introduction by S. G. Lofts. Foreword by Donald Philip Verene. New Haven: Yale University Press, 2000.

Cassirer, Ernst. 1979. *Symbol, Myth, and Culture: Essays and Lectures of Ernst Cassirer, 1935–1945.* Edited by Donald P. Verene. New Haven: Yale University Press.

Celan, Paul. 1961. "The Meridian. Speech on the Occasion of the Award of the Georg Büchner Prize." In *Selected Poems and Prose of Paul Celan.* Translated by John Felstiner, 401–414. New York: W. W. Norton.

Chaplin, Adrienne Dengerink. 2020. *The Philosophy of Susanne Langer: Embodied Meaning in Logic, Art and Feeling.* London: Bloomsbury Academic.

Cheng, François. 2006. *The Way of Beauty: Five Meditations for Spiritual Transformation.* Translated by Jody Gladding. Rochester, VT: Inner Traditions, 2009.

Colapietro, Vincent. 1989. *Peirce's Approach to the Self.* Albany: State University of New York Press.

Colapietro, Vincent. 2018. "The Actuality of Philosophy Thought over Once Again." *Journal of Speculative Philosophy* 32, no. 1: 3–20.

Coleman, Earl L. 1978. *Philosophy of Painting by Shih Ta'o.* The Hague: Mouton.

Corrington, Robert 1997. *Nature's Religion.* Foreword by Robert C. Neville. Lanham, MD: Rowman and Littlefield.

Corrington, Robert. 2013. *Nature's Sublime.* Lanham, MD: Lexington Books.

Corrington, Robert. 2016. *Deep Pantheism.* Lanham, MD: Lexington Books.

Corry, John. 1984. "TV Review: Views of Weisskopf on Science and Morals." *New York Times,* April 3. https://www.nytimes.com/1984/04/03/arts/tv-review-views-of-weisskopf-on-science-and-morals.html.

Crosby, Donald A. 2002. *A Religion of Nature.* Albany: State University of New York Press.

Crosby, Donald A. 2008. *Living with Ambiguity.* Albany: State University of New York Press

Crowther, Paul. 1989. *The Kantian Sublime.* Oxford: Clarendon Press.

Crowther. 1993a. *Art and Embodiment.* Oxford: Clarendon Press.

Crowther. 1993b. *Critical Aesthetics and Postmodernism.* Oxford: Clarendon Press.

Daive, Jean. 2020. *Under the Dome: Walks with Paul Celan.* Translated by Rosmarie Waldrop. San Francisco: City Lights Books.

Deleuze, G. 1993. *The Fold: Leibniz and the Baroque.* Translated and with a Foreword by Tom Conley. Minneapolis: University of Minnesota Press.

Dewey, John. (1896) 1998. "The Reflex Arc Concept in Psychology." In *The Essential Dewey,* vol. 2, edited by Larry A. Hickman and Thomas M. Alexander, 3–10. Bloomington: Indiana University Press.

Dewey, John. (1908) 1998. "Does Reality Possess Practical Character?" In *The Essential Dewey,* edited by Larry A. Hickman and Thomas M. Alexander, 1:124–133. Bloomington: Indiana University Press.

Dewey, John. 1916. *Essays in Experimental Logic*. Chicago: University of Chicago Press.

Dewey, John. (1922) 1988. *Human Nature and Conduct*. Critical edition. Edited by Jo Ann Boydston. With an Introduction by Murray G. Murphey. Carbondale: Southern Illinois University Press.

Dewey, John. (1925) 1988. *Experience and Nature*. Critical edition. Edited by Jo Ann Boydston. With an Introduction by Sidney Hook. Carbondale: Southern Illinois University Press.

Dewey, John. 1929. Letter to Samuel Alexander. John Rylands University Library, Manchester/Alexander Papers, ALEX/A/1/1/78.

Dewey, John. (1930a) 1998. "Qualitative Thought." In *The Essential Dewey*, edited by Larry A. Hickman and Thomas M. Alexander, 1:195–205. Bloomington: Indiana University Press.

Dewey, John. 1930b. Letter to Sidney Hook. Sidney Hook/John Dewey Collection, Special Collections, Morris Library, Southern Illinois University at Carbondale.

Dewey, John, 1930c. Correspondence to Corinne Frost. John Dewey Papers. Box 25, Folder 8. Special Collections, Morris Library, Southern Illinois University at Carbondale.

Dewey, John. 1931a. "Affective Thought." In *Philosophy and Civilization*, 117–125. New York: Putnam.

Dewey, John. (1931b) 1998. "Context and Thought." In Larry A. Hickman and Thomas M. Alexander, eds., *The Essential Dewey*, 2:206–216. Bloomington: Indiana University Press.

Dewey, John. 1931c. *Philosophy and Civilization*. New York: Putnam.

Dewey, John. (1934a) 1998. *Art as Experience*. Critical edition. Edited by Jo Ann Boydston. With an Introduction by Abraham Kaplan. Carbondale: Southern Illinois University Press.

Dewey, John. 1934b. *A Common Faith*. New Haven: Yale University Press.

Dewey, John. (1935) 1998. "Peirce's Theory of Quality." In Larry A. Hickman and Thomas M. Alexander, eds., *The Essential Dewey*, 2: 371–376. Bloomington: Indiana University Press.

Dewey, John. (1938) 1986. *Logic: The Theory of Inquiry*. Critical edition. Edited by Jo Ann Boydston. With an Introduction by Ernest Nagel. Carbondale: Southern Illinois University Press.

Dewey, John. 1946. "Peirce's Theory of Linguistic Signs, Thought, and Meaning." *Journal of Philosophy* 43, no. 4: 85–95.

Dreon, Roberta. 2012. *Fuori dalle Torre d'Avorio: L'Estetica inclusiva di John Dewey Oggi*. Genova-Milano: Marietti.

Dryden, Donald. 2001. "Susanne Langer and William James: Art and the Dynamics of the Stream of Consciousness." *Journal of Speculative Philosophy* 15: 272–285.

Dufrenne, Mikel. (1953) 1973. *The Phenomenology of Aesthetic Experience*. Translated by E. S. Casey, A. A. Anderson, W. Domingo, and L. Jacobson. Northwestern University Studies in Phenomenology and Existential Philosophy. Evanston, IL: Northwestern University Press, 1973.

Ehrenzweig, Anton. 1965. *The Psycho-analysis of Artistic Vision and Hearing*. 2nd ed. New York: George Braziller.

Ehrenzweig, Anton. 1971. *The Hidden Order of Art*. Berkeley: University of California Press.

Eliot, George. 1900. *The Mill on the Floss*. New York: Athenaeum Club.

Elkins, James. 1999. *What Painting Is*. New York: Routledge.

Emerson, Ralph Waldo. 1992. *The Selected Writings of Ralph Waldo Emerson*. Edited by Brooks Atkinson. New York: The Modern Library.

Epstein, Russell. 2004. Consciousness, Art, and the Brain: Lessons from Marcel Proust. *Consciousness and Cognition* 13: 213–240.

Felski, Rita. 2020. *Hooked: Art and Attachment*. Chicago: University of Chicago Press.

Freud, S. (1913–1914) 1955. *Totem and Taboo and Other Works* Vol. 13 in the Standard Edition. Translated by James Strachey. London: Hogarth Press, 1955.

Gadamer, Hans-Georg. (1960) 1991. *Truth and Method.* Translated by Joel Weinsheimer and Donald Marshall. 2nd rev. ed. New York: Crossroad.

Gadamer, Hans-Georg. (1964) 1977. "Aesthetics and Hermeneutics." In *Philosophical Hermeneutics.* Translated and edited by David E. Linge, 95–104. Berkeley: University of California Press.

Gadamer, Hans-Georg. 1977. *Philosophical Hermeneutics.* Translated and edited by David E. Linge. Berkeley: University of California Press.

Gadamer 1986a. "Art and Imitation." In *The Relevance of the Beautiful and Other Essays.* Translated by Nicholas Walker. Edited with an Introduction by Robert Bernasconi, 92–104. Cambridge: Cambridge University Press.

Gadamer, Hans-Georg. 1986b. "Composition and Interpretation." In *The Relevance of the Beautiful and Other Essays.* Translated by Nicholas Walker. Edited with an Introduction by Robert Bernasconi, 66–73. Cambridge: Cambridge University Press.

Gadamer, Hans-Georg. 1986c. "Intuition and Vividness." In *The Relevance of the Beautiful and Other Essays.* Translated by Nicholas Walker. Edited with an Introduction by Robert Bernasconi, 155–170. Cambridge: Cambridge University Press.

Gadamer, Hans-Georg. 1986d. "The Relevance of the Beautiful: Art as Play Symbol, and Festival." In *The Relevance of the Beautiful and Other Essays.* Translated by Nicholas Walker. Edited with an Introduction by Robert Bernasconi, 3–53. Cambridge: Cambridge University Press.

Gadamer, Hans-Georg. 1986e. *The Relevance of the Beautiful and Other Essays.* Translated by Nicholas Walker. Edited with an Introduction by Robert Bernasconi. Cambridge: Cambridge University Press.

Gadamer, Hans-Georg. 1993. *The Enigma of Health.* Translated by Jason Gaiger and Nicholas Walker. Stanford, CA: Stanford University Press, 1996.

Goodman, Nelson. 1976. *Languages of Art.* Indianapolis: Hackett.

Goodman, Nelson. 1978. *Ways of Worldmaking.* Indianapolis: Hackett.

Grange, Joseph. 1999. *The City: An Urban Ecology.* Albany: State University of New York Press.

Hausman, Carl R. 1984. *A Discourse on Novelty and Creation.* Albany: State University of New York Press.

Hausman, Carl R. 1989. *Metaphor and Art. Interactionism and Reference in the Verbal and Nonverbal Arts.* Cambridge: Cambridge University Press.

Hecht, Anthony. "At the Frick." *Painters and Poets,* March 9, 2013, http://www.paintersandpoets.com/2013/03/hecht-and-bellini-at-frick.html.

Hegel, G. W. F. 1807. *Phenomenology of Spirit.* Translated by A. V. Miller. Oxford: Clarendon Press, 1977.

Henry, Michel. 1988. *Seeing the Invisible: On Kandinsky.* Translated by Scott Davidson. New York: Continuum Books, 2009.

Hofmann, Hans. 1967. *Search for the Real and Other Essays.* Edited by Sara T. Weeks and Bartlett H. Hayes, Jr. Cambridge, MA: M.I.T. Press.

Hollander, John. 1995. *The Gazer's Spirit: Poems Speaking to Silent Works of Art.* Chicago: University of Chicago Press.

Hudson, W. H. 1918. *Far Away and Long Ago: A History of My Early Life.* New York: E. P. Dutton and Co.

Hustvedt, Siri. 2005. *Mysteries of the Rectangle: Essays on Painting*. New York: Princeton Architectural Press.

Ibri, Ivo Assad. 2009. "Reflections on a Poetic Ground in Peirce's Philosophy." *Transactions of the Charles S. Peirce Society* 44, no. 3: 273–307.

Ibri, Ivo Assad. 2010. "Peircean Seeds for a Philosophy of Art." In *Semiotics: The Semiotics of Space*, edited by K. Haworth, J. Hogue, and L. G. Sbrocchi, 1–16. New York: Legas Publishers.

Ibri, Ivo Assad. 2017. *Kósmos Noetós: The Metaphysical Architecture of Charles S. Peirce*. Cham: Springer Nature.

Ibri, Ivo Assad. 2020. *Semiótica e Pragmatismo: Interfaces Teóricas*. São Paulo/Marilia: FiloCzar.

Ingold, Tim. 2000. *The Perception of the Environment*. London. Routledge.

Ingold, Tim. 2013. *Making: Anthropology, Archaeology, Art and Architecture*. London: Routledge

Ingold, Tim. 2015. *The Life of Lines*. London: Routledge.

Ingold, Tim. 2017. *Lines: A Brief History*. London: Routledge.

Innis, Robert E. 1977. "Art, Symbol, Consciousness." *International Philosophical Quarterly* 17, no. 4: 455–476.

Innis, Robert E. 1983. "Dewey's Aesthetic Theory and the Critique of Technology." *Phänomenologische Forschungen: Studien zum Problem der Technik* 15: 7–42.

Innis, Robert E. 1985. *Semiotics: An Introductory Anthology*. Bloomington: Indiana University Press.

Innis, Robert E. 1987. "Aesthetic Rationality as Social Norm." *Phänomenologische Forschungen* 20: 69–90.

Innis, Robert E. 1994. *Consciousness and the Play of Signs*. Bloomington: Indiana University Press.

Innis, Robert E. 1998a. John Dewey et sa glose approfondie de la théorie peircienne de la qualité. *Protée* 26, no. 3: 89–98.

Innis, Robert E. 1998b. Pragmatism and the Fate of Reading. *Transactions of the Charles S. Peirce Society* 34, no. 4: 869–884.

Innis, Robert E. 2001. Philosophy and the Play of Life. *Focaal: European Journal of Anthropology* 37: 121–142.

Innis, Robert E. 2002. *Pragmatism and the Forms of Sense*, University Park: Penn State University Press.

Innis, Robert. 2005. "The Tacit Logic of Ritual Embodiments." In *Ritual in Its Own Right*, edited by Don Handelman and Galina Lindquist, 197–212. New York: Berghahn Books.

Innis, Robert E. 2007a. "Dimensions of an Aesthetic Encounter." In *Semiotic Rotations: Modes of Meaning in Cultural Worlds*, edited by SunHee Kim Gertz, Jaan Valsiner, and Jean-Paul Breaux, 113–134. Charlotte, NC: Information Age Publishing.

Innis, Robert E. 2007b. "The Making of the Literary Symbol: Taking Note of Langer." *Semiotica* 165, no. 4: 91–106.

Innis, Robert E. 2008. "Language and the Thresholds of Sense: Some Aspects of the Failure of Words." *Journal of Speculative Philosophy* 22, no 2: 106–117.

Innis, Robert E. 2009. *Susanne Langer in Focus: The Symbolic Mind*. Bloomington: Indiana University Press.

Innis, Robert E. 2011. "The 'Quality' of Philosophy: On the Aesthetic Matrix of Dewey's Pragmatism." In *The Continuing Relevance of John Dewey: Reflections on Aesthetics, Morality, Science, and Society*, edited by Larry A. Hickman, Matthew Caleb Flamm, Krzysztof Piotr Skowroński, and Jennifer A. Rea, 43–60. Amsterdam: Rodopi.

Innis, Robert E. 2012. "Signs of Feeling: Susanne Langer's Aesthetic Model of Minding." *American Journal of Semiotics* 28, no. 2: 43–61.

Innis, Robert E. 2013. "Peirce's Categories and Langer's Aesthetics: On Dividing the Semiotic Continuum." *Cognitio* 14, no. 1: 35–50.

Innis, Robert E. 2014. "On Not Beating One's Wings in the Void: Linking Contexts of Meaning-Making." In *Cultural Psychology and Its Future*, edited by Brady Wagoner, Nandita Chaudhary, and Pernille Hviid, 131–150. Charlotte, NC: Information Age Publishing.

Innis, Robert E. 2016. "Energies of Objects: Between Dewey and Langer." In *Das Entgegenkommende Denken*. Edited by Franz Engel and Sabine Marienberg, 21–38. Berlin: de Gruyter.

Innis, Robert E. 2017a. "America as Assemblage of Placeways: Toward a Meshwork of Lifelines." *Journal of Speculative Philosophy* 31, no. 1: 40–62.

Innis, Robert E. 2017b. "Dewey's Peircean Aesthetics." *Cuadernos de sistemática Peirceana,* 139–160. Bogotá: Centro de sistemática Peirceana.

Innis, Robert E. 2017c. "Pragmatism and the Challenge of a Cosmopolitan Aesthetics." In *Cosmopolitanism and Place*, edited by Jessica Wahman, José Medina, and John Stuhr, 59–75. Bloomington: Indiana University Press.

Innis, Robert E. 2018a. "Affectivating Signs: On Semiotic Interruptions." In *I Activate You to Affect Me,* edited by Carlos Cornejo, Giuseppina Marsico, and Jaan Valsiner, 47–70. Charlotte, NC: Information Age Publishing.

Innis, Robert E. 2018b. "Pragmatism and the Language Animal." *Cognitio* (São Paulo) 19, no. 1: 145–159.

Innis, Robert E. 2018c. "The Lost Trail of Dewey: Eco's Problematic Debt to Pragmatism." *European Journal of Pragmatism and American Philosophy* 10, no. 1. https://doi.org/10.4000/ejpap.1159.

Innis, Robert E. 2018d. "Peirce's Aesthetics and the 'Way of Beauty.'" In *Sementes de Pragmatismo na Contemporaneidade: Homenagem a Ivo Assad Ibri,* 47–57. Edited by Eluiza Bartolotto Ghizzi, Lúcia Ferraz Nogueira de Souza Dantas, Marcelo S. Madeira, Maria Eunice Quilici Gonzalez, and Monica Aiub. São Paulo: FiloCzar.

Innis, Robert E. 2019. "Peirce and Dewey Think about Art: Quality and the Theory of Signs." *Semiotica* 228: 103–134.

Innis, Robert E. 2020a. *Between Philosophy and Cultural Psychology*. Cham, Switzerland: Springer.

Innis, Robert E. 2020b. "Peirce's Aesthetic Confession and Its Analytical Consequences." *The Bloomsbury Companion to Contemporary Peircean Semiotics,* Edited by Tony Jappy, 155–184. London: Bloomsbury Academic.

Jackson, Philip W. 1998. *John Dewey and the Lessons of Art*. New Haven: Yale University Press.

Jakobson, Roman. 1988. *Language in Literature*. Edited by Krystyna Pomorska and Stephen Rudy. Cambridge, MA: Belknap Press.

James, William. (1890) 1983. *The Principles of Psychology*. Introduction by George A. Miller. Cambridge, MA: Harvard University Press. 1983.

James, William. 1911. *Some Problems of Philosophy*. Reprint. Introduction by Ellen Kappy Suckiel. Lincoln: University of Nebraska Press.

James, William. 1971. *Essays in Radical Empiricism and A Pluralistic Universe*. Introduction by Richard J. Bernstein. New York: E. P. Dutton.

Jankélévitch, Vladimir. 2003. *Music and the Ineffable*. Translated by Carolyn Abbate. Princeton: Princeton University Press.

Jappy, Tony. 2003. *Introduction to Peircean Visual Semiotics*. London: Bloomsbury Academic.

Jappy, Tony. 2017. *Peirce's Twenty-Eight Classes of Signs and the Philosophy of Representation*. London: Bloomsbury Academic.

Jappy, Tony, ed. 2020. *The Bloomsbury Companion to Contemporary Peircean Semiotics*. London: Bloomsbury Academic.

Johansen, Jørgen Dines. 2002. *Literary Discourse: A Semiotic-Pragmatic Approach to Literature*. Toronto: University of Toronto Press.

Johnson, Galen, ed. 1993. *The Merleau-Ponty Aesthetics Reader: Philosophy and Painting*. Translated by Michael Smith. Evanston, IL: Northwestern University Press.

Johnson, Mark. 2007. *The Meaning of the Body: Aesthetics of Human Understanding*. Chicago: University of Chicago Press.

Jullien, François. 2000. *Detour and Access: Strategies of Meaning in China and Greece*. Translated by Sophie Hawkes. New York: Zone Books.

Jullien, François. 2004. *In Praise of Blandness: Proceeding from Chinese Thought*. Translated by Paula M. Versano. New York: Zone Books.

Jullien, François. 2007a. *The Impossible Nude: Chinese Art and Western Aesthetics*. Translated by Maev de la Guardia. Chicago: University of Chicago Press.

Jullien, François. 2007b. *Vital Nourishment: Departing from Happiness*. Translated by Arthur Goldhammer. New York: Zone Books.

Jullien, François. 2009. *The Great Image Has No Form, or On the Nonobject through Painting*. Translated by Jane Marie Todd. Chicago: University of Chicago Press.

Kandel, Eric. 2016. *Reductionism in Art and Brain Science*. New York: Columbia University Press, 2016.

Langer, Susanne K. 1942. *Philosophy in a New Key: A Study in the Symbolism of Reason, Rite, and Art*. 3rd ed. Cambridge, MA: Harvard University Press, 1957.

Langer, Susanne K. 1953. *Feeling and Form: A Theory of Art*. New York: Scribner's.

Langer, Susanne K. 1967. *Mind: An Essay on Human Feeling*. Vol. 1. Baltimore: Johns Hopkins University Press.

Langer, Susanne K. 1974. *Mind: An Essay on Human Feeling.*Vol. 2. Baltimore: Johns Hopkins University Press.

Langer, Susanne K. 1982. *Mind: An Essay on Human Feeling*. Vol. 3. Baltimore: Johns Hopkins University Press.

Langer, Susanne K. 1988. *Mind: An Essay on Human Feeling*. Abridged by Gary van den Heuvel. Foreword by Arthur C. Danto. Baltimore: Johns Hopkins University Press.

Lauschke, Marion. 2007. Ästhetik im Zeichen des Menschen: Die äesthetische Vorgeschichte der Symbolphilosophie Ernst Cassirers und die symbolische Form der Kunst. Hamburg: Felix Meiner Verlag. Sonderheft 10, der *Zeitschrift für Ästhetik und Allgemeine Kunstwissenschaft*.

Lauschke, Marion. 2016. "'Experience Comes Whole.' Zum Rhythmus der Kunsterfahrung." In *Das Entgegenkommende Denken*, edited by Franz Engel and Sabine Marienberg, 75–86. Berlin: De Gruyter.

Liszka, James Jakób. 1996. *A General Introduction to the Semeiotic of Charles Sanders Peirce*. Bloomington: Indiana University Press.

Lucid, Daniel P, ed. 1977. *Soviet Semiotics: An Anthology*. Translated and with an Introduction. Baltimore: Johns Hopkins University Press.

Lyotard, Jean-François. 1991. *Lessons on the Analytic of the Sublime*. Translated by Elizabeth Rottenberg. Stanford: Stanford University Press, 1994.

Lysaker, John. 2017. *After Emerson*. Bloomington: Indiana University Press.

Lysaker, John. 2018a. "Giving Voice to Philosophy." *Journal of Speculative Philosophy* 32, no. 1: 131–150.

Lysaker, John. 2018b. *Philosophy, Writing, and the Character of Thought*. Chicago: University of Chicago Press.

Maclagan, David. 2001. *Psychological Aesthetics: Painting, Feeling and Making Sense*. London: Jessica Kingsley.

Maran, Timo. 2020. *Ecosemiotics: The Study of Signs in Changing Ecologies*. Cambridge: Cambridge University Press.

Matejka, Ladislav, and Irwin R. Titunik. 1976. *Semiotics of Art: Prague School Contributions*. Cambridge, MA: MIT Press.

May, Rollo. 1985. *My Quest for Beauty*. Dallas: Saybrook.

McDermott, John. 1976. *The Culture of Experience*. New York: New York University Press.

McDermott. John. 1987. *Streams of Experience*. Amherst: University of Massachusetts Press.

McDermott, John J. 2007. *The Drama of Possibility: Experience as Philosophy of Culture*. Edited by Douglas R. Anderson. New York: Fordham University Press.

Merleau-Ponty, Maurice. 1945. *Phenomenology of Perception*. Translated by C. Smith. International Library of Philosophy and Scientific Method. London: Routledge and Kegan Paul, 1962.

Milner, Marion. 1957. *On Not Being Able to Paint*. Foreword by Anna Freud. Los Angeles: J. P. Tarcher.

Murdoch, Iris. 1970. *The Sovereignty of Good*. London: Routledge.

Murdoch, Iris. 1974. *The Sacred and Profane Love Machine*. New York: Viking Press.

Murdoch, Iris. 1992. *Metaphysics as a Guide to Morals*. London: Penguin Books.

Nöth, Winfried. 1990. *Handbook of Semiotics*. Bloomington: Indiana University Press.

Pallasma, Juhani. 2005. *The Eyes of the Skin: Architecture and the Senses*. Chicester: John Wiley and Sons.

Pallasma, Juhani. 2009. *The Thinking Hand: Existential and Embodied Wisdom in Architecture*. Chicester: John Wiley and Sons.

Peirce, Charles S. 1931–1958. *Collected Papers*, 8 vols. Edited by C. Hartshorne, P. Weiss (vols. 1–6), and A. Burks (vols. 7, 8). Cambridge, MA: Harvard University Press.

Peirce, Charles S. 1976. *The New Elements of Mathematics*. Vol. 4. Edited by Carolyn Eisele. The Hague: Mouton.

Peirce, Charles S. 1977. *Semiotic and Significs: The Correspondence between Charles S. Peirce and Victoria Lady Welby*. Edited by C. S. Hardwick. Bloomington: Indiana University Press.

Peirce, Charles S. 1992. *The Essential Peirce: Selected Philosophical Writings*. Vol 1. Edited by Nathan Houser and Christian. Kloesel. Bloomington: Indiana University Press.

Peirce, Charles S. 1998. *The Essential Peirce: Selected Philosophical Writings*. Vol. 2. Edited by the Peirce Edition Project. Bloomington: Indiana University Press.

Pérez-Gomez, Alberto. 2016. *Attunement: Architectural Meaning after the Crisis of Modern Science*. Cambridge, MA: MIT Press.

Pinheiro, Marina Assis, and Livia Mathias Simão. 2020a. "Creativity and Fiction: Interpretative Horizons on the Emergence of the New in the Relationship between Individual and Culture." *Integrative Psychological and Behavioral Science*. https://doi.org/10.1007/s12124-020-09583-8.

Pinheiro, Marina Assis, and Livia Mathias Simão. 2020b. "Fiction." *The Palgrave Encyclopedia of the Possible*. Cham: Springer Nature. https://doi.org/10.1007/978-3-319-98390-5_95-1.

Polanyi, Michael. 1958. *Personal Knowledge: Towards a Post-Critical Philosophy*. Chicago: University of Chicago Press.

Polanyi, Michael. (1966) 2009. *The Tacit Dimension*. Garden City, NJ: Doubleday. Reprint with a new Foreword by Amartya Sen. Chicago: University of Chicago Press, 2009.

Polanyi, Michael, and Harry Prosch. 1975. *Meaning*. Chicago: University of Chicago Press.

Proust, Marcel. 1982. *Remembrance of Things Past*. 3 vols. Translated by C. K. Scott Moncrieff and Terence Kilmartin. New York: Random House.

Queré, France. 1995. *Le Sel et le Vent*. Paris: Bayard.

Randall, John H., Jr. 1958. *Nature and Historical Experience: Essays in Naturalism and in the Theory of History*. New York: Columbia University Press.

Rasmussen, Steen Eiler. 1959. *Experiencing Architecture*. Cambridge, MA: MIT Press, 1959.

Richards, Richard A. 2019. *The Biology of Art*. Cambridge: Cambridge University Press.

Ricoeur, Paul. 1976. *Interpretation Theory*. Fort Worth: Texas Christian University Press.

Robinson, Sarah and Juhani Pallasmaa, eds. 2015. *Mind in Architecture: Neuroscience, Embodiment, and the Future of Design*. Cambridge, MA: MIT Press.

Rosenblatt, Louise M. 1994. *The Reader, the Text, the Poem: The Transactional Theory of the Literary Work*. Carbondale: Southern Illinois University Press.

Rosenblatt, Louise M. 1995. *Literature as Exploration*. 5th ed. With a Foreword by Wayne Booth. New York: Modern Language Association.

Rothenberg, David. 2011. *Survival of the Beautiful*. London: Bloomsbury.

Sallis, John. 2015. *Klee's Mirror*. Albany: State University of New York Press.

Santayana, George. 1905–6. *Reason in Common Sense*. Volume 1 of *The Life of Reason*. New York: Charles Scribner's Sons.

Santayana, George. (1896). 1988. *The Sense of Beauty: Being the Outlines of Aesthetic Theory*. Coedited by William G. Holzberger and Herman J. Saatkamp, Ju. With an Introduction by Arthur C. Danto. Critical Edition. Cambridge, MA: MIT Press.

Sartwell, C. 2004. *Six Names of Beauty*. New York: Routledge.

Schapiro, Meyer. 1994. *Theory and the Philosophy of Art: Style, Artist, and Society*. New York: George Braziller.

Scharfstein, Ben-Ami. 1989. *The Dilemma of Context*. New York: New York University Press.

Scharfstein, Ben-Ami. 2009. *Art without Borders: A Philosophical Exploration of Art and Humanity*. Chicago: University of Chicago Press.

Seel, Martin. 2005. *The Aesthetics of Appearing*. Translated by John Farrell. Stanford, CA: Stanford University Press.

Sennett, Richard. 2009. *The Craftsman*. New Haven: Yale University Press.

Sennett, Richard. 2018. *Building and Dwelling: Ethics for the City*. New York: Farrar, Straus, and Giroux.

Sheriff, John K. 1989. *The Fate of Meaning: Charles Peirce, Structuralism, and Literature*. Princeton: Princeton University Press.

Sheriff, John K. 1994. *Charles Peirce's Guess at the Riddle: Grounds for Human Significance*. Bloomington: Indiana University Press.

Short, T. L. 2004. The Development of Peirce's Theory of Signs. In *The Cambridge Companion to Peirce*. Ed. Cheryl Misak. Cambridge: Cambridge University Press.

Short, T. L. 2007. *Peirce's Theory of Signs*. Cambridge: Cambridge University Press.

Shusterman, Richard. 1997. *Practicing Philosophy: Pragmatism and the Philosophical Life*. New York: Routledge.

Shusterman, Richard. 2000. *Pragmatist Aesthetics: Living Beauty, Rethinking Art.* 2nd ed. With a special Introduction and a new chapter. New York: Rowman and Littlefield.

Shusterman, Richard. 2002. *Surface and Depth: Dialectics of Criticism and Culture.* Ithaca, NY: Cornell University Press.

Shusterman, Richard. 2008. *Body Consciousness: A Philosophy of Mindfulness and Somaesthetics.* New York: Cambridge University Press.

Shusterman, Richard. 2010. "Dewey's *Art as Experience:* The Psychological Background." *Journal of Aesthetic Education* 44, no. 1 (Spring 2010): 26–43.

Shusterman, Richard. 2011. "The Pragmatist Aesthetics of William James." *British Journal of Aesthetics* 51, no. 4 (October 2011): 347–361.

Shusterman, Richard. 2012. *Thinking through the Body: Essays in Somaesthetics* Cambridge: Cambridge University Press, 2012.

Shusterman, Richard. 2018. *Aesthetic Experience and Somaesthetics.* Leiden: Brill Academic Publishers.

Spuybroek, Lars. 2016. *The Sympathy of Things: Ruskin and the Ecology of Design.* London: Bloomsbury.

Spuybroek, Lars. 2020. *Gravity and Grace.* London: Bloomsbury Visual Art.

Stendhal. 1822. *On Love.* Translated and with an Introduction and notes by Philip Sidney Woolf and Cecil N. Sidney Woolf. New York: Brentano's, 1920.

Stjernfelt, Frederik. 2007. *Diagrammatology.* Dordrecht: Springer.

Stjernfelt, Frederik. 2014. *Natural Propositions.* Boston: Docent Press.

Stuhr, John. 2015. *Pragmatic Fashions: Pluralism, Democracy, Relativism, and the Absurd.* Bloomington: Indiana University Press.

Stuhr, John. 2018. "Lost, Looking Around, Looking Ahead." *Journal of Speculative Philosophy* 32, no. 1: 35–49.

Tallis, Raymond. 2010. *Michelangelo's Finger: An Exploration of Everyday Transcendence.* London: Atlantic Books.

Tallis, Raymond. 2014. *Summers of Discontent: The Purpose of the Arts Today.* With Julien Spaulding. London: Wilmington Square Books.

Teresa of Avila. 1988. *The Life of St. Teresa of Ávila, by Herself.* Ed. J. M. Cohen. London: Penguin.

Tinio, Pablo, and Smith, Jeffrey. 2017. *The Psychology of Aesthetics and the Arts.* Cambridge: Cambridge University Press.

Tuan, Yi-Fu. 1977. *Space and Place.* Minneapolis: University of Minnesota Press.

Valsiner, Jaan. 2019. *Ornamented Lives.* Charlotte, NC: Information Age.

Walter, E. V. 1988. *Placeways: A Theory of the Human Environment.* Chapel Hill: University of North Carolina Press.

Weil, Simone. 1942. Letter to Joë Bousquet, April 13, 1942. In Simone Pétrement, *Simone Weil: A Life.* Translated by Raymond Rosenthal. New York: Pantheon, 1976.

Weil, Simone. 1951. *Waiting on God.* Translated by Emma Craufurd. London: Collins.

Wentworth, Nigel. 2004. *The Phenomenology of Painting.* Cambridge: Cambridge University Press.

Wiley, Norbert. 1994. *The Semiotic Self.* Chicago: University of Chicago Press.

Wittgenstein, Ludwig. 1984. *Culture and Value.* Translated by Peter Winch. Chicago: University of Chicago Press.

INDEX